Patricia Neal

As I Am

'Celebrated names flash on and off these pages like a slide show. We catch brief, bright glimpses of Lillian Hellman, Dashell Hammett, Eugene O'Neill, Vivien Leigh, Sir Laurence Olivier, Paul Newman, her cohorts at the Actors Studio and, of course, the Hollywood crowd. . . . The ruthless honesty with which Ms. Neal examines her own feelings is often moving. . . .''

—*The New York Times Book Review*

'*AS I AM* is a courageous and controversial book. . . . Neal's life was to take on the dimensions of a Greek tragedy, and that's what makes her autobiography as intriguing as it is shocking, as heart-warming as it is heartbreaking, and as controversial as it is inspirational. . . . People may love or hate Patricia Neal after reading *AS I AM*, but they will never forget her.''

—*Marlboro Enterprise / Hudson Daily Sun*

'Patricia Neal's life since the irrevocable decision that she and Gary Cooper part company has been like a Eugene O'Neill drama. She overcame one setback after another, proof of her phenomenal guts. . . . *AS I AM* is what she *is*—totally honest—and this candor is reflected on every page. . . .''

—*The Hollywood Reporter*

'*AS I AM* takes the famously troubled life of this adventuresome, formidably talented, deliciously 'actressy' actress, and makes it the reader's own experience. . . .''

—*Washington Times*

'Patricia Neal has lived and loved as few women have. . . . What a lady. What a book. What a thrill. . . .''

—*Chattanooga Times*

'HONEST AND REVEALING. I COULDN'T PUT IT DOWN.''

—*Detroit Free Press*

A LITERARY GUILD FEATURED ALTERNATE SELECTION
A DOUBLEDAY BOOK CLUB ALTERNATE SELECTION

Patricia NEAL

AS I AM

POCKET BOOKS

New York   London   Toronto   Sydney   Tokyo

The author is grateful for permission to reprint excerpts from:

"I Could Have Danced All Night," by Alan J. Lerner and Frederick Loewe, © 1956 by Alan J. Lerner and Frederick Loewe. © copyright renewed and assigned to Chappell & Co, Inc. International copyright secured. All rights reserved. Used by permission.

Excerpt from lyrics of "A Pretty Girl Is Like A Melody," by Irving Berlin, © copyright 1919, Irving Berlin. © copyright renewed 1946, Irving Berlin. Reprinted by permission of Irving Berlin Music Corp.

"Review: Garden District," *by Kenneth Tynan, reproduced by permission of* The Observer, *London.*

The Story of My Life, *by Helen Keller, © 1954. Reprinted by permission of Doubleday & Co, Inc.*

POCKET BOOKS, a division of Simon & Schuster Inc.
1230 Avenue of the Americas, New York, NY 10020

Library of Congress Catalog Card Number: 88-1990

ISBN: 0-671-67437-4

First Pocket Books printing May 1989

10 9 8 7 6 5 4 3 2 1

POCKET and colophon are trademarks of
Simon & Schuster Inc.

Printed in the U.S.A.

RL-2047

TO MY BELOVED
LADY ABBESS OF REGINA LAUDIS
ON HER GOLDEN JUBILEE
FOR INSISTING THAT I REMEMBER
IT ALL

ACKNOWLEDGMENTS

My friends at Angel Entertainment, thank you for professional guidance in helping me turn my journals into a manuscript; and my fine publishers, Simon and Schuster, thank you for the extraordinary spirit in which you have received and present my book.

CONTENTS

A GREETING

Have you ever been at sea in a dense fog, when it seemed as if a tangible white darkness shut you in, and the great ship, tense and anxious, groped her way toward the shore with plummet and sounding-line, and you waited with beating heart for something to happen? I was like that ship before my education began, only I was without compass or sounding-line, and had no way of knowing how near the harbour was. Ours is not the stillness that soothes the weary senses. It is the inhuman silence that severs and estranges. It is the silence not to be broken by a word of greeting or the song of birds or the sigh of a breeze. It is the silence which isolates cruelly, completely. It is to live long, long days and life is made up of days. It is to live immured, baffled, impotent, all God's world shut out. It is to sit helpless, defrauded, while your spirit strains and tugs at its fetters. One day I felt approaching footsteps. I stretched out my hand . . .

—HELEN KELLER
The Story of My Life

I got pregnant with my son Theo the night *The Miracle Worker* opened on Broadway. It was 1959. I was playing the role of Helen Keller's mother. It was just another

3

part for me, but a relationship with Helen Keller was also seeded deep within me that I have treasured ever since. Helen has strengthened me in my own personal, private darkness for years. I speak of her often. I quote her in my speeches around the country. Her words spring forth as my own continual sign of life and hope.

Frequently my life has been likened to a Greek tragedy, and the actress in me cannot deny that comparison. It was only an impetuous moment when the young nanny strolling my son in his pram went for that green light. His beautiful head, his beautiful future, were crushed in an instant. I have had my own ides of March. My thirty years of marriage suddenly dissolved on a crisp November day, the seventeenth of November, in 1983. Another November 17 was the date of my beloved first child's death. My Olivia died, only seven years old, from measles, in 1962. Five years later, again on November 17, my mother-in-law died, a strong woman, a cherished remnant of the Dahl family. What day in November was it when I hung up the phone on my love for the last time?

Then the fateful "seventeen" struck its most artful blow, one that changed my entire life. On February 17, 1965, as I was bathing my little daughter Tessa, I was stricken with a cerebral aneurysm. The stroke was quick, simple and decisive. The target was demolished.

Thirteen years later the ruins still had not been completely reclaimed. In 1978 I was doing a film in France. The company was lodged in a hotel at Nice. It was a lovely hotel and I was getting expense money. I love expense money. My husband thought the hotel was too good for me, and like an idiot, I went against my better instincts and said, "All right, Papa." I found a cheaper hotel. They served only breakfast, and no English was spoken. I could not sleep all night long and the next day I went back to my fine hotel. They took me back and promised me another room.

While I was waiting I had tea in the hotel bar, and something made me look up toward the door. A very beautiful young woman walked into the bar and swept the room with a glance, looking for someone. She did not

4

see me. She turned to leave and I was drawn to my feet. I followed her to the desk and called her name. She looked at me for an eternity before she knew me, and then she gasped, "Oh my God!"

"I would love to buy you a drink," I said. "I would love to speak with you."

"I can't now," she apologized. "Are you staying here? I will call you."

I watched her leave. So tall. So slender. The eyes and mouth so like her father's. His child, carrying the genes that had once called to me for continuity.

One miraculous meeting had already taken place between us. I was grateful for another. Maria and I talked more. We saw each other every day in my room. The fact that I was facing another major struggle in my life could not have been known to her. But there is a knowledge that passes between persons because of a mysterious bond. Our bond is a loved one who lives in my heart and in hers. His name is Gary Cooper. He is one of the most beautiful things that ever happened to me in my life. I love him even now, and what is more important, I am now able to love any person who also loved him.

Maria told me about an abbey that had become very significant in her life. We did not have to discuss why I had to go to this abbey. I simply knew I had to.

So it was Maria Cooper who introduced me to the nuns at the Benedictine monastery of Regina Laudis. And it was the nuns who encouraged me to begin to sort out my past, step by step, skipping nothing, to speak my memories into a tape recorder, to keep a journal. To piece together the fragments of my life.

But why write a book? To capitalize on relationships and make money? The thought crosses my mind with no small bite. I have a great fear of growing old and becoming poor and dependent. To make apology to those whom I have hurt or even damaged through my own ignorance? For my friends, my children, my Roald? They all deserve whatever missing pieces I can now dig up.

Or—for me?

To reach back and try to reclaim the past that was

5

stolen? Perhaps that is the heart of it. To reach back for the sake of the reach itself, and hope that in remembering, I can at last know there is sense to all of this. Because I do still exist. I do still have faith in life. And I do still believe in love.

At the abbey there is a special "willow cabin at the gate," where I could allow memories to return and invite old friends to join me and help me remember. It was to be my sanctuary for many years.

Remembering was laborious. Remembering was humbling. It was painful beyond all words, and then, finally, remembering was purifying, and it began to give me peace.

YELLOW
WATERMELONS
1926–1946

CHAPTER ONE

Packard, Kentucky, is a ghost town now—gone, gone forever —even the house where I was born. But it was once a fertile and thriving boomtown, just below the Mason-Dixon line, nurturing many families like ours on the deep veins of coal that wound down into the bowels of the earth. In 1926 the town was about three hundred wooden houses along a web of dirt roads that etched their way through knobby grasslands over the rolling hills. The church and the general store were the hubs of activity, as they were in every small town in America. The men, when they were not working, would gather at the storefront and swap tales. It was like a village green except the front of the store was just a slab of cement, the only sidewalk in town. There was a well where you could pump water. There was one boardinghouse and a schoolhouse. And, of course, a Baptist church.

Only a few decades away from the Civil War, the Old South still clung to its cobwebs and conventions. Women and men, blacks and whites, bad and good. Everyone had his or her place. The railroad tracks separated the sheep from the goats among the townsfolk with a biblical severity. Women were never permitted to enter the mine shafts, a primal territory of the male. The church unquestionably chose sides. The whites sat on the ground floor and the blacks were restricted to "nigger heaven."

My family did not venture firsthand into the mine

shafts, but the aura was there—dark miner, covered with soot—white miner, covered with the details of management.

My father moved through our town like a white god in a native village. He was manager for the Southern Coal and Coke Company and totally beloved and respected by all his friends and all who worked for him. At harvest time the local farmers could not wait to give him their first melons and corn. They would never allow other hunters on their land, but gave him permission to enter their sanctuary for quail or pigeon as if his gun did not kill. His physical dimensions can only be described as—shall I say it?—fat! He was a great fat man. But it was absolutely right. His body complemented an immense spirit that seemed to wrap itself around everyone. When I am asked why I wanted to be an actress, I always say, "I don't really know, I just did." But I think I wanted to have everybody love me, the way they loved my Daddy.

His name was William Burdette Neal, but he was called "Coot" by all. As a baby he was very "cute" and the description became a nickname that stuck to him for life. I loved my father. I looked for his faithful response in the eyes of many men. None could say "forever" as he did.

My father had long roots in the South, five generations that I know. He was born in 1895 in Pittsylvania County, Virginia. His mother was Lucy Fitzgerald and his father was William David Neal. They owned a tobacco plantation between Chatham and Danville, Virginia, and had one daughter and five sons.

My mother was Eura Mildred Petrey. She was the daughter of Pascal Gennings Petrey, who was the town doctor in Packard. In my parents' relationship two very American strains met—the tobacco farmer and the country doctor.

Eura caught her first sight of William at a railroad depot during the closing days of World War I. She had gone to meet a friend and Daddy had just returned from his mother's funeral with his sister, Maude. Later, Mother was invited to a game of rook, a hot card game of that era, that was sponsored by a local schoolteacher named Bertha Snyder. Mother never let us forget that name. Coot was invited to attend on the arm of this hostess, who had set her consoling eyes on the young Virginia boy. But it was love at first sight across the rook board for Mother and Daddy. She said she saw it in his great brown eyes, and it was sealed forever as he spoke in his thick Virginia accent, "No faya tawkin' 'cros th' boawd!" So they got up and *tawked* in the garden. They started dating immediately. The number-one hit tune of the time was a Hawaiian melody with the meaningful sentiment, "Your big brown eyes have such linger lovely." Mother played that song to death on her Victrola.

The Petreys enlarged their family to four daughters when my mother was sixteen. My mother's new baby sister, Virginia Siler, was the light of her eyes and awakened her young maternal heart. She doted on her, changed her, dressed her up every day and curled her hair, and mourned her as deeply as any mother when the baby tragically died at eighteen months. Mother never returned to school after this incident, perhaps to my advantage, for she was then available to the courting ways of my father. He and Mother got married on November 5, 1918, the week that the Armistice was signed.

Mother and Daddy anticipated their firstborn, Margaret Ann, with elaborate preparations and great emotion. Mother borrowed a bassinet that had come all the way from a friend in Toledo, Ohio. It might as well have come from Paris. It was trimmed with dainty lace and a bridal veil net that went clear to the floor. Margaret Ann was a gorgeous baby and the nurses triumphantly wheeled her all over the hospital. Daddy wept with pride.

I didn't have the advantage of such a debut. I was born at home, with only our doctor present. On January 20, 1926, totally out of character, I slipped quietly into the world. Mother says I was her easiest birth, but she was distressed by my totally bald head. When Margaret Ann toddled into the room, she took one look at me in the bed with my mother and said, "Well, if it isn't *Bill!*" I was, fortunately, christened Patsy Louise by my Aunt Ima's

11

choice, but for many years Bill was my name. Wasn't that good of her?

My maternal grandfather, Dr. Petrey, whom we called Pappy, had his office in back of the general store. Pappy was an astonishing man. I enjoyed him so much. I'd sit with him on the porch swing, trying to absorb his talk about the black-eyed pea crop, the nutritious value of corn bread or the new president-elect, Franklin Delano Roosevelt. He was very religious and often gave homilies in church. Frequently he had his Bible out to talk to me about God. "Patsy, remember what the psalmist says: 'He changes a desert into pools of water, and streams of water into a dry land . . . a fruitful land into saltness for the wickedness of them that dwell in it.' " My eyes would grow as big as saucers and he would see that I had been duly affected. "Never forget the wisdom of the Bible, Patsy Lou."

"But how can I possibly remember all that?" I would ask quite sincerely.

"Never mind," he would scowl. "Get a bookmark."

My mother and my aunts, Ima and Della, adored Pappy. The three daughters courted his darling, affectionate nature by spoiling him to death. When he returned home hot and tired, one of them would come to wipe his face with a cool cloth, another to comb his hair, and the third to fetch him cold lemonade. He thrived on being the center of so much devoted attention.

He came from German farm people. He was reared in a family of eleven and they worked hard. Any son who left the farm had to be very determined, and Pappy had set his sights on medical school. He got a teaching job to support himself and finally earned a diploma from Louisville Medical College, first in his class. He set up practice in Packard.

Pappy took his Hippocratic oath as a religious vow and gave his life for it. When I was ten years old he was operated on for a prostate condition. He was cautioned not to risk a night call for at least three months. One of the farmers called him in the wee hours, begging him to come and treat his sick child. "Just this one time," said

Pappy, and off he went in the buggy. The next night he became desperately ill himself and was rushed to the hospital. The doctor was not an ideal patient. "They are giving me too much of this newfangled shot. If only I could treat myself. I have had such marvelous luck with pneumonia patients." He was put under an oxygen tent, but he stayed alert in those last days. The nurse noticed that he was trying to brush his hair. It was beautiful, black with a few gray streaks, and he wore it in a pretty pompadour in the fashion of the day. The nurse asked, "Oh, are you getting all fixed up today?" He answered, "Why shouldn't I? This is Sunday." It was almost as if he were expecting a caller. When the visitor came, it was not a death anyone might have expected. Pappy's expression changed. His face beamed with an unearthly recognition and he cried out in such joy, "My mother! Oh, my mother!" Then he went to her.

My grandmother, Flora Jane Siler, came from neighboring Williamsburg, Kentucky, where the English Silers had gravitated. She was related to almost everybody in that town. Mammy, as she was called, and the young country doctor produced a family of daughters. The first was Della, next came Eura, who was my mother, then Ima and, many years later, the beloved baby sister, Virginia Siler. I am told the girls were named after the Hoggs, an oil-rich Texas family whose children were called Ima Hogg, Eura Hogg and Bea Hogg, who was, unfortunately, a boy. Mammy was a fine seamstress. She made embroidered blankets, really beautiful work. She kept a flock of chickens and she would wring their necks herself with her bare hands. The half-dead things would run around the yard for about five minutes before they dropped. We would have those to eat. The more fortunate birds laid eggs and were kept for loftier purposes—Mammy's glorious angel food cake. If they eat cake in heaven, it must be her recipe.

But Mammy was not a heavenly lady. My mother never remembers Mammy picking her up or offering her any manifestations of love. She describes her as being cold as a cucumber. When Mammy punished, she took a

13

whip. It was horrendous how she would whip my mother. Mammy cast a strong, hard shadow and Mother still shivers in the coldness of that shade. Mammy was not a tender grandmother, either. She stayed with us quite a lot after Pappy died. I remember when my sister would sit on the porch with her beau, Mammy was always at the window with her eyes peering through the blinds to see what was happening. She was always thinking that we were thinking dirty thoughts.

Still, I liked her very much. We did seem to speak the same language. She may have sensed that I was straining at the fetters that had shackled her all her life. Then again, maybe I liked her because she never spanked me.

Once a year we would visit Grandpa Neal's farm in Virginia. Grandpa Neal grew tomatoes, cucumbers, sweet potatoes and all kinds of vegetables, but his main crop was tobacco. The immense barns were perfect for hide-and-seek, and running and jumping onto the stuffed wagons was paradise. I still treasure a photograph of my brother, Pete, taken when he was two or three, standing in his play yard—a wagonload of tobacco.

I remember summer vacations, when Grandpa's watermelon patches would yield their harvests of pink and yellow fruit. I do say yellow! There *is* such a thing! The black families in service would pack a whole wagonload onto a cart and bring them into the backyard. We would cut the melons and eat just the heart out of them. The rest was cast away.

The farmhouse was white wood. Its central sitting room was shrouded with sheets and was never used by anybody but elegant friends and the vicar because it was "too good." The house had a great porch swing where we would sit on sultry summer evenings and rock back and forth, watching the fireflies. Sometimes the only breeze was created by the gentle to-and-fro of the swing. Hot. Hot. Hot. So hot that it was almost ecstatic.

The center of the household at that time was my grandfather's new wife, Miss Mollie. My real grandmother, Lucy Fitzgerald, had died suddenly from a heart attack. She was an enormously fat, enormously beautiful woman

14

who worked like a man and ate like a man. She just dropped over dead one day while she was sitting on a chair in the kitchen. She left a tremendous gap in my grandfather's life, and her picture over his bed. Miss Mollie was at least fifteen years younger and hardly a beauty. Her chin stuck out and she wore thick glasses. She would always call him with a certain majestic air: "Mistah Neal, Mistah Neal!" I think it is astonishing to go to bed with your husband, still call him "Mistah" and have Lucy Fitzgerald Neal looking on.

Miss Mollie was a fabulous cook. The coal stove crackled early in the morning with kingly portions of bacon, sausages, eggs, hot biscuits and grits. She and Grandpa Neal would rise early to share in the chores of the farm. At noon she would summon everyone with a weighty bell to come to a bountiful dinner of smoked ham or roast possum and vegetables from the garden, which was right next to the family graveyard.

The farm also boasted an exotic form of life I have seen only in this part of the South. There were tiny holes in the earth, and whenever we saw one, we would burst into a kind of singsong: "Doodle bug, doodle bug, hurry back home, your house is on fire and your children will burn." The ground around the hole would swell as a tiny creature ruptured the earth in a frenzy of panic. To our delight, they would surface one by one, great round bugs from some secret hiding place. With godlike blessing we would allow them to return to their holes unmolested. Why does my mind jump suddenly to the hand of my Uncle Fitz's wife slamming an insulting blow on a Negro face? The vulnerable bodies of those tiny frightened bugs and the eyes of the black woman darting in contempt— flashes of the soul of my southern childhood. The fragrant perfume of the mimosa with its fernlike fingers . . . the voluptuous roses . . . the joyfully vulgar sunflowers. And those plump yellow watermelons, oozing with a sweetness and a promise that eating alone could never satisfy.

* * *

Life in Packard was very good. My parents were officials in the mining camp. The officials had the rare privilege of electricity, which they made themselves, and we were among the elite who had a telephone. There were three phones in town. The general store had one, Daddy's office had one, and so did our house. My terrible telephone habits started early, for I teethed on one before most people knew what they were.

Daddy ran his job as if he owned the company, which he did not. His boss would say, "As big as Coot Neal is, he is worth his weight in gold." Above Daddy's desk was a motto that he quoted throughout his life: "Organization is the art of getting men to respond like thoroughbreds. When you call upon a thoroughbred he gives you all the speed, strength of heart and sinew in him. When you call on a jackass, he kicks."

Once a sudden absence in the company personnel prompted an invitation quite uncommon to the times. It was suggested that Coot Neal enlist his wife to help out in the office, which he did. It disclosed a unique trust between Mother and Daddy and a capacity to work together that lasted throughout their married life. From that time on Daddy split his salary willingly with his marriage partner. That same lady was also a full-time housewife and mother. No matter how hard she worked in his office, our rooms were cleaned, our clothes were washed, and our meals were cooked.

Of course, she didn't have to fret too much about the menu. Daddy loved fowl. He simply adored eating chicken and even begrudged the dog an occasional liver. Once he went out and bought an extravagant thirty-five dollars' worth of fryers—one hundred live chickens. Mother thought, *Well, I am going to get the boy this time. I am going to feed him chicken until he has had his fill.* One by one she killed them and dressed them and let them sit overnight in salt. She fed Daddy a chicken a day for fourteen weeks. He never tired of it, and said every day what a wonderful supper it was.

The Neal house had electricity but not plumbing. Every morning the black handyman, whom everybody alled "Pip," would fill the water tank by the stove. Then Mother would feed him before he went to the mines. He could devour a breakfast of country ham, four eggs and a pan of hot biscuits and drain a six-cup percolator of hot coffee. When he finished he would send up a volley of praise: "Thank you, Miss Eura, thank you. The Lord will bless you. The Lord will bless you." And she would always say, "He already has. He already has." Mother used to say that Pip "flunkied" for us. When we had company he would take us out, my sister and me, playthings and all, to a treasured spot under the trees and model to us. I guessed it was not a bad thing to be a flunky if it meant being old Pip!

Mothers are flunkies, too. My mother was. Her own needs easily took second place to those of her husband and children. The joy in her children's eyes was her reward and she thrived on it. In her hands Christmas was fabulous. Through the coal company Mother had access to wholesale catalogs from Marshall Field, Carson Pirie Scott and dozens of other stores. We spent our last Christmas in Packard when I was almost three. Mother had arranged a whole sleighful of toys for Margaret Ann and me in our living room—dolls, buggies, just about anything that could come through mail order. Christmas morning, she waited by the tree in happy anticipation of our throwing open the door and rushing to our fantastic heap of gifts. But Margaret Ann and I just stood at the door, frozen in complete awe of the display. We didn't touch a thing. Our young mother left the room and cried and cried and cried.

Mother already knew it was to be our last Christmas in that dear mining camp, so perhaps her tears flowed from a deeper well. My father had been offered a much better job in Knoxville, Tennessee, and although he had not yet decided whether to take it, Mother had. She was afraid that if we stayed in a small town, the time would come when her children would inevitably leave to get their education in the big city. Mother had lived in a school dormitory, separated from her own father, and she did not want the same fate for us. We were, of course, still ba-

17

bies, but already she envisioned our move to Knoxville as a way to keep the family together. She would not ever think of approaching my father on the subject because he loathed the idea of a move. So she wrote him a letter:

> I missed my father through the years, not having been with him and away at school. I want my children to be with you and for that reason I think we should make this move, so they don't have to be away from you to get their education.

My mother sent the letter and waited.

She did not have to wait long. The next evening my father was sitting in the outhouse, when suddenly the seat collapsed and the whole thing fell through, including all two hundred sixty pounds of Daddy. I was never told who pulled him out or whether he climbed out himself, but he was furious, and covered, covered, covered with shit! The next day he accepted the new job. He never mentioned the letter to Mother, and she never mentioned it to him.

CHAPTER TWO

t was 1929. The Neal family was trying to adjust to its new home in Knoxville. That city on the Tennessee River was then a sooty industrial town. The people were not "folks" the way they were in Packard. Knoxville was "citified," and everybody was a stranger. The change was terrible for us. Twice a month we would pile into the car for the three-hour ride "home" to Packard. Before we left to go back to the city, Pappy would always press a few coins into my hand. I was pulling in nickels and dimes from Pappy from the time I could toddle. I loved the feeling of those coins and the sense of security they gave me when I could hear them jangling in my pocket. It is a feeling that has stayed with me all my life. I am sure that growing up in the midst of the Depression affected me, but I am even more certain that those coins from Pappy made a very deep impression on me. When I could fight for nothing else, I could always fight for money.

Our first Easter in Knoxville, I went to the department store with Mother. I saw a coat just my size. It was blue like the sky, and at the bottom the blue darkened to look like water. Tiny yellow ducks floated along the hem. There was a cap to match. I went absolutely wild for it and begged my mother to buy it for me. "No, it is too much money, Patsy," was her answer. But I was going to have that coat. Reaching into my pocket, I produced

my precious coins. Mother looked at me for a long, long
time, and then she took the money from me and dis
creetly added the needed bills. It was the first time I paid
my own way for something I wanted.

It would not be the last.

Mother did enjoy Margaret Ann and me and took every
opportunity she could to bring us into town. People al
ways stopped to admire the precious little Neal girls.
Margaret Ann was a beautiful dark brunette and I was
her younger blonde counterpart. But that was the extent
of any resemblance between us. My sister was already
showing strong signs of Mother's lean, Protestant sensi
tivities. I was surely going to be Daddy's girl all the way.
From the earliest days of my childhood I had his sense of
curiosity and a way of just walking into any situation with
a hearty *here I am*.

I had long been intrigued by a drawer in Mother's bed
room. One afternoon when she had gone uptown, I
slipped into the empty room and climbed up on the chair
to the bureau. I pulled the drawer open and was dazzled
by a box of beautiful beads. It must have been a broken
strand of a necklace. The bright objects sparkled and I
immediately grabbed one and put it directly into my ear.
I pressed it down as far as it would go, and when I could
no longer reach it, I was triumphant. When Mother re
turned, I greeted her with my wonderful news. "I put a
bead in my ear! A blue bead!" Mother and Aunt Ima held
me upside down and shook me like a piggy bank, but the
bead held firm. Finally they whisked me off to the emer
gency room at the hospital. The doctor picked me up and
carried me around, and even showed me the birds he had
in a cage. He told me I would go to sleep for a while and
then it would all be fine. When I woke up from the anes
thesia I was yelling "Gosh! Gosh! Gosh!" It was the only
strong word I knew. Mother was so embarrassed. For
days she fretted, "I just wonder what kind of a home he
thinks Patsy comes from?"

I had a special cousin named Jack Kuhn. Jack was a
naughty fellow. He was always getting a beating for one
thing or another. Like the time we took his mother's paint

tubes and squashed out their bright oily innards all over
the walls and all over each other. When Aunt Della came
home she beat the daylights out of him. She thought *I*
was just an innocent bystander.

It was Jack who introduced me, at a very early age, to
my first bad habit. Our Aunt Ima was the only lady in the
family who smoked. In those days, they had boxes that
held a hundred cigarettes. Jack stole one of Aunt Ima's
boxes and a few books of matches one afternoon and
convinced Margaret Ann and me that it was time to grow
up. We found a spot beside the house, out of sight, and
sat down to our smoking lesson. We each lit up a cigarette and, after one puff, threw it away. We did this with
all one hundred of them. Jack got another beating. I was
just about five years old, but I must say, the lesson took
well. I smoked on and off for the next forty-three years
before I gave it up for good.

Jack evened the score. One of my great passions as a
little girl was dolls. A friend of the family had presented
me with a beauty. She was special because her head was
made of glass. One afternoon I introduced her to Jack.
He snatched her from my arms and raced off with her. I
ran after him, panicked, until we reached the cellar door.
Suddenly, he grabbed for the handle, flung the door open
and hurled my precious doll down the steps. I heard the
sickening shatter of glass. Down the wooden stairs in the
semidarkness I could see the small form. The beautiful
head was shattered into a million tiny pieces of colored
glass.

Jack and I still played together after that day. I certainly grieved over my doll. Living through the tragedy
of losing one's doll is a hard lesson. The amazing thing
was that I don't remember ever hating my cousin for
what he did. He was just being Jack.

I remember that he and Margaret Ann would tease a
neighbor girl. They would taunt her and run away, and
she would chase them. One day I tried to run with them,
but I was so much smaller, I could not possibly keep up.
The girl caught me by the throat. "I'll just choke you,
young lady," she snarled, and she began to throttle me. I

set up such a howl. I screamed my lungs out until my mother separated us and sent my attacker on her way. Mother still insists that that is why I have such a deep voice.

The most glorious memory of my young life in Knoxville still brings a great smile to my face. That tough little girl continued to torment me. I just kept out of her way, but one day I looked up and saw her coming at me. It was clear that she was going to kill me. I looked around for *something,* and what did I see but a rotten half of a grapefruit lying in the grass. I picked it up and threw it at her. I hit her, a soggy bull's-eye right in the center of her face. To this day, when I want to feel good I remember that. *Smack!* She went home screaming. It was the greatest thing I ever did.

When Mother sat me down to explain that I had to have my tonsils out, she said if I behaved real good she would tell me a thrilling secret. She knew I could be bribed. When I came out of the operation she confided that in three months I would have a baby sister or brother.

Of course, Mother did not tell me where our new baby would come from. Sex was not discussed in our house. Margaret Ann and I learned the difference between boys and girls the way most kids in our neighborhood did. We took a friend's little brother down cellar and made him take off his pants. Even our own bodies were not explained. An older girl down the street got me into the bathtub to explore. Mother was offended. "You mustn't touch yourself, Patsy." I got a spanking, and I discovered there would be things in my life I could not tell Mother.

Anyway, it was Aunt Ima who was delegated to discuss intimate matters with Margaret Ann and me. So I was told that the new baby would come from my mother's tummy. I was fascinated. I asked her whether the baby would be a boy or a girl. She took out one of those round things, like a kaleidoscope, and peered into it. Its patterns, she said, revealed that it would be a boy.

I knew about girls, but the only boy I really knew was Daddy. I was sure it would be all right if it was a boy.

William Petrey Neal was born on December 22, 1935,
most in time for my tenth birthday. I was so excited to
see him I thought I would burst. Margaret Ann and I were
ally permitted to go to the hospital. He was a beauty.
real live doll of my very own—only Mother handed
m to Margaret Ann! I reached out to take him. "No,
atsy, don't." Mother's "don'ts" drove me crazy. Like
was too stupid to know what to do. I was crestfallen.
learly, the new baby boy belonged to Mother and Mar-
aret Ann.

I held on to my resentment for having been treated so
adly even after Mother allowed me to look after him.
laring into his cherubic little face, I sneered, "You
-E-V-I-L!" spelling out each letter with all the venom I
ould muster. He smiled back at me, gleefully repeating,
D-B-L, D-B-L."

That night when Daddy came home I overheard
Mother say to him, "The baby has learned something
ew, Coot. He keeps saying 'D-B-L.' I do wonder what
e means by that." For weeks I lived in terror that they
ould make sense out of it. But at the same time I en-
oyed it when Pete would use this secret code, which only
knew was a naughty word. Pete and I were going to
ave a fine relationship after all.

One day my tiny pupil, who was now walking, looked
p and announced, "Fuck-oh-fuck."

Mother nearly perished. "Pete Neal, where did you
ver hear that?"

He chirped back brightly, "Pat-Pat!"

Pete's private tutoring abruptly ended.

I really wanted my sister Margaret Ann to be my
riend, but at our tender age, twenty-two months was a
uge difference. So I was the flunky. NiNi, as Pete nick-
amed her, was a born librarian. A favorite game of hers
vas to play library in the garden. She was in charge of
he library, of course, and I was always the person who
ame for a book. I would dutifully say, "I would like a
ook, please," and she would ask, "What sort of a book
lo you want?" I would tell her something and she would
ive me two books and stamp them. I would go away for

23

about five minutes and she would ring a hand bell a[nd]
say, "Time's up! Bring them back!" Then we would [go]
through the same thing over and over and over aga[in.]
Each time I would create a different story about the bo[ok]
I wanted and why I wanted it. Each time I would get t[he]
same two books and five minutes to pretend I'd re[ad]
them.

When the library game was over we would switch [to]
baseball, to my absolute delight. This was one place[I]
could shine. One bright afternoon I went up to bat, rea[dy]
to send that darling ball right out of the empty lot into o[ur]
backyard two houses away. I could already hear the ki[ds]
cheering. NiNi wound up and pitched. A shock of pa[in]
stabbed me in the nose and I whirled to the ground. Blo[od]
poured out of my nose. Margaret Ann had beaned m[e.]
Just that day in school we had been studying *Julius Ca[e-]
sar*. I staggered to my feet and fell again, just like t[he]
dying emperor. "I am dead! I am dead! You have kill[ed]
me!" I cried. My audience was greatly impressed.

I think that may have been my first public perfo[r-]
mance.

I was growing taller than the other girls, but I was n[ot]
yet too tall for the boys. The boys at school had alwa[ys]
liked me and used to vie for my attention. A fat fell[ow]
who sat behind me would tap me on the shoulder, a[nd]
when I looked around he would pull a long strand of sn[ot]
from his nose, which sent me into a giggle fit. It w[as]
really just accordion-pleated yellow paper, but he got m[e]
every time.

After school, young gentlemen would walk me hom[e,]
one on either side of me. Each would try to do crazi[er]
things than the other. Once one of these young compa[n-]
ions showed up on my doorstep with an older boy who[m]
I did not know. "Hi! Patsy, I just told my friend what [a]
beauty you are and I wanted him to see you," he said.

I threw my hands over my face and turned awa[y]
squealing "No! No! I am not! I am not!" I ran to m[y]
room and hid. So much attention from the opposite se[x]
actually embarrassed me. I was not exactly sure what [I]
could do with it. Then.

It bothered me that NiNi had a best friend. I so much wanted girls to like me, and to have a best friend myself.

One afternoon NiNi and her friend were leaving the house together and I started after them. Daddy was on the porch and NiNi implored him, "Please make Patsy go back!" For NiNi, asking Daddy to take her side was nothing new. But the curtness of his reply stunned me: "You come back here!" I set my jaw and said, "No! I won't!" He marched me back to the house and smacked me right across the face. My nose began to spurt. I could tell the sight of blood did him in. Oh boy, it got him! So I kept the poor thing bleeding all day. I didn't care what I had to do to my nose to make him feel sorry.

One day we moved to a new house and Mary Emma Thompson became my new playmate. We would take all our dolls and things and make our own house and spend the entire day being little mothers. Then Charlcey Adcock moved into the neighborhood. I wanted both Mary Emma and Charlcey to be my *best* friend, but *they* became best friends and I was just a *plain* friend. I was always the third one. Even then.

If one thing in my young years motivated me strongly, it was anger when someone took what was mine. I remember I was going to buy a pair of shoes and had been entrusted with ten whole dollars, which I brought with me to school. At one point during the day I checked my little purse, and, sure enough, the crisp bill was gone. I swung around to the girl sitting behind me. I just knew she was the only person who could have taken it. Very sternly I said, "I would like my money back." She protested that she had not taken it, but I insisted she open her purse and let me check. She flushed nervously and then admitted she had taken my money, but only to tease me. The girl was poor and we were not, though I didn't really understand what that meant. I did understand that taking what belonged to someone else was wrong. I found as I grew older that I could endure many things, like being a fifth wheel in a friendship or feeling second-rate with my mother, but I simply *could not handle* being stolen from. It was something I would carry with me my whole life.

CHAPTER THREE

Mary Emma, Charlcey and I shared many adventures, not the least of which was the forbidden pleasure of smoking. We usually partook of this vice at Mary Emma's. She had her own bedroom with a window right over her bed. We would sit on the bed, light up, and the smoke would sail right out the window, leaving no telltale evidence. We spent a lot of time in Mary Emma's bedroom.

There was to be a big revival meeting at the Magnolia Avenue Methodist Church. Mary Emma and I decided to go. Mother and Daddy, even though they were Baptists, allowed me to go to the Methodist church because my friends went. I was not what you would call a model parishioner. I usually giggled or found some distraction like watching people who were sleeping or reading a hidden paperback during the sermon. I certainly wouldn't claim the preachers were not telling Gospel truth, but their talk always made me feel sorry and not good. Still, I dutifully went to Sunday school. In the last resort, I wanted to be on His side.

But walking into the Methodist church that evening, this ten-year-old was completely astonished. The most beautiful lady was standing at the altar. She was dressed in a pure white robe. She would have captured me by her looks alone, but when she spoke, her voice wrapped around me. It embraced me. "God is not a law, God is

ot somebody out there who is keeping a score. God is
a your heart and in mine. Come. Come. Come to God,
ho is Love.'' She spread her hands and the shimmering
obe opened wide in appeal. I had never been talked to
bout God like that. I watched her standing there with
er arms stretched out and the people going up to her.
Oh, I wanted to go up with them, too. But I couldn't. I
ust couldn't budge. I simply had to go back the next
ight, and she was just as wonderful, but I still could not
nove when she said, "Come!" I went back a third night,
nd this time I gave in to my pounding heart. I went up
o the altar and stretched out my hand to her, and I wept
nd wept. She smiled at me with such tenderness. I didn't
now why I was crying or what I was reaching for. It
vould take me almost a lifetime to find out.

That night, I reluctantly climbed into the bed beside
Mary Emma. She switched out the lamp and we sat in
he moonlight while she lit up a cigarette and pushed it
oward me. "All right now, smoke!" she whispered.

"I can't," I stammered. "I can't. Really. I found
God.''

"You are going to smoke this cigarette, Patsy Neal, or
lse I am going to kill you."

I conceded and took a puff. The smoke curled up and
ut the open window.

Suddenly, we heard the voice of doom. "Mary Emma,
ut out that cigarette!" I smashed the butt into the win-
lowsill and Mary Emma dived under the covers. We
vaited for her mother's footsteps to come down the hall,
ut all was silent. In minutes I heard Mary Emma's heavy
reathing. She had fallen off into blissful sleep. I lay
awake for hours. All night long I was tormented. I felt so
guilty. I had found God—and then given Him up for a
cigarette.

Jane Hunter was not a special friend of mine. She was
ust a girl at school. But the day her appendix burst she
ecame famous. She was whisked off to the hospital, and
hen we learned that she had died. Jane was one of the
eople I had watched in church. She was very serious in
er prayers and I thought something special must be

going on between her and God. The whole school went to her funeral. I was so upset, the only thing I could think of doing was going to speak to her mother. Mrs. Hunter was a lovely woman who had birthed her daughter late in life. She told me that she had been with her little girl in the hospital. Jane had said, "Oh, Mother, look! The angels are coming. They're coming after me." And then she died.

"Where do the angels come from?" I asked, and Mrs. Hunter told me they lived in heaven. It was a beautiful city with golden streets.

For days I moped around the house. All I could think of was dying. It all seemed so utterly sad. Finally, my mother couldn't take it any longer. "Patsy," she said, "just what in this world is going on with you?"

"It's not this world, Mother," I sighed. "I want to die and see the golden streets of heaven."

My distressed mother took her concern to our good neighbor, Cornelia Avaniti, who was also my teacher at school. Mother knew I thought the world of her and asked her to help.

At school the following day, Miss Avaniti asked me to walk with her. "Patsy," she said gently, "death is just a deep sleep. Jane was ill. She was suffering. You are young and healthy and have so much to live for, but Jane needed this sleep. On Judgment Day there will be great trumpets blown in heaven and everybody who is sleeping in death will be aroused. You have parents who love you, and a sister who loves you, and I love you. There are so many things you want to do. Now do them!"

I was very pleased to hear Miss Avaniti say that she loved me and that my parents did, too. I was not convinced about my sister. As for the rest, I was relieved to hear that Jane would wake up again and I liked very much the idea of a great trumpet blowing anywhere.

Cornelia Avaniti's influence in my life was to be far more significant than either of us could have imagined. She gave dramatic readings and book reviews around Knoxville. I had never seen her do this until after the Women's Christian Temperance Union speech contest.

Cornelia had given such an impassioned speech against the demon alcohol that was ruining family life in Knoxville that she was invited to repeat it for a Christmas program, an evening of monologues in the basement of the Methodist church. As I listened to her recite from the world's great literature, I was utterly thrilled. I could do that! I knew I could! This, I said to myself, is what I want to do all my life.

At the end of the evening I rushed up to her. "Oh, Miss Avaniti!" I cried. "You were just wonderful. I want to do that, but I know I can never be as good as you."

"Of course you can, Patsy Lou," she said. "I will probably be listening to *you* one day."

There was a mirror on my closet door, and I could catch my sister's disgusted look in its reflection as I practiced expressions that would be suitable for any kind of monologue. Daddy for sure had no idea what was hatching in my head when he casually mentioned to my mother, "By the way, Eura, did you know that Mr. Mahan's daughter Emily is back from New York? She's starting up a drama school for herself." That was the most fabulous news in the world. There was someone right here in Knoxville who could teach monologues and she was my daddy's boss's daughter, and, even better, my Aunt Maude had married into the Mahan family when she wed Emily's Uncle Will.

It was just before Christmas 1936. That very night I took the cardboard from Daddy's laundered shirt, wrote a message and placed it in my sock over the fireplace:

Dear Santa,
What I want for Christmas is to study dramatics.
Please.

CHAPTER FOUR

Kathryn Stubley had the greatest figure I had ever seen in my life. Her bosoms just stuck out by themselves and she didn't even need a brassiere. Anne Fonde was a cheerleader and champion tennis player. Gloria Lucas was a poet and an honor student, and single-handedly got me through Latin. I was not a great scholar in high school. I could not play tennis. Nobody asked me to be a cheerleader. But I would be special, too, and I knew it. My new teacher said I had talent.

Emily Mahan was very rich and very strict and she knew how to teach drama. Two times a week I would take the bus right after school to Miss Mahan's studio, which was a great loft over a filling station. She would choose monologues that I would take home and memorize and then present to her at the next class for her criticism and help. I would be amazed at how much she could give in one hour and how much I could learn, considering how little I got in an hour of school. If I skimped in my other studies, I did my best for her. She gave me confidence in my natural gifts and even revealed unsuspected assets. "I know, Patsy, that you feel entirely too tall for your age, which I admit you are, but when you get older you will realize it is a great advantage."

My enthusiasm for dramatics was becoming contagious. I would present my monologues to the neighborhood kids, and soon anybody who could walk, crawl—or watch—was eligible to become part of my own little theater group. I would get my friends to sing and dance and even act—always with me. Our shows would be presented out in the front yard and on our porch and in our basement. We could have continual afternoon and evening performances, rain or shine. Mother and Daddy, the whole family in fact, but especially Aunt Maude, were heroic audiences. Even my sister took an interest.

My plots were always very complex, and the gorier the better. One afternoon I set up my two featured players in the window of a bathroom. Only their heads were in view above the sill. Then I wrapped a bright red ribbon around their bare necks and dipped a huge butcher knife into tomato ketchup. I gave my actors their directions and told them I would be back as soon as I could find a willing audience. A little neighbor girl was walking up the street and I knew this was my catch. "I have something amazing to show you," I said temptingly. When we got back to the stage, I grabbed her by the arm and swung my dripping butcher knife over her head. "You are going to die!" I cried out. "Say your prayers!"

The two heads picked up their cue and popped into view. "Don't do it! Don't do it! Oh! Look what she did to us!"

The effect was sensational. She was utterly horrified. She wrenched herself free, her dress blotched with ketchup stains, and ran home as fast as her legs would carry her. I was absolutely thrilled with myself. I did feel sorry, though, that the little girl's mother would never again let her daughter come near the Neal house. She had no appreciation for the arts.

Things were changing around me now, things that I had taken for granted would always be the same. Even visits to Packard were over now that Pappy and Mammy had died. Aunt Ima met the man of her dreams, R. E. Lee, and moved out to her own home. And we finally bought our own house. Things were changing inside me as well. When I spent the weekend with Aunt Ima and her new bridegroom, my first period arrived. That night, R. E.

came to me in my dreams and made passionate love to me. I was finding there were things I could not tell Aunt Ima, either.

My monologues graduated from the front yard to Aunt Maude's drawing room, and my audience was growing. I was becoming quite popular and the Knoxville Social Club invited me to give a reading. I carefully prepared my best monologues. There would be sketches from various plays and *The Wingless Victory*. But I would need a dramatic surprise for my encore. I had seen *Gone With the Wind*. Surely I could find something in Scarlett O'Hara that would be properly dramatic and even a little shocking. I had my nose in that book every spare minute.

The occasion called for an evening dress. I had never worn one before. Aunt Maude bought it for me. Daddy thought I was beautiful. The club thought I was sensational. They applauded and called me back for more. Then I hit them with my encore: "Lawdy, Lawdy, Miss Scarlett . . . I don't know nuthin' 'bout birthin' babies!"

I surprised them all right, those prim and proper ladies. Their fans began to quiver. "My land, she's doing a nigra!"

But they not only applauded, they cheered.

That night Aunt Maude started the first of many scrapbooks on me. On the first page she pasted the program. In big letters at the top it said: MISS PATSY NEAL READER IN RECITAL.

I did not have a big social conscience, but I knew I hated to see anybody get stepped on. In those days, buses in Knoxville were still segregated. I felt so disgusted every time I would get on one and sit down in the front and see other people herded to the back like they were contaminated. It was just plain wrong. So one day I gathered all my courage, stood up and marched to the back of the bus, and sat down among the blacks and waited for the impact. Not a single white turned around. Not one of the blacks even looked up. At my stop I quietly slipped off the bus. I guess no one took me seriously except when I was onstage.

After my triumph at the Knoxville Social Club, every

club in the city began to call on me. Aunt Maude became my manager, adding names to the list of places where I had appeared. The Y Men's Club, the University of Tennessee Faculty Players, the TVA Technical Men's Club, the Fountain City Sanders, and one that gave her particular pleasure, Cumberland College, her alma mater. I did *Open House* by Florence Ryerson and Colin Clements for Cumberland College and won the Tennessee State Award for dramatic reading. We were all disappointed that I could not go to the national meet, but it was canceled because of the war.

These appearances gave me a new sense of confidence that carried over at school. I entered speech contests and won awards for dramatic readings, and even took on directing the High School Thespians in their big production of *Jane Eyre*. I was blossoming physically, too. I could now out-bosom Kathryn Stubley.

I was not a member of the elite at Knoxville High. The girls who belonged to the grand families also belonged to the oldest club in school. No one got in without a blood test and it had to be blue. Mary Emma, Kathryn, Charlcey, Gloria, Sarah Bryer and I were *not* asked to be members, so we decided to establish a club of our own. We called ourselves "The Sophilites." We were like a gaggle of geese with one concerted purpose, to give one another social confidence.

I was absolutely thrilled when I got an invitation to my first school dance. The boy was shorter than I, but I did not mind in the least. Daddy gave me money for a new dress and I told all my girlfriends. I was ecstatic. Then, four days before the dance, Charlcey told me that this boy was planning to take another girl.

"He is not! How do you know?" I cried.

"Everybody knows," she said. I fled for home.

How dare he invite me and then chicken out and invite somebody else! There I'd be, all dressed up in my brandnew dress and he wouldn't come. No, if he said he was going to take me, then he was going to do it, even if we had the worst time of our lives. I decided the only thing to do was call his mother.

"He should do what he said! He is not going to step on me!" I cried into the phone. "I have my new dress. Make him take me to the dance!"

And she did. You have never seen such an angry boy. It *was* the worst night of our lives.

Thank God for Frank Ball. I met him during summer vacation in the Great Smoky Mountains. Frank was a year older than I. He was a member of the ROTC, great fun, a little plump and perfectly acceptable to mothers. He gave me my first sweet kiss. Later when he went to the University of Tennessee, he gave me his Sigma Chi pin.

The momentous decision to be *an actress* and not just a monologuist came while I was watching a play put on by the Tennessee Valley Players, the local little theater group. I confess it was not their art that attracted me. It was their leading man. Wesley Davis was his name. He was gorgeous, and I vowed to become part of their group. Mother and Daddy were agreeable as long as it did not interfere with my schoolwork. With the help of my friend Gloria, I was sure I could pull in passing grades. I got a part at once, the lead in a romantic comedy opposite my intended. It was such a perfect setup for romance. But offstage my hero didn't give me a tumble. He already had a girlfriend.

Knoxville High School's Patsy Neal made her debut with the Tennessee Valley Players and just about walked off with the show. She had grace and poise; her reactions were well timed and natural; her reading was nicely pointed, and her voice projection was splendid.

Malcolm Miller was the most important theater critic in Knoxville. He not only encouraged me through his lovely reviews, he actually offered to help. He suggested that I set my sights on the Barter Theatre in Abingdon, Virginia, during my next summer vacation. He himself would write to Robert Porterfield, the Barter's director, and plead my cause.

CHAPTER FIVE

Everybody in show business knew about the Barter Theatre. It was a very successful group that Robert Porterfield had started during the Depression. The audiences at that time had no money so they brought ham or fish or corn-on-the-cob as their admission fee, hence the name.

That summer of 1942, I had just finished my junior year at Knoxville High and, thanks to Malcolm Miller's persistence, was to be an apprentice at the Barter. Mother and Daddy showed their approval by gifting me with a grand suitcase. It was to be the first time I had been away from home alone.

I was not the least bit homesick. I was in the magical aura of a kind of royalty—real theater people. Among them were Margaret Phillips, Elizabeth Wilson and Phyllis Adams. Phyllis's daddy was very rich and had a fabulous New York apartment.

Within a short time I was totally involved in the activities of the group. I started out moving props and then I held the prompting book and was even assistant stage manager. Then I did small parts. Finally, I got the lead in Robert Ardrey's fantasy *Thunder Rock,* which Frances Farmer had done on Broadway.

Broadway! Oh, how I wanted to know about Broadway! I hounded anyone in the group who had worked there, even if they only had walk-ons. I *had* to go to New

York. I would have to figure out a way to spring that one on the family. Phyllis and I began cooking up a plan for me to visit her.

Barter Theatre productions sometimes went on the road and—I could not believe it—we were going to play *Thunder Rock* in Knoxville.

Mother and Daddy invited the whole cast to our new home for dinner. Mother worked for days adding every little touch she could think of to make it fancy. After all, the *theater* was coming! When the immense bus finally pulled up in front of our apartment building and we piled out, Mother's smile dissolved like a crumbling cookie. We had just come from putting up the set and looked like bums tramping into a soup kitchen. Still, Mother and Daddy were perfectly darling and made us feel welcome. One of the girls leaned over and, within earshot of Daddy, quipped, "I don't know what you were talking about the other day, Pat. I think you have a very *good* family!" I was mortified. Like a typical teenager, I had talked my family down. Nothing really terrible. I think I felt they weren't sophisticated enough, that my new theater friends might find them a little "country." Nevertheless, I decided not to bring up New York just yet.

My girlfriends from Knoxville High were very impressed seeing me come home in such distinguished company. But secretly, they had only one burning question. Alone and on my own for the first time, had I done *It*? Petting was as far as any respectable girl would ever go at KHS in 1942. But we loved to *talk* about going all the way. I had made up my mind even before going to the Barter Theatre that I was going to find out a little more about this business of sex. I had fancied the experience in my imagination and was sure it would be the greatest thrill of my life. I had heard the facts of life from Aunt Ima and gotten the spice from the girls at school, but the cold truth was I had never seen a male unclothed except the undiapered Pete and that one little boy down in the cellar. I certainly had never slept with one, clothed or unclothed, and the thought was as fascinating as it was frightening.

One of the young actors had caught my eye. I had been mooning over him all season and I just couldn't stand it any longer. I went to his room late at night after the performance and we sat and talked about the theater. We continued this for over a week. He didn't once try to kiss me. I felt like I was failing completely. One night when I knocked, the boy was already in bed. I took off my shoes and crawled in with him.

When I asked nervously if it was all right if I stayed, he answered, "Well, sure, Patsy, you can stay if you want, but I do have to get some sleep." Before I left the theater that summer I learned that he did not like girls. I had heard about homosexuals at school, but had never met one in Knoxville.

The Barter season ended. It was a wonderful experience. For fifty-five cents—or the equivalent in food, for the theater still honored its original policy—people saw me in *French Without Tears*, *Letters to Lucerne*, *Family Portrait* and *No Boys Allowed*.

I went back home, and outwardly my life was much the same as it had been. Except for some very sad news.

"Patsy, do you know who just died? That man from the Tennessee Valley Players. The one you liked so much." I couldn't believe it. That beautiful Wesley. Cornelia's lovely promise of trumpets awakening the dead from their sleep didn't help now.

The only thing that helped was to talk to Wesley's mother. I liked her very much and talking about him seemed to take away the terrible sting of his absence. After his funeral I visited her often.

One night when I returned home after a suppertime talk about Wesley, I lay in bed a long time listening to the sound of my own breathing. What was death like? Would you see nothing? Hear nothing? Wesley's body would be cold now. I felt such aloneness. It seemed unreal because my own body was so alive. I put my hand to my breast and felt it, warm and living. I allowed my hand to caress my body. I had never done that before. I could almost hear my mother: "You mustn't touch yourself, Patsy."

* * *

I continued to go to school and do my monologues, but inside I was burning to go to New York. I remembered Phyllis's plot to have me visit her during spring break. But how could I get Mother and Daddy to agree? Emily Mahan provided the key. She told Daddy it would be a good experience for me. After all, Emily had been to New York herself. And he agreed.

When my train pulled into Grand Central Station I thought I had finally arrived on those golden streets. It seemed to me that everyone I had met at Barter was there. Phyllis's home was exactly like the millionaires' homes in the movies. Fifteen rooms! Carpets so plush you almost lost your balance. Gold picture frames and real silk sheets. And butlers! I was astonished that food was served from a tray and not passed.

The theater district blazed with the names of Ingrid Bergman, Helen Hayes and Katharine Cornell. I sent a silent message to my daddy: I will write my name in those lights and I will bring you to New York to see it.

The most gorgeous moment for me was seeing Katharine Cornell in *The Three Sisters*. I was absolutely shaking after the performance. I knew I had to find a way to meet her. I headed for the stage door and somehow got past the guard. I stepped onto hallowed ground—backstage of a Broadway theater. I located the star's dressing room and knocked. She answered the door herself!

"Hello, I'm Patsy Neal from Tennessee, Miss Cornell. Everyone says I look like you."

The great lady eyed me for a moment, then smiled delicately and said, "Well—perhaps a little younger."

After I returned home, going *back* to New York was the only thing I could think about or talk about. Mother and Daddy were equally determined that I would go to college first. That seemed utterly ridiculous to me. Going to *school* to learn acting! *My* classroom could only be the real theater. We made a deal. I could go for the summer to the Priscilla Beach Theater Group in Plymouth, Massachusetts, if I would look into a college for the fall. They conceded that I could major in speech.

Northwestern was suggested. It had an excellent

speech program and it was relatively close to home. It was late to submit an application and I secretly hoped I would be turned down. Evanston, Illinois, seemed a roundabout way to my dream.

But I was accepted.

En route to Plymouth, I stopped in New York City. Absolutely everyone there had the same message for me. "Stay away from Plymouth! They just want people to carry scenery up there, Patsy. You'll waste your time." The Priscilla Beach Theater Group did not seem the place to be that summer. My good friend Gloria Lucas was now living in Brooklyn with her aunt and uncle. She came up with a brilliant idea. "Why don't you ask if you can stay with me this summer and see if you can land a job?" I called Mother and Daddy and I begged. Rather effectively. Six weeks in New York was a risk, but they would take it, especially since I would be staying with Gloria's family. I neglected to mention that this living arrangement would be temporary. Gloria and I were already scouting for an apartment in Greenwich Village.

I was really going to be an actress now. I had my résumé ready. Someone must be looking for a five-foot-eight-inch, hazel-eyed brownette beauty, 135 pounds in the right places, who could act any range from sixteen to sixty.

At the crack of dawn I got out of bed as if I were in Olympic training and began my rounds. I went from casting office to casting office, from agent to agent and heard what all beginning actors hear. The agents said they couldn't see me unless I had a part. The casting directors said they couldn't see me for a part unless I had an agent.

That summer I traipsed up and down Madison Avenue, Broadway and Fifth Avenue from Eighth Street to Eightieth. And I never got a job.

I might still be on Minetta Lane if NiNi hadn't come to visit. She took one look at the Village and immediately told Mother and Daddy.

I was sent for at once.

CHAPTER SIX

My love affair with New York was put on the back burner when, at seventeen, I entered Northwestern and saw what the university offered.

Since I had registered late, I could not get into the main dormitory. It was a hidden blessing because I was put into McFarland House, a small residence for freshmen, with only sixteen other girls.

My sister had prepared me for the first important decision of university life—joining the right sorority—and of course it would be hers, Delta Delta Delta. "Each sorority gives an open house," she told me, "and all the freshmen come. There is a little book by the door and you are invited to sign it *if* they like you." Rush week came. I dressed to the teeth and began my rounds of sorority teas. I went from house to house, charming them all, but my sights were trained on Kappa Kappa Gamma. Deep down I felt disgusted by the sorority caste system, but not because I was excluded. I got invitations from almost every house. Kappa Alpha Theta wanted me, Delta Delta Delta wanted me, Pi Beta Phi wanted me. Every house but Kappa Kappa Gamma. It was the only one that declined. The best had turned me down. I was furious. I finally settled for Pi Beta Phi, and once I gave myself to the pledge, I felt there was no other sorority in the world. So, up yours, Kappa Kappa Gamma!

I faithfully sent letters to my dear Frank Ball, whose pin I still had, and who was now in the army. I wrote him all about the terrible snowstorms we were having and how great everybody was to loan me boots and extra heavy woollies, and about the hairy episodes of college life, like spring-cleaning the freshman house from top to bottom. I even wrote about dating this or that fellow, always careful to explain it was only social from my side.

Frank answered often, but part of one letter really hit home. "Patsy," he wrote, "don't you know there's a war going on?"

Frank was very right. I was conscious of the war, but I really did not know what was going on. I knew the buses and streetcars were constantly crowded with boys in uniform and we had to use ration stamps for everything. We were deprived just enough to feel heroic, not enough to suffer. I also knew that so many young men never returned from service. We constantly saw lists of those killed in action. But Frank was right. How few of us at home realized what war really meant.

It was April 16, 1944. The excitement of the sorority initiation had been dampened by sudden tragedy. The girl across the hall from me had lost her mother in a car crash. We all sat talking to her for hours in that gripping web of pain that draws people together when death strikes close to home. Then each of us went to bed, and I lay there a long time wondering what I would do if it had been my mother.

I was just falling asleep when I heard the telephone ring in the dormitory. It was midnight.

Somehow, I just knew it was for me.

"Hey, Patsy! Phone!"

I walked out into the dark hallway and down the stairs. At the landing I began to tremble. I lifted the receiver, and before I heard the words, I felt the piercing blow.

"Patsy, your daddy died tonight." I remember when my mother said that, my heart leapt out of me, hit the wall and came back. The words made no sense. What she said could not be true. "It was very sudden. A heart

41

attack. He died on his way to the hospital in an ambulance." My heart just kept going from my chest to the wall and back again. She could not possibly be talking about my father. My daddy!

The housemother and two of the girls got me onto a train. I would meet Mother at Aunt Maude's house. I would not meet Daddy there. Every click of the train wheels said "Daddy." I would fall asleep and wake again into the lulling monotony of this strange new prayer, "Daddy-Daddy-Daddy."

In Williamsburg I took the familiar turn to Aunt Maude's, from the main street up to the split in the road and past the church—that's where Daddy would be tomorrow—and down the left fork to her house. Mother was waiting in the room where I had given my monologues. She was standing by the window all alone. The afternoon sun had finally broken through and haloed her black hair. She looked so young. She was only forty-four.

Whenever anyone died, I always went to the mother. This time it was my own. I put my arms around her and she began to sob quietly. "Oh, Coot—what will I ever do without you?"

Everyone in town came to Coot Neal's funeral. I was stunned by the overwhelming display of flowers. The people were familiar faces. I knew most of them. It took a long time for all of them to file by the open coffin. Then it was my turn.

I had never seen a dead person before, except long ago, in an accident on the road in front of our house. But that was a stranger. Not my daddy. I pressed my fingers against those great cheeks and they didn't give now. This great fat man was now an enormous stone. He was a rock.

After the service we all went back to Aunt Maude's house. I saw Grandpa Neal and it broke my heart to watch that old man weeping for his young son of only forty-nine. It might have helped him to find his grandson Pete in the church, but Aunt Maude would not hear of the little boy having to face such an ordeal. How wrong she was.

The table was laden with food. It is fantastic, the cooking that takes place in those southern houses when people die. I made such a pig of myself it was appalling. My heart was broken and I ate and ate to kill the pain.

My only consolation was Frank Ball. He came home on furlough during summer vacation. I would talk to him for hours about Daddy and then bury myself in his arms. Frank was the kindest man. That summer I grew to love him.

Back at school I wrote:

Dearest Mother,

I guess that life is just a series of dreams—bad and good intermingled. Daddy was just the first to awaken. So now we must be brave and go on doing the things that he would want us to do. Maybe someday we can accomplish the thing he lived for and dreamed of for us. How can we fail? For years we had the most beautiful, lovable, kind and faithful inspiration that anyone could hope for. God gave to me the great gift—the great honor of being your and Daddy's child; in every way I must repay him.

I will not believe that my Daddy died. Men like "Coot" Neal do not die. They live on in every heart, in every place, in every thing that they have touched. He is my "rock of ages," the rock upon which anything good about me has been built. All I have ever known is, "Do it for Daddy."

I love you,
Patsy

CHAPTER SEVEN

Whi hen I met her in 1944, Alvina Krause was a vital force at Northwestern. Her acting classes were reserved for sophomores and upperclassmen. I had looked forward for a whole year to my first day in one of those precious classes. "Do you have any idea what it means to be an actor?" she challenged. "An actor must be a little more and a little better than anyone else. He must be able to play a genius today and a fool tomorrow and understand both. And do it on cue. I teach for those who want to be professional. If you are looking for glamour or fun, this is not the place for you." I certainly had nothing against glamour or fun and I knew I was talented, but I also knew that was not enough. I was ready to work my tail off for a career. I had found my champion.

By early spring I was a member of the University Theater and the Radio Playshop, and something called the Wildcat Council. I was also a model for the *Purple Parrot* campus magazine. My sorority chose me to be its candidate for the junior prom Syllabus Queen contest. George Petty of "Petty Girl" fame was going to be the head judge on a panel of illustrious radio personalities that included Don McNeill of "The Breakfast Club," Franklin McCormack of NBC and Virginia Payne of the "Ma Perkins" show.

Dearest Mother,

Well, I guess I was born under a lucky star. I wish you could have been here. I was so shocked. I really looked good, but when I saw how beautiful everyone else looked I didn't think I had a chance. I guess the reason I got it was I happen to be gifted with a string of gab. I had a marvelous time talking with the judges. And I can put on a good show occasionally, too.

Everyone looked scared and their smiles were forced. And—you know me—at that time I was sure that I hadn't won and I was gonna make them all sorry—so I came out with perfect posture, head held high, and the best smile that I have.

When they said "Miss Pat Neal, Pi Beta Phi," I nearly collapsed. Gosh, it was wonderful!

Now—I can tell you. Shirley, my roommate, is in the hospital with the mumps. Have I ever had them?

Much love,
Patsy

When the reporters for the *Knoxville Journal* called my mother, she said, "I am more than delighted that Patsy won the honor, because she was chosen for her personality and poise as well as her beauty." That was Mother. I like to think I won for my sex appeal.

After the contest, the Chicago Fashion Industries voted me one of their ten best-dressed women. I thought that was a bit much myself. I really did not have that many clothes and I never thought I put things together all that well. But I guess I had gotten a lot of publicity, so they put me on their list. The thing I liked best about the article they wrote was that they said I looked like Katharine Cornell.

Helen Horton was the queen of the drama department when I entered as a lowly freshman. I looked up to her and was really overjoyed when, during my sophomore year, we both landed parts in Claudia Webster's production of *Twelfth Night*. Helen was cast as Viola and I got

45

to play Olivia. From the moment we first met, it worked between us. A bond was set that would last a lifetime.

Tennessee Williams's masterpiece *The Glass Menagerie* played at the Civic Theater in Chicago prior to its Broadway opening, and the university's publicity department decided to cash in by arranging for Helen and me to be photographed backstage with its star, Eddie Dowling. We would be in our Shakespearean costumes, supposedly seeking advice from the veteran actor. I thought the idea was ridiculous. But the shot got published all over.

There was a side benefit to the trip that made that day memorable. I got to see Laurette Taylor in *Glass Menagerie*. It was, and is, the finest performance I have ever seen in my life. Absolutely inspiring. I prayed I could be that good.

For years Alvina Krause had nurtured a dream of starting a theater of her own. She found an old building standing empty near the mountain resort of Eagles Mere, Pennsylvania. The opening season's company would be limited. I was last in rank, but I knew Alvina liked my work. I was elated to see my name on the list.

That summer was fun. I spent a lot of time running around town getting furniture for props and making tuna casserole as a member of the kitchen team, but those duties did not keep me from acting. I worked like a dog to lose my southern accent for Noel Coward's *Blithe Spirit*.

Talent scouts found their way to Eagles Mere and flashed temptations of Hollywood, but I wanted only the real thing, the theater. I was more interested in an offer made to a girl in the company who was even taller than I was. She must have been about six feet. One of the scouts said he would suggest her name to the Theatre Guild for Eugene O'Neill's *A Moon for the Misbegotten*. The main character was just her size, and there would be auditions soon. I couldn't believe it when she said she didn't want to go to New York. She had to be crazy. Wouldn't *I* love to show up for that audition in her place!

My most vivid memory of Eagles Mere had nothing to do with theater.

A local couple, a photographer and his wife, approached me and asked to take some photographs. It never occurred to me to ask for the photographer's credentials. I was simply very flattered. A few days later, by a lovely stream, I posed and posed while he snapped away.

My head was completely turned when they wanted me for a second sitting. His wife said, "My dear, you are so gorgeous. You know, all really fine art is best expressed in the nude form. And you would be a work of art." I told her I could never take off my clothes in front of anybody, but the lady insisted. "You must understand. My husband is a master photographer. This is not taking your clothes off. This is revealing your body as a thing of beauty. I'll stand up on the road and make absolutely sure no one can possibly see you."

I struggled. I was terrified to show myself naked. A good southern girl would never do it. But I knew my figure was beautiful, and the glory of being immortalized by such an artist was too much to resist. By the time he finished I had quite lost my nervousness.

"We have accomplished something beautiful together," he said. "Let us consummate this moment forever." And then he grabbed for me. I dashed for the bushes and my pile of clothes.

During the ride back with them I was so embarrassed I could not look up. I kept wondering if his wife knew what he had said.

That evening I cried my eyes out. I felt utterly stupid. One of the students, Priscilla Weaver, saw my red eyes and asked what was going on. I spilled out the whole dreadful story. She said there was only one thing to do—get those negatives and destroy them.

The photographer was not as unpleasant as I expected. With only the slightest resistance, the man destroyed the negatives, cutting up strip after strip right before my eyes. "Oh, thank you! Thank you!" I cried. And left, comforted.

47

"Did you get the negatives?" Priscilla demanded.

"Oh, he cut them up! I watched him do it!"

She was aghast. "How do you know they were *your* negatives? Did you actually *see* them?"

For months, for years, really, I was terrified that someday pictures of Patricia Neal in the nude would pop up from the murky depths of my past. They have not. Yet.

My Eagles Mere summer ended with greater pain. Mother sent me a copy of a letter. The original had gone to Frank Ball, Sr., from the headquarters of Second Battalion, 21st Infantry. It was not an unusual letter. Many families had received one just like it between 1942 and 1945.

Oh my God, my brave lieutenant, my beautiful Frank. I always knew I couldn't keep from being hurt badly by the war. I thought my life was over. I cried for months. Our family had gotten a letter, too. My cousin Fitz Neal, Jr., had been shot down in his tiny plane. I wept for them and for Daddy and for the unfairness of God to take them all with no warning.

Aunt Maude was willing to continue my tuition at Northwestern. But I really did not want to return to school, and there was little reason to go home. I began to think about that part for a tall girl.

I got my train ticket and went directly to New York. I did not even go home for clothes.

CHAPTER EIGHT

his time New York was home ground, and I had $300 in my pocket. The first thing I had to do was find a cheap place to stay. Helen Horton was sharing an apartment on the West Side with three other girls. They needed one more to make the rent and I moved in.

The second thing was to call the Theatre Guild to find out when auditions were scheduled for *A Moon for the Misbegotten*. Not for a while, I was told. So I began the regime of making the rounds, smile by smile, flirt by flirt. Flirting was a tool of the trade and I was becoming an expert. I usually ate in Horn & Hardart or the Genius Club, where all the out-of-work actors hung out. I had learned that if you wanted to know what was going on in town, you had to be in touch with this underground network. It was also a good way to meet actors who needed scene partners for auditions.

Three of my new roommates were from Northwestern. Natalie Brown worked as a proofreader for *The New Yorker*. Natalie would wake me up every morning as she was leaving for work. But since she did it with a "Get up, beauty!" we got on. Irene Petroff was "Petey" to everyone. She kept the purse and did all the shopping. The staples were doughnuts, cheese, soda crackers, peanut butter, popcorn and tuna fish. I can't for the life of me remember anything about the fourth girl, except that she had once worked in a defense plant in California. There were four beds in the bedroom and a sofa in the sitting room. The last person home at night got the sofa.

Even though $300 went a long way in 1945, it didn't go far enough. I did not want to write home for money, and I did not want to face Petey with the slightest hint that I could not pay my part. I had a few callbacks for readings, but that was all. Hardly a nibble professionally. I did help a young actor do a screen test, but of course, there was no money in it. The only answer was to get a job that would not interfere with my real work—making rounds, taking classes and seeing, free if possible, every play I could.

I started slicing pie and scooping ice cream in a Greenwich Village luncheonette. That added $5.50 a day to the kitty. Dinner dates helped—somebody else paid.

About six weeks later I got an unexpected call from the agent who handled the actor I had worked with on the screen test. He thought he could get me a job.

The Voice of the Turtle had been a major hit on Broadway; it was a comedy about a young actress who fills in for an older friend on a date and ends up falling in love with the guy. The producer was looking for an actress who could understudy both the leads, Martha Scott and Vicki Cummings. There were masses of us trying out. I read bits of both parts to the handful of shadowy figures in the front row of the empty theater.

That evening, my "new agent," Maynard Morris, called. I had gotten the job.

It seems that of all those people out front, Alfred de Liagre was the only one who had wanted me. John van Druten, who was staging his own play, didn't think I was right for either role. Even Mr. de Liagre's fiancée thought her future husband had quite lost his sanity. Fortunately for me, Alfred de Liagre was producing the play.

I was delirious with joy. I would be making $150 a week!

Mr. de Liagre's interest continued. "Pat Neal," he mused. "It shouldn't be 'Pat.' You should be 'Patricia.' That's a beautiful name."

I became Patricia Neal.

And I was about to fall in love.

There was just enough nip in the air as I walked along briskly toward Walgreen's. I scanned the counter for my friend, another struggling actress. She was up for a good part. I hoped she would have good news.

But the look on her face was desolate. "Did you lose the part?" I asked.

"Oh, Pat, I am in *real* trouble," she said. My friend was pregnant and wanted to get an abortion. The word shook me to the bone. At home you would never even say it out loud. "It happened just once. Just one time. You know what I mean?"

"Sure," I said, but I didn't know what she meant at all. For all my flirting and big talk, I had been faithful to Mother's morality.

My girlfriend had no money for an abortion, but had heard of a doctor who arranged for them. The girls would then work for him afterward to pay for it.

"What an evil man," I blurted out, but she stopped me.

"You're dead wrong. He's a good man. Some girls just might go off and do something really stupid, like kill themselves."

The hospital room, however, would cost $300. We would get the money somehow, I promised. I was already planning to find an excuse to wire Aunt Maude.

The money order came. The whole thing was over a few days later and soon my friend was at her job in the medical office. I discovered that the doctor in question was a general practitioner, and many young actresses saw him because he didn't charge much and gave terms for payment. One evening I came by to pick her up and was in the waiting room when a young man came in. His eyes met mine immediately. They were beautiful, and his smile was handsome. He sat down next to me and introduced himself. He was the doctor's son and was interning at a local hospital. We talked until my friend approached, and I stood up to leave. He asked if he could call me and

51

I gave him my number. I turned to my girlfriend as we walked down the hall and said, "Isn't he just gorgeous?"

"Yes," she replied, smiling, "everybody's in love with him."

During my first months in New York I went out with a lot of men. I was always "making contacts." That is part of the business of breaking into the business. You went out once or twice with anybody who asked you and kept them all on a casual string that someday might be attached to something important. I was not going to sleep with any jerk who came along and certainly would never do it to get a job, which had as much to do with my pride as my virginity. I believed in my talent. And I knew I wanted *that* experience with somebody I really loved.

My young doctor and I began dating, and I found myself falling in love for the first time since Frank Ball.

During the day I was making the rounds again. Helen couldn't understand it. "Heavens, Pat, you *have* a job!" True, but I was always sure there was a better one around the corner.

One afternoon at the Genius Club I heard that the Theatre Guild was finally holding readings for *A Moon for the Misbegotten*. I phoned the Guild and said that a talent scout at Eagles Mere had told me to call. I got an appointment to meet Dudley Diggs, the director.

I was ushered into a large, bare room. Mr. Diggs looked up at me and smiled. "I'm sorry, Miss Neal, you're too young and really too short." It may have been the only time in my entire life that I heard that. As I got up to go, two men and two women came into the room. To my surprise, Mr. Diggs made introductions. In that lucky moment, I met Miss Theresa Helburn and Mr. Lawrence Langner—they *were* the Theatre Guild—and Mr. and Mrs. Eugene O'Neill!

"Oh!" I said. Face to face with the greatest playwright of his time—and all I could say was, "Oh!"

When I got home there was a message waiting. I was to call for an appointment to read for Eugene O'Neill.

I met with Mr. O'Neill several times before the actual reading. He was tall and thin, getting old of course, but to me he looked sensational. And I loved his plays. I showered him with attention and he liked me. His interest was not for a zealous fan or even a promising professional. I think his interest was personal and he just hoped I was talented, too. He even invited me to have supper sometime with him and his wife, Carlotta.

One meeting took place on my birthday. I was twenty. As we were leaving the Guild, I impulsively said to him, "It is my birthday today. Why don't you take me for a chocolate soda?"

"It has been a long time since I had a soda, Pat," he answered.

"Please, please," I persisted.

"All right, I guess O'Neill can afford a soda," he laughed.

We went to Schrafft's down the street and found a booth in the back. After we ordered I remember pulling out my cigarettes. I started to go for a match, but he caught my hand and reached into his pocket for his own. He struck one, but as he put it to the tip of my cigarette, his hand shook so badly that it went out. He struck another match and again it went out. I became aware that the shaking must be an illness. Again and again he tried. I sat there and waited until finally he lit the cigarette. He carefully put the matches away and smiled. "You know," he said, "if I were young, I would love you very much."

When the audition was over, I knew I would not get the part. I said goodbye with no deep regrets. I had made a very special friend.

I walked downstairs, collapsed on a chair and had a smoke. My attention was taken by a man at the phone. He was talking about a play that was going to be done in Westport, Connecticut, during the summer, and he was describing one of the characters. "She should come from the Ozarks." My ears perked up. "Yeah, a hillbilly type." When he finished I approached him.

"I'm a hillbilly. Will I do?" He looked me up and down.

"You just might!" He took my number.

* * *

The young doctor and I were together constantly now. We had already said all the lovely flowery things, and one night the inevitable moment came.

"Pat," he whispered softly, "will you come home with me tonight?"

I froze with fear. "I really can't," I stammered.

"It's a beautiful thing to have happen."

"It's just that in our family you should be married."

Every argument I could think of he cunningly wiped away. Still I resisted, and he reluctantly agreed to take me home. We walked in silence.

After several blocks, I stopped and asked, "Do you love me more than anyone?"

"I do, Pat," he whispered, "yes, I do."

"Let's go to your apartment."

I stood in the middle of the room not knowing what to do and feeling very awkward. I could not bring myself to remove my clothing. He began to unbutton my top. "It's the most normal thing in the world. It's the way God intended it to be." He kept talking until I was naked with him under the covers.

It would be very easy to say that my young doctor had talked me into losing my virginity, but that would hardly be honest. I *wanted* to get talked into it. Virginity did not mean purity or innocence to me. It meant my mother still had the screws on me. God was *pleased* when I did not eat this or did not drink that or did not go there or did not talk to that person or did not feel a certain way in my body. No, guilt for a loss of virtue never occurred to me. I had found sex. I had found love. I was going to be the doctor's wife.

Our romance bloomed. I was not thinking about how I might handle a marriage and a career. We loved each other and that would make it all come together. I was also not worrying about getting pregnant. I had met his father, who had casually suggested that I come to see him on a professional visit "just to be sure everything is all right." I made the appointment.

After a few questions he began his examination to fit

me for a diaphragm. Then the disinterested motions of his professional hand stopped. I felt his touch. He was purposely arousing me. I knew I should not allow this. I didn't know what to do. I kept my eyes shut tight until it was over. He told me dryly that he just wanted to be sure I was clinically capable of orgasmic release. He gave me instructions for using the diaphragm and said, "There is no bill."

I left the office and shock finally turned to anger. I spilled out the story to my friend. "Don't let it get you," she laughed, "the old lizard gets his kicks with all the girls that way." I never spoke to my young doctor about it.

My agent called with a double dose of good news for my career. I would be understudying *Turtle* in the road company. And when I returned I would be doing two weeks of stock. The Theatre Guild wanted me for *Devil Takes a Whittler*. It was that hillbilly part. I remembered the man on the phone: "You just might do." He just happened to be the director.

During the days before the tour my young doctor seemed distant. I thought he was just reacting to my going away, so I didn't give the matter too much thought until I got back to New York. There was no message at the apartment and he did not call. I called him. He was pleasant, but his voice was strained. I could not imagine what was wrong. At last I asked him point-blank. There was a long moment of silence, which he finally shattered.

"Pat, I got married last week."

After I hung up, I was sick. I ached so badly with hurt, with betrayal. I needed to know why. I went to his small room at the hospital.

"Just tell me what happened," I pleaded. "I need to know."

"It was one of those family things, Pat," he tried to explain. "She's a childhood sweetheart, just right to be a doctor's wife. I never slept with her before we got married. I never did it with her while I was with you. I want you to know that."

"That's very consoling," I said.

"But it's not like it was with you. I just feel so frustrated." We sat in silence. I felt everything loving and beautiful in me twist into a hard knot. He finally said what was on his mind. "I want to give you beautiful sex once more. Please, Pat, I need you."

I didn't answer him. My humiliation and hurt turned to hard thoughts. *You lying bastard. I swear I'll never let myself believe again. But this is one way to get even with you. And her.* He got up and locked the door. I heard the click.

Beautiful sex. Why not, I thought. I started to unbutton my blouse. *Why the hell not?*

CHAPTER NINE

t was a stormy Tuesday when the stage doorman greeted me with, "You'd better get dressed. It looks like you're going on."

"Which one? I mean, which part?" I asked.

It was Vicki. She wasn't sick, she was caught in a blizzard. This is it, babe, I thought to myself as I applied the eyeliner just a little heavier than usual. I could feel nerves swell inside. It may have been only a few weeks since I had gotten the job, but I had been waiting for this moment forever. I knew I was ready. The stage manager called, "Five minutes." I tried to powder away the perspiration oozing through my makeup and took my place in the wings. Suddenly the stage door swung open. And there she stood.

"Oh no, Vicki, it can't be you!" I cried.

The dripping lady began to smile. "You break my heart, kid. You want to go on? Go on!"

I was about to give Vicki the biggest hug in the world when I suddenly realized that I had never rehearsed with Martha. "What about the leading lady?"

I shouldn't have asked. Vicki went to check. I could hear Miss Scott answer, "No, Vicki darling, I want *you* to go on. We'll hold the curtain."

I took off my dress, trying to hold back my tears. I was so upset, not only for losing the chance to go on, but for that burdensome conscience of mine that always made me blurt out the truth.

Vicki Cummings went down in my book as the rarest of actresses—an unselfish one—and a damned good human being.

I was starting to date a young actor named Bruce Hall when notice came that I was going to join the touring company of *Turtle* in Chicago. Bruce was going to the Coast anyway, so whatever romance was brewing would have to brew long-distance.

A few days after Christmas 1945 I arrived in the Windy City. Waiting for me was the best present since Daddy gave me drama lessons. I wrote home to Mother and Aunt Maude:

The most exciting day of my life! I was going shopping with K. T. (K. T. Stevens plays "Sally" and Hugh Marlowe plays "Bill" and Vivian Vance plays "Olive"). I called her and she told me that Vivian was leaving the show and that I was playing that night, New Year's Eve. You can imagine—the old pulse just stopped. I had a rehearsal with the stage manager and then one with Hugh and K. T.

Then I went on. I was *numb*! Somehow I gave a damn fine show. Helen was the only person I knew in the audience. She said to me afterward, "You know that part where you put your foot up on the ottoman? Well!! You have such an enormous hole in your right shoe!" They were my own shoes. I couldn't fit into Vivian's.

We had a special Tuesday matinee. I wasn't quite as good then and that night I was pretty bad. I don't know what happened but I rushed through it at one hundred miles per hour. I could have kicked myself.

Last night I redeemed myself with a *really good* performance. *Now* I *know* what I am doing! Not just stabbing in the dark. Hugh and Katy [K. T.] were awfully pleased. They decided I was ready for all the intricate little details. So after the show we went to Katy's room, had sandwiches, and rehearsed parts of it.

I can't begin to tell you how nice they have been to me. They have helped me every inch of the way.

It is really smart to have everyone like you in a show.

Mr. de Liagre will be here with the replacement next Tuesday, I think. So, I will play it until then. He will watch me play it. I've got to be good.

Katy and Hugh want him to let me go to California with them—just covering "Olive"—but all of us know he won't. He won't pay two understudies and the other girl has a run of the play contract. They don't like her and they (me, too) know she can't act.

Yesterday Hugh and I went to see *The Hasty Heart*. I loved the play. All the other casts were there. I met the cast of *Anna Lucasta*. They are wonderful! Wonderful actors and highly intelligent people. We are all going to have dinner together next Wednesday. That is an all-colored cast—so someone won't tell you and shock you.

Mother, after I talked to you I asked Katy about California. She said, "No, don't go, Pat. Get yourself a name first. Make them really want you for your talent. You're pretty enough to get a small contract with anyone, but you will be miserable. Go out there under good conditions." If anyone should know, Katy should. You know her father is Sam Wood, the big director. Katy changed her name and went onstage to do it on her own. He could have set her up in Hollywood.

I have to go to dinner now. I just wanted you to know how perfectly wonderful everything is. I think that I am the luckiest girl in the world. "I ain't afraid of nothing!" I think the gods are on my side.

Much Love,
Pat

P.S. I had to have new shoes so I bought really good ones, since Mr. de Liagre was footing the bill. I bought a pair of Delmans. I get to keep them after I am through.
P.P.S. Oh yes! I signed my first autograph last night —I signed *two*.

I played Chicago for two and a half weeks and Bruce was calling me long-distance all the time. It looked as if we were becoming a hot romance. Between the Chicago and Cincinnati runs I went home to Knoxville for a couple of days. NiNi was now dating a divine fellow named George Vande Noord. They seemed serious. I hoped so. For all the nagging between NiNi and me, we loved each other.

While I was in Knoxville my agent called to tell me that I had landed a part in a Broadway show called *Bigger Than Barnum*. The stars were Benny Baker and Chili Williams, and I would have fourth billing. I was thrilled and gave Mr. de Liagre my notice.

Bigger Than Barnum opened and closed in Boston the same week, which was no surprise, considering that the best line in the show belonged to a parrot. He would whistle, "Oh, say can you see?" as a girl's bra strap broke and her costume fell down. All of the women except me wore practically nothing. I was dressed in a high-necked tweed suit that made me look like someone in drag. I was more than grateful to see the whole tasteless mess go down the drain out of town. The night we closed I received a most welcome telegram. It was from Alfred de Liagre: YOUR JOB WITH THE TURTLE IS STILL OPEN. I was so happy and deeply touched. During my first year in New York, every time I left Alfred de Liagre's company to explore something else, he always asked me back. I was never without a job, thanks to his great kindness.

But I was still making only $150 a week and was still just an understudy. I found another cheap apartment a block away from Helen and Petey—a fourth-floor walk-up that looked out onto a wall. Cockroaches were always darting around the floor and in the bed, too. We *never* had bugs at home. The bathroom was down the hall and it was so revolting that one could only slip in and out as quickly as possible for the bare necessities. I would have to pass by an old hag on my floor who was always lurking like a giant bug in a nightgown. I felt so repulsed every time I saw her. I think that this is when I got my fear of growing old, poor and alone, a fear that persists to this day. And as soon as I saw the bathtub, I immediately made an arrangement to use my friends' tub whenever possible. Theirs had a board over it, making it into a table by day.

Bruce was back and we made a date to meet in the Astor Bar before I was due at the theater. For all our impassioned love letters and fevered phone conversations, the two of us just sat there looking at each other with absolutely nothing to say. Finally, Bruce broke the agonized silence. "Look, I don't like you much and you don't like me much, so let's call it off." I was so relieved.

Many months later I ran into Bruce on a street corner near the Astor and he invited me for a drink. He had a surprise for me. He wanted me to meet his bride, a girl he had met in California, an actress. Well, my curiosity was piqued. I couldn't wait to get a look at her. When we all sat down to tea she refused me a smile, even a glance, and I knew she must have thought I was still interested in him. It was, of course, impossible to explain at the time that there was no love lost between her bridegroom and me—and it would be almost sixteen years before Kim Stanley and I would meet again.

One afternoon, Helen asked if another Northwestern girl could stay with me. I had met Jean at school, but I didn't know her well, in spite of the fact that people used to tell us we looked like sisters. She was bright and funny, a good comedienne. She was also very lucky. The famous writer Charles MacArthur adored her, gave her a job as an understudy, and changed her last name from Verhagen to Hagen. I always liked her real name much better.

Jean and I hit it off right away and decided to move to another place about two blocks up that was bigger and brighter. It had its own bathroom, but the tub was always clogged with water, so we took sponge baths in the sink. The cockroaches had moved with us, too. But somehow we didn't mind.

The character Sally has a great line in *The Voice of the Turtle*. I never got to say it, but it was true: "It's when you're *out* of work, you need a nice place to live."

CHAPTER TEN

n *Devil Takes a Whittler,* I played a backwoods temptress who calls on the devil to help her take the whittler away from his wife. Miss Helburn and Mr. Langner of the Theatre Guild and Eugene O'Neill watched rehearsals and said I was great in the part. Mr. O'Neill thought I was good enough to suggest we talk about his new play, *A Touch of the Poet.* I had never gone to his house for that supper. Plans had been made, but were mysteriously canceled at the last minute. I always suspected it was Carlotta O'Neill who disinvited me.

Devil Takes a Whittler had only a two-week run in Westport, but those two weeks may have been the most important of my entire life, because Richard Rodgers and Lillian Hellman came to see the play.

My new agent called to say that Mr. Rodgers wanted me to come in for an interview. Rodgers and Hammerstein were producing a play called *Happy Birthday.* It was a comedy with masses of people in it. I was not right for any of them, but Mr. Rodgers invited me to have lunch sometime.

Several nights later, he dropped backstage at *Turtle,* where I was now waiting for Beatrice Pearson to break her neck. He stopped me on the stairs and whispered an invitation to lunch the following day.

It was a lovely lunch—somewhere at Radio City, I

think. The following night he was backstage, whispering again. We lunched the next day, and the day after that. By the third lunch, I was dead sure I knew exactly where he was heading, so I cut through the small talk with a good-natured jab.

"Mr. Rodgers, I know that you want to sleep with me, but I really can't sleep with you because you are a married man and I like your wife."

"How could you be thinking such a thing?" he sputtered.

"*I* am not thinking such a thing, *you* are." There was silence. "*Aren't* you?"

"What I want to talk to you about is a new play I'm doing. It's called *John Loves Mary*."

It was true, he did. The reading for *John Loves Mary* went very well and Mr. Rodgers wanted me for the lead. A date was set for contract signing.

The night before, however, Lillian Hellman's agent came backstage with an invitation for me to read for Miss Hellman's new play, *Another Part of the Forest*. I thanked her but told her that there was no reason to audition, because I had a firm job offer.

The lady was aghast. "*I* am *not* telling Miss Hellman no. *You'll* have to tell her no yourself."

"Okay, okay," I agreed obediently, "I'll audition."

Who knows? I thought. This might be that better job around the corner.

There was the usual line of girls waiting backstage at the Fulton Theater. "Oh, no!" a familiar voice cried out in despair. "No one will stand a chance at this audition." It was Helen Horton. I started to sit down next to her, but the stage manager called me to the front of the line. "I don't want to see you," Helen hissed, "not for some time." She was serious. She was angry with me!

I did not see Lillian Hellman out front, but I was absolutely sure she was there somewhere. Someone handed me the script. I was asked to read the part of Regina Hubbard. It was the same character Tallulah Bankhead had made famous in *The Little Foxes*, only in *Forest*, Regina was twenty years younger. As I scanned the character description the stage manager whispered, "Regina wouldn't do anything more underhanded than cut your throat."

Kermit Bloomgarden, the play's producer, was on-stage right after I finished reading. His first words were, "We want you."

I was stunned. Two Broadway offers in twenty-four hours! I knew immediately, instinctively, which part was the one for me. Regina, sight unseen, had more range and potential. Besides, I wanted to be a dramatic actress and I feared that once you got typed in comedy, it would be very hard to break away. And frankly, I didn't think I was very funny.

The next day I faced Mr. Rodgers and told him I had another job and was turning him down. He was flabbergasted. But then, so was I.

What are the odds that two roommates in Manhattan would get into the same show? Just days after I was cast, Jean breathlessly announced that she was also going to be in *Another Part of the Forest*. We hugged and cried and both sensed it was more than luck.

Jean and I decided to celebrate with our first lunch at the famous Sardi's.

We were hysterical, walking down Madison Avenue looking into every jewelry store window, every dress store, every furrier. "Maybe I should buy that for the opening?" I would laugh.

"No! No!" Jean would shriek. "You'd look better in chinchilla than mink."

We passed a smart lingerie shop and something caught my eye. "Jean," I cried, "do you see that? Isn't it great?" I really had to have it. Jean started to disapprove but I was already on my way into the store. When we arrived at Sardi's I was wearing my new bra. A flesh-colored number. With the tips cut out. In diamond shapes!

We walked into the sacred precincts and were abruptly taken upstairs to a table in the tourist section. I remember we flipped a coin for the bill, and I lost.

After lunch Jean and I parted in front of the restaurant and I headed back to the apartment. Suddenly I heard someone call my name. It was the director of *Whittler*. He congratulated me on my great new part and insisted we have a drink to celebrate. "I have a ballerina friend who has a flat just around the corner and I've got the key," he said. "Let's go up for a while."

I knew he was married. I even knew the ballerina was his mistress. And I knew what he had in mind. But I was feeling great. "Sure!" I said and followed him up to the apartment. We had a couple of drinks, and I heard those same words inside me. *Why the hell not?*

Afterward, I was disgusted with myself. I was disgusted with him. I was even disgusted with the ballerina. The whole damn thing was so sordid. I never saw the man again.

CHAPTER ELEVEN

Dearest Aunt Maude,

I am still so up in the clouds I can't eat, sleep or think. You know Lillian Hellman is just about the most wonderful American playwright. She and O'Neill and a couple of others. Following Bankhead is quite a task, too.

I am going to send you and Mother the book of Lillian Hellman's plays so you can read *The Little Foxes* for yourself. Our play is about the same characters when they were younger and shows how they got to be so mean.

We go into rehearsal Monday and we are so excited. The play is wonderful and we have just *got* to be good. Maggie Phillips (from Barter) is in it too, you know.

I am so glad that I signed with the agency that I did after the play in Westport. They really took care of my business well. I think that my salary is wonderful, considering that I have never done a Broadway show before. I am getting $300 a week the first year and $460 the second if I am still in it. If it is a hit I can't get out for two years unless Mr. O'Neill wants me to do *Touch of the Poet.*

I am so happy that you are going to be here for the opening. Mother sent your letter on. I doubt if anyone will want to come anyway—but you know it is almost impossible to get tickets for an opening. Especially to one that will arouse as much interest as this. The press and all the theatrical people and friends of the management have to come then. So I don't know how many tickets I will be allowed. But I will find out as soon as possible.

I got the wonderful package of food. I haven't opened the peas yet 'cause I am saving them for company. Are they Miss Mollie's and when did she start using fancy cans?

I have to go now. But I do want to thank you for all that you have done for me all my life. No one could have an aunt who has been so interested, so encouraging and generally helpful. I appreciate so much everything that you have done for me and said to me.

> Much Love,
> Pat

Monday morning Jean and I arrived at the Fulton Theater promptly at 9:30 ready to begin. We met our cast.

The very lovely Mildred Dunnock was my mother in the play. From the very first rehearsal, I could feel her maternal eye on me, in and out of character. I knew right off Mildred Dunnock was the stuff of which great actresses are made. Millie never gave me advice, but when she gave her approval it meant the world to me. Percy Waram played my father. I was usually annoyed with him because he was always forgetting lines. Scott McKay played one of my brothers and Leo Genn played the other. Leo was a tattler. He was always telling Lillian what everyone said behind her back.

It was clear from the very first moment that Lillian Hellman was going to dominate every aspect of this play. Although it was the first time she was directing, Lillian had the *air* of a great director. Before we began rehearsing, I anticipated the unveiling of secrets and mysteries that would transmit her genius to my talent. When we got on the stage, however, all she did was point and shout. It seemed I was getting nothing from her that made my imagination work, but Lillian's instinct was right and I trusted it. If she said something worked, I believed her. She couldn't show you how to do it, but she certainly could tell you if you had done it.

Having a first fitting for a Broadway show was like getting a letter on your school sweater. I had absolutely no idea what a "fitting" meant.

"Just strip down to your slip," the girl said. "Mr. Stroock will be here in a moment."

I gasped, "But I don't have a slip on!"

"That's okay, honey," she said, "they've seen a girl before. Bra and panties will be fine."

The five mirrors on the wall reproduced five images of me undressing down to my underpants and—of course—the peekaboo bra. I saw ten pink teats peeking out of their diamond-shaped holes just as James Stroock and his entourage came into the room. The costumer pulled out her tape measure and called to an assistant: "Shoulder to shoulder, seventeen inches, shoulder to waist, seventeen and a half inches . . . elbow to wrist . . . knee to ankle . . ."

By the time she had worked around to "nipple to nipple" I thought Mr. Stroock's blue eyes would pop right out of his head. When they finished, he said, "After you dress, Miss Neal, would you please come to my office? I've a personal matter to discuss with you."

In his office, he spoke with a fatherly tone. "You know, I liked you the moment I saw you," he began. "You don't have a family in the city, do you?"

"No," I admitted nervously.

"Somehow I get the feeling you need a friend."

Here it comes, I thought.

"I'd like you to come to my house and meet my daughter. She's just about your age." As he spoke, he wrote down his number. "My wife's name is Bianca," he said, erasing any question he might have seen on my face, "ask for her."

The Stroocks became a second family to me in New York. Gloria Stroock and I became great pals and have remained so throughout our lives. Her sister, who changed her name to Geraldine Brooks, went to Hollywood to be in films before I did.

We all knew that Lillian did not have the last act written. So no one knew exactly what we were going for. I, of course, was hoping she would come up with a glorious third act for me. After about a week's rehearsal, she came up with a glorious third act all right, but it was glory for Millie, Percy and Leo. I was practically not in it at all. I was really down about it and complained bitterly to Jean. "All I do is come in at the end and realize that my father had been blackmailed out of his money by my brother, and I say, 'Go jump in the lake, Daddy-boy, I'm playing ball with Ben.' "

Jean's eyes flashed. "You're not the only one with problems, Pat," she said pointedly, and walked out of the room. I didn't know she was in serious trouble and close to being replaced.

The next day a gossip column carried the item that Lillian Hellman was going to fire Jean Hagen. When we got to the theater, Lillian was in a rage. "Who the hell gave that out without my permission? Jean will not be replaced as long as I'm running the show. I'll rehearse her until she's great." She did and Jean was. Nobody knew who had given out the story, but I'm sure I was not the only one who suspected Leo.

Lillian's friend Dashiell Hammett was frequently out front during rehearsals, sometimes in a stupor. But Lillian adored him, drunk or sober. I saw that the first day he joined us for lunch. If he wanted the saltshaker and it was within his reach, she would go for it first and hand it to him. If he said the sky was blue, she would call him a poet. If he predicted rain, she would hail him as a prophet.

But Lillian's gentle, tender side was obvious to few. Most people saw only her impetuous temper and never the woman beneath the fire. Instinctively, I understood her and knew that when I got an angry swat, all I had to do was duck and wait it out. Being annoyed was her way of being Lillian Hellman.

We had several weeks of out-of-town tryouts in Wilmington, Baltimore and Detroit. By the time we got to Boston our reviews were so great we thought we had the hit of the world.

I sent every one of them to Aunt Maude and she called me the moment she read them. "Patsy, it's what we've waited for ever since you gave those monologues in my front parlor. Why, you're going to be the loveliest thing ever. They said that you were better than Tallulah *Banks*."

"I don't think they said better, Aunt Maude, I think they said I sounded like her sometimes."

"I just wish your daddy could be there to finally see your name in lights."

Well, my name wasn't in lights, but I did indeed sorely miss my daddy.

"God bless you, Patsy, and keep you safe for opening night." And He did.

The only thing that even God could not protect me from was my mother. She arrived with Pete three days before the opening. At the last minute, Aunt Maude had to cancel the greatest moment of her life because Grandpa Neal died.

Jean and I knew it would never work to crowd my family into our apartment, and Mother wanted to be near me and the theater. The Algonquin was the solution. We stepped inside the tiny hotel elevator and I bragged, "This place has housed every famous actor and author who has ever come to New York." But Mother was not listening. She was more concerned that the chugging lift might get stuck between floors.

Between last-minute costume changes, unexpected rehearsals, interviews and a late November snowfall, I thought I would perish in the most frantic three days of my life.

"Patsy," Mother would complain, "it is just terrible that they keep you up until two A.M. rehearsing like that before a big performance! Don't they know you have an opening to face?"

And when I came home from dress rehearsal, still in makeup: "Oh, Patsy, did people on the street see you looking like that?"

By four o'clock on the afternoon of the opening, I thought I was going to lose my mind. I was in the bathtub weeping my head off. Mother poked her head in.

"Oh, Patsy! They have just worn you out."

"I'll be all right, Mother. It's normal for an opening."

"Well," she sniffed, "I never realized how difficult it was to be in show business."

Opening night was both the most frightening and most wonderful night of my life. I was the next thing to catatonic, but at the final curtain, when we were flooded with applause as only a New York audience can give, the Broadway opening was everything I had ever hoped it would be. I knew for certain that the reason I wanted to be an actress was for that moment. Applause was love. It was approval by everybody and I bathed in it.

Lillian had a huge party at her house on Eighty-fifth Street, where we waited for the reviews. Loads of celebrities who didn't even have anything to do with our show were there. That was the first time I saw Dorothy Parker, who overwhelmed me with her praise. Then I overheard her being perfectly vicious about Percy's performance, just moments after she had told him how marvelous she thought he was. I wondered what she really thought about me.

As far as the reviews went, I was a hit in my first Broadway show. If only my daddy could have known. In fact, everyone in the cast got raves. Only Lillian's reviews were mixed, and perhaps only she really anticipated what that might mean for the future of our run. *Another Part of the Forest,* for all our expectations, was not to finish out the season on Broadway.

When I got back to the hotel, Mother was so excited for me, and so proud. She had collected eighty-six telegrams of congratulations. She also vowed that she would never, ever, let me go through such a difficult thing alone again. Pete thought I was a "real trouper," but Mother scowled. "He embarrassed me so much, Patsy. Why, I didn't see till we got to the theater, but he wore cowboy boots to your opening!"

Overnight I was the toast of New York. I was totally charmed. I have always loved being admired. It was thrilling to walk down the street for the first time in my life and have people, complete strangers, come up to me and say, "You were wonderful in that play."

Being known had its quick rewards, too. Jean and I were now seated downstairs at Sardi's.

Hollywood people began currying my favor and I found myself on every party list in town. Producers like George Stevens, Samuel Goldwyn and David Selznick invited me to supper to discuss my future career plans. One night Mr. Selznick took me to the Stork Club, or maybe it was "21"; they all seemed very much alike to me. Gregory Peck and his wife made up our foursome. Mr. Peck was gracious and charming and such a perfect gentleman that he convinced me that the tales I had heard about Hollywood were false. Mr. Selznick proved that everything I had heard about Hollywood was true. He got very drunk, told me how much he loved Jennifer Jones, and then tried to get me into bed. I nearly pushed the poor man down the stairs.

Relieved of the tension of rehearsals, Lillian generously invited the cast to her home in the country on Sundays. She had a real farm where she and Dashiell raised chickens and pigs. Both of them were very adept at handling the farm, even down to slaughtering those animals themselves. They had a great pond on the property where we went ice-skating in the winter and swam when the weather turned warm. Lillian and Dash were the ice skaters. It was fun to watch them together. I spent most of my time just trying to stand up on the skates.

Jean and I decided to move to a very fancy apartment on Riverside Drive. We got monogrammed matches, stocked Champagne, and sent our laundry out. But we did not keep house any better than we had in the dump. It got so bad that Nancy Hoadley, another Northwestern actress friend, used to sneak in and clean the place for us. We were the darlings of the press and all the papers seemed to be interested in us. Nancy simply couldn't bear for them to see how messy we were.

Right after Christmas, *Life* magazine put me on its cover and *Look* gave me an award as Broadway's brightest newcomer. Before the play closed in May, I had also received the Donaldson Award, the Drama Critics Award and the first Antoinette Perry Award ever given. It was an engraved compact, which I still have.

Eugene O'Neill won the Drama Critics Award the same year for *The Iceman Cometh*. I sat down and wrote him a fan letter.

The night of my twenty-first birthday the whole cast got together and sang "Happy Birthday." Lillian appeared at my dressing room with a bottle of brandy. Beside her was Millie holding a huge birthday cake. I caught a glimpse of the woman standing behind them and I could not believe my eyes. It was Katharine Cornell. She congratulated me on my performance. I tried so hard to remember all the lovely things she was saying that I forgot everything. If she recalled our first meeting, she graciously did not say so.

Millie Dunnock had another surprise for me. She invited Tallulah Bankhead to see our play and made sure she would come backstage to meet me. I was so impressed, not only that the legend came back, but that she was dressed in trousers, which women did not do in those days. "Well, darling!" she said. "You were wonderful, and if I told you that you were half as good as I was, it would still be a hell of a compliment!"

But the best was a simple square blue envelope that contained a note.

Dear Pat Neal,
    I was delighted to hear that you liked *The Iceman Cometh*. It was charming of you to write and tell me so. It was also good news to hear of your success. This was no surprise to me as I know you will, one day, be one of our best.
    All best! Keep up the good work!

                                        Very Sincerely,
                                        Eugene O'Neill

During the last months of our run I kept the most exhausting schedule. *Redbook, Life, Vogue* and *Harper's Bazaar* all did features on me. I went to every luncheon in town. I plugged the March of Dimes campaign and did practically everything but run for mayor. But life was not busy enough. I started a love affair with Victor Jory.

CHAPTER TWELVE

Victor Jory was about twenty-five years my senior, and married. Although we had several mutual friends—K. T. and Hugh and Jean Hagen's new boyfriend, Tom Seidel—we had not met until his Actors' Benefit performance. Victor was trying to make a go of a national theater group, one of several springing up to provide a working arena for otherwise unemployed actors. Unfortunately, it didn't last the year.

I went backstage to congratulate him. I thought he was gorgeous. He was half American Indian—thin, tall, with those severe features that made every kid in America tremble when they saw him in *Tom Sawyer* and women quiver at his faerie king in *A Midsummer Night's Dream*. He was amusing, and obviously a ladies' man. That very evening he made sure I was aware that his wife and children were in California. I, in turn, let it drop that the Marlowes had given me the use of their apartment while they were on tour. He called the next day.

Jean and Tom and Victor and I soon became a foursome. We would meet after our shows for a late supper and then would go out until one or two in the morning. It was no surprise when Victor and I wound up together one night at the apartment. So began our routine: all night on the town, going to bed together at five in the morning and staying in the sack the whole day. We would get up in time to make it to our respective theaters, give our performances and then start all over again. This went on day after day for six months. When I think back on it, I can't imagine how I lived through that horrendous schedule, much less poor darling Victor.

During those months Victor filled a lovely charm bracelet he had given me with dozens of gold trinkets, all with fantastic little working parts. I loved it. That's what I was to Victor. A lovely little charm with working parts.

Our love affair stayed amazingly quiet. We did not make a point of keeping out of the public eye, but there was never anything about us in the newspapers. Everybody at the theater knew, but they took it in stride. Lillian didn't care as long as I got to work on time. If Victor's wife knew, he never told me. It was plain that I was no more a threat to his marriage than the many others who had preceded me. In the end, Victor always went home to his wife.

My family was aware of Victor but only as one of my many wonderful friends in New York, as reported by Aunt Maude, who had met him. She did not tell anyone, I'm sure, that he had gotten her tipsy for the first time in her life at the Stork Club.

When I wasn't with Victor, I was usually in acting class or else out making the rounds. Casting people could not believe it when they saw me coming. "My God, you've got a job! Will you *please* stay home?" But I couldn't. I was driven to see if something better might be around the next corner.

I was also hearing rumblings about the formation of a new actors' workshop. Its goal was to develop a community of actors with a committed state of mind about their craft. Not since I had worked with Alvina Krause had I felt as excited as I did by the vision of The Actors Studio. Millie Dunnock and I talked about it at length, and we both wanted to be part of it.

Another Part of the Forest closed the first week in May. Plans called for the cast to reassemble in September to take it on the road. My agents arranged for me to spend the summer at the venerable Elitch's Garden Theater in

Denver. There was no better summer stock company in the country.

Elitch's fifty-sixth season would bring me everything I could hope for, and then some.

I played Saint Joan, Elizabeth Barrett, the wife in *State of the Union,* and the title role in the mystery drama *Laura,* as well as the lead in a farce on infidelity called *Made in Heaven,* all with the company's leading man, a handsome actor named Peter Cookson. I had not seen Peter on Broadway that past season, but he had been voted the year's most promising actor by the critics. One look at him and I knew Victor had to go. I placed a call to California.

"Victor, I am so sorry, it's over."

"Do you really mean it?" he said, sounding utterly relieved.

Peter was also married, and in the process of a reconciliation with his wife when rehearsals began. I asked him over for a drink. The second time he came, he stayed the night. When his wife found out he was sleeping with me, she took their young children and left him for good. It was the only time in my life that I wrecked a marriage, but in those days I had no conscience.

Stock was a real challenge. There was no staying in bed all day. We were up and rehearsing early in the morning. We would rehearse one play during the day and perform another at night. After rehearsals Peter and I would race to the local amusement park and ride the hell out of the roller coaster so we could be "fresh" for the night's performance.

Once we stopped for readings at a fortune-teller's in the park. Peter was delighted because she said he would marry a very rich woman. We didn't know what to make of what she saw for me. She said I would have trouble with my head.

I had been in Denver only a few days when an old friend contacted me. It was Anne Fonde, the cheerleader from Knoxville High. She was married now, living in Denver, and was expecting her first child. Anne and I saw a lot of each other that summer and I loved watching her grow rounder and rounder with her child. I loved seeing this fantastic miracle called pregnancy happen right before my eyes. In my heart, I desperately wanted that experience for myself. It made me know that acting would not be the most important thing in my life.

At the end of the season, I went back to New York to begin rehearsals for the tour of *Another Part of the Forest*. Peter had returned before I did to do *The Heiress* on Broadway. He found us a cheap hotel room near the theater district. He was supporting a family, and neither of us had been too careful with our money. But it would do for the short time I'd be in town. The tour would start at the end of the month in Philadelphia, en route to California.

But the most exciting news that awaited Peter and me was an invitation to become members of The Actors Studio.

Elia "Gadge" Kazan, Cheryl Crawford and Robert Lewis were the founders. They set up the first classrooms in a rented building on Manhattan's West Side. I was thrilled to be asked into Lewis's advanced class along with Peter, Herbert Berghof, Marlon Brando, Anne Jackson and Eli Wallach, Maureen Stapleton and Millie.

About eighty members showed up for the opening sessions. I remember Kazan spoke with fire. He had me in the palm of his hand. How I regretted he would not be my teacher. I regretted it even more after my first encounter with Robert Lewis. It was deadly between us. Real hate. According to him, everything I did was wrong. But actually, I was not in New York long enough to take much of his abuse, only long enough to get a nibble of the prestige that went with being a founding member of The Studio.

The tour of *Another Part of the Forest* began at the best possible time. Peter was becoming too serious, while I was starting to feel that we just could not last. He was moody, which I found difficult, and penniless, which did not appeal to me at all. This was not what I wanted out of life. I should have told Peter the truth then, but I kept the poor man hanging on, even letting him join me for weekends on the road. He would take off right after his Saturday-night performance, fly to whatever city I was in, spend Sunday and Monday and return to New York in time for that night's show. I loved him for it, but I felt more than a little guilty. Jean, however, was delirious. She and Tom had gotten married and they were carrying on the honeymoon by phone. They'd call each other several times a day. I would hear her purr into the receiver, "Kiss-kiss, kiss-kiss, kiss-kiss." That was the extent of their conversation during the whole road trip.

On opening night in Chicago, I was emoting my heart out during the first act when I sensed someone in the wings. There was Lillian, her hand cupped to her mouth.

"Louder!" she whispered. So I spoke louder.

"Louder!" she repeated vehemently. I began to speak at the top of my lungs.

Nothing deterred Lillian. "Louder! Louder!"

She kept it up until I was sure the people out front could hear her. I was so angry by the time the curtain came down, I could hardly contain myself. I stomped offstage to find her.

"Lillian," I snapped, "I *heard* you! Every time you said it. I heard you!"

"Well, then," she growled, "you should have nodded!"

Another Part of the Forest did not go west as we had expected. The tour ended after six weeks on the road. I went back to my one room with Peter and assessed my future. For months Hollywood had been beckoning, but I had insisted I would not succumb to any offers because I wanted to establish a stage reputation first. But there were no plays on the horizon. There seemed to be little reason now to resist.

Resist, hell! I wanted it—bad!

It was like the old sorority days, except there was no Kappa Kappa Gamma this time. Goldwyn wanted me. Selznick wanted me. Metro-Goldwyn-Mayer and Twentieth Century–Fox and Paramount wanted me. My agent made the decision. Warner Brothers wanted me, too, and they offered an added incentive: the lead in their newly acquired Broadway hit, *John Loves Mary*. I was thrilled. I was going to have my cake and eat it, too.

Peter had also received movie offers, but he was tied up with *The Heiress*. He insisted that, for now, his main attraction on the West Coast was going to be me. He saw me off at Grand Central and promised to join me as soon as he could.

I had left home early in the fall of 1945 and by the end of the year had gotten my first job as an understudy. A year later I had opened on Broadway. There was no doubt about it, success had come to me overnight, and if I had not felt the dizziness of the leap while I was in New York, the change of altitude hit me when I stopped in Tennessee en route to California.

"Oh, Patsy, you have not changed one bit!" was the "compliment" repeatedly offered. How strange, I thought, for if I had come home really the same, everyone would have felt disappointed, even sorry.

I quickly learned that you must be forgiven your success by those who stay behind. And you must hang on every word said to you lest you appear "uppity." And you must ask the questions before they are asked of you. "How many kids do you have?" I would quickly inquire before anybody could bring up Broadway. As long as people talked about themselves to me, they thought I was just great and had not changed one bit for the worse.

But with close friends there was a definite shared joy in my triumph in the big city. Frank Ball's daddy met me at the station and was as proud of me as if I were his own daughter. So was darling Malcolm Miller, who had reported my every career move in his column. My wonderful Emily Mahan felt rightly that her lessons had blossomed and borne fruit. If I had been able to hire a skywriter I would have done so, to spell out a huge "thank you" to my family and friends. I felt they were all part of my incredible good fortune and I wanted them to know it. I still do.

It was a perfect family Christmas, my last at home as

far as I can recall. We all went to Mommy and Poppy Shipman's, who were as close as family, for a great turkey dinner, not only to celebrate the feast, but also to say a kind of southern farewell.

I presented Mother with an enormous box, a gift I had brought from New York. It was a fabulous beaver coat. When she opened it, her face fell. I thought she was disappointed and I started to cry. Then she began to cry because she thought she had hurt me. She put on her coat and we both cried some more. Mother gave me a gorgeous blue-gray pin-striped suit to wear to Hollywood. There was a matching hat designed to look like a Salvation Army bonnet, which I loved. Mother made plans all the way to the depot for her and Pete to join me on the Coast just as soon as I could arrange for it.

Amid the goodbyes and all the kissing, I caught sight of dear Mr. Ball, who had come to see me off. He loaded my suitcases and then lifted me onto the coach. One last hug as the train gave a lurch and he whispered in his honeysuckle drawl, "Men will do you harm, Patsy. Do not succumb to them. Morals are very important. *They* will be with you always."

CHAPTER THIRTEEN

I t was my longest trip by far.

Seasoned travelers familiar with the three-day journey across the country shaded their eyes from the changing landscape and got comfortable in their seats. But I spent hours walking the train, chatting with anyone who would listen—especially the lady who said she worked for Louella Parsons—or gaping out the windows. I was coming to Hollywood as I had come to New York City, ready to set the town on fire.

I stepped onto the train platform and my eyes swept the sea of people for a familiar face. It was my first time in California, yet instinctively I looked for a face that I knew.

"Miss Neal?" It wasn't a familiar face, but an earnest one belonging to a young lawyer from my agency, MCA. Our destination that morning was the Hotel Bel-Air, located above Sunset Boulevard beyond Beverly Hills. A few morning residents were out walking their dogs. In shirt-sleeves and shorts! It was just after Christmas.

Christmas in Hollywood! I wanted only one thing, one gift. I wanted to be the greatest actress ever to appear on the screen.

We pulled up to the Bel-Air, where I was greeted by two fabulous swans in a perfectly manicured landscape of gardens and ponds pretending to be in their primal state. I could never have believed on that balmy December day, as I crossed the little bridge into such a fairyland, that I was walking into the heart of one of the deepest struggles of my life.

2

WITHOUT DIGNITY, WITHOUT REGRET
1947–1953

CHAPTER FOURTEEN

K. T. Stevens had been very right to insist that I not come to Hollywood as a starlet looking for a job. Jack Warner felt it was a coup to sign me. My acceptance of his offer over the competition had given him a leg up in town. I had a seven-year contract, starting at the magnificent sum of $1,250 a week and escalating to $3,750, with a clause that permitted me to return to New York for a play. I still had *A Touch of the Poet* tucked into my brain. Warner seemed genuinely pleased that I was joining his stable and I, in turn, found him to be utterly charming. Because he believed in my future, everyone at Warners seemed to believe in me, too. They wanted me to become the Katharine Cornell of the movies. I hoped they were right. Because it felt *fantastic*.

John Loves Mary would not start for several weeks, and apart from wardrobe fittings and publicity interviews, I was given complete freedom to do as I pleased. But since I did not yet know anyone in town, I spent weekends lying around the pool, which was just outside my door, and eating supper alone at night in my room. As liberated as I thought I was from ties to home, I phoned there often.

It hardly seemed possible that Daddy was dead four years. I deeply sympathized with my mother's loneliness and felt a growing responsibility for her.

So we made plans. Mother and Pete would come out from Tennessee, Cousin Lenore McGimpsey driving them to Hollywood in the brand-new Buick I had purchased in Knoxville and returning home after a few days of sightseeing. We three Neals would get an apartment together. Mother would cook and run the house and I'd continue to provide for Pete's education as I had done since Daddy died.

I was quickly introduced to the Hollywood mainstream at a grand New Year's Eve celebration. The studio publicity department arranged a date for me, as they often did for their people. Masses of movie stars were there. Everybody I met was utterly divine to me, with the divided intimacy that I quickly learned was the style of Hollywood parties. One eye is fixed intently on the person you are talking to while the other scans the room to see whom you *should* be talking to.

Early in the evening, a very robust and handsome man took my hand. "I'm Ronnie Reagan," he said. "We're going to do this *John Loves Mary* together. I'm very happy to meet you." What a lovely, cheerful man, I thought. The next time I caught sight of him, it was at the stroke of midnight. He was on the terrace with an older woman, weeping into her arms. I later learned that he and his wife, Jane Wyman, were divorcing.

A movie set seemed an absolute fantasyland on my first day. I had so much energy and curiosity that I was everywhere, investigating everything. The main set of *John Loves Mary* was surrounded by a forest of lights, reflectors, cranelike sound booms and recording equipment. Wires and cables laced the floor like huge octopus tentacles that trailed high up into the rafters, connecting the whole stage to some secret energy source in the sky.

We did only one scene that whole day. It took hours to fix every detail. This was the Golden Age of Hollywood, and we were obliged to appear without any blemish that would expose us as merely human. I was so impressed with the stars of the film, Ronald Reagan and Jack Carson. They knew what to do in front of a camera. In fact, everyone on the set was experienced but me. But I was too excited to be afraid. That night I returned to my hotel

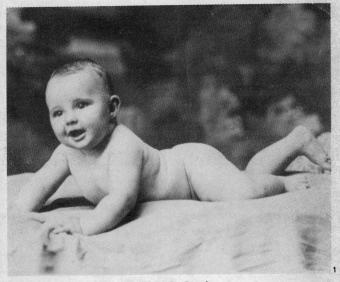

My only nude photo—published, that is.

At five months, with Pappy.

The Neal girls: Patsy Lou and Margaret Ann, ages three and five.

William Burdette "Coot" Neal. My daddy.

My mother, Eura Mildred Petrey Neal.

At seventeen.

Northwestern's 1946 Syllabus Queen. The line forms on the left, Mr. Petty.

My first New York
résumé photo.

Mother and Pete in
New York for my
Broadway debut.

Another Part of the Forest, with Percy Waram and my second mother, Millie Dunnock.

11

As Maxwell Anderson's *Joan of Lorraine* at Elitch's Garden Theater.

Arriving in Hollywood in my new suit and Salvation Army bonnet, ready to set the town on fire.

John Loves Mary, with Ronald Reagan and Jack Carson. No beginner could have been in better company.

12

13

14

Meeting Hedda Hopper, the queen of the columns. We all bowed just enough.

15

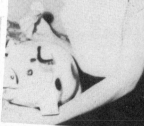

16

17

18

19

Gary Cooper.

20

21

The Fountainhead.

22

23

My favorite picture of Gary and me. It was taken during a photo session for *The Fountainhead*, but we weren't posing.

En route to London with Joan Caulfield, Billy De Wolfe, Virginia Mayo and Michael O'Shea, Sue Ladd and—way over there—Alan.

The Hasty Heart, with Richard Todd. Heavenly actor.

**Relaxing in London with the future president.
Ah, that smile.**

**With Kirk Douglas. The Champion—and he certainly
was to me.**

Three Secrets, with Eleanor Parker. It doesn't look it here, but no one made me laugh the way Eleanor could.

On the beach at La Jolla in the red-and-white polka-dot dress.

30

Bright Leaf.
My second
film with
Gary.

31

During rehearsals of *The Cocktail Party* at the La Jolla Playhouse, with Reginald Denny and Vincent Price.

with my head pounding. I called Peter. "*This* is acting and a roller-coaster ride all wrapped into one!" Exhausted, I fell onto my bed and conked out into a dead sleep.

If the aim of the Hollywood movie of the forties was to re-create paradise, going to rushes was purgatory. Never before had I seen myself on the screen, and I was horrified. I thought I looked so bad. I was a caricature in false eyelashes and forties lips. My hair was pulled straight back on my head. I didn't know that on-screen one photographs a little heavier. I could see that I would have to keep a strict diet. I thought my acting was equally overdone. I had no technique and my voice and gestures, geared for a Broadway house, were way too big. David Butler, a darling fat man, was the director, and although he loved and encouraged me, he did not know how to teach me anything about film acting.

Within a week I was on a first-name basis with every cop at the studio, every waitress in the commissary and virtually anybody I saw on the street more than once. In those days, being under contract was like being part of a family, but it was no ordinary family, not with Joan Crawford, Barbara Stanwyck, Ann Sheridan and Bette Davis. I thought Miss Davis certainly had it made. She had her own studio car.

Jack Carson was a dear. It was always fun and games with Jack, who was everybody's good fellow. Pretty soon the fun and games included lunch together at the Golf Club near the studio, where he could get a drink. He had two martinis and I had two before going back to work. It was the only time in my life I ever showed up on a soundstage a little tipsy. He started inviting me out and sometimes we would end up at his house. One night we wound up in bed together. But we were both too smashed to do anything except pass out.

I had found an apartment before Mother and Pete arrived. Mother and I moved into one bedroom and Pete had the other. I immediately enrolled him in school, filled up the larder, and settled down to blissful illusions that this new beginning would magically erase all the old "don'ts."

It was absolute disaster. Not only were the old problems still there, but new ones turned up. Pete simply could not fit in with the sophisticated California kids and was constantly teased about his southern accent. He would arrive home from school blubbering with anger. I learned to drive, but Mother could not face the Los Angeles traffic, so she spent her time at home cooking delicious meals that I could not eat because I was desperately trying to stay on my diet. Mother was sure that Hollywood had no moral parameters, and its free sexual climate revived her determination to continue forming me in her image. "Patsy, be careful. Patsy, don't." The prognosis for our living situation was clear: terminal.

I met a writer named Harry Kurnitz, who became my occasional escort to the endless round of rather predictable Hollywood evenings, which usually started with drinks and a formal dinner followed by a private screening of a new film at the home of one of the moguls.

It was at such a supper that I met John Gunther. I found him very cultured and amusing. He offered to drop me off at my apartment. As I started to get out of his car, he suddenly lunged at me. The refined Dr. Jekyll had become an amorous Mr. Hyde. "Oh please! Don't!" I gasped.

His enthusiasm melted. "I'm so sorry. I didn't know you were a lady."

"I'm not being a lady. You scared the hell out of me." And he really had.

John and I settled for a good friendship. He almost introduced me to another lady friend of his. He invited me to meet him at his hotel, and when I arrived, Greta Garbo was just leaving. She shot past and said "Go-o-o-odbye" as if I had been part of their day. I nodded and she grinned. Garbo didn't smile, she grinned.

Darling Peter had been fanning the flames of our romance by mail, but I was putting off thinking about *us* at the moment. Until he announced that he had finally gotten his wife to agree to a divorce. Then I knew how unfair I had been. I wrote the poor fellow a letter: "I am so sorry, Peter, I really am, but it's not right and we're not right." I don't know if he was heartbroken, because I did not hear from him again. Fortunately, he was about to go on the road with *The Heiress* and its new star, Beatrice Straight. Not too long after that, they married. I remember thinking how amazing it was of God to put Beatrice there for him.

When *John Loves Mary* finished, I got nervous. I did not know how to act in films, and I knew it. Like many women I confided in my hairdresser. He was studying to be an actor and told me he was working with a wonderful coach, a Russian colleague of Michael Chekhov whose name was George Shdanoff. I had heard of this famous teacher and his wife, Elsa Schreiber; both had become acting coaches for some of the greats of the movie world, including Robert Stack, Leslie Caron and Gregory Peck.

It was love at first sight. He said I was the most talented thing that had ever walked into his studio and he thought I was divine, and I thought he was divine for thinking so. I really needed the encouragement because I had just received a "Dear John" letter of my own from Robert Lewis, the new head of The Actors Studio. I don't remember the exact words, but I took it as "Don't come back—no talent." It was a staggering blow.

An invitation to come to Jack Warner's private luncheon room was a major event for any new player on the lot. The lavishly set table seated about thirty, usually all very important people. I had been invited several times during my early days at Warners. Pretty young actresses were always a complement to the elegant setting.

The latest summons came on a lovely spring day, which meant it was even warmer than Christmastime. Errol Flynn was one of the guests that day, but it was not the dashing Mr. Flynn who made shivers go up my spine.

Jack Warner made the introductions. "Gary, this is Patricia Neal."

"How do you do, Miss Neal?"

I looked up into the ravishingly handsome face. "How do you do, Mr. Cooper?"

He moved away to greet another guest. There were no other words between us that day; in fact, he did not even look my way again.

But, for me, there was no one else in that room.

CHAPTER FIFTEEN

Afew days later at the studio, a man riding a bicycle suddenly stopped at my side. "Patricia Neal?" he called brightly. "I'm King Vidor." He was a major director there. Everyone knew he was planning one of the biggest films of the year. It was *The Fountainhead* by Ayn Rand, a best-selling novel during my days at Northwestern. Its hero, Howard Roark, had been in bed, page after blazing page, with every American coed in the forties.

We chatted for a few moments before he got to his point. Would I be willing to test for the part of Dominique, the female lead in the film? It was one of the plums of the year and Barbara Stanwyck had her sights trained on any competition. Gary Cooper had already been cast in the lead. I had never thought of Howard Roark as Gary Cooper, but I certainly would not argue this now. As for Dominique, no one else would get this part but me. I determined that even before I said yes to Mr. Vidor's invitation to come to his office to talk about it.

I got my dog-eared copy of *The Fountainhead* off the shelf. I had brought it with me from Knoxville. Again I pored through the familiar story of the architect who refuses to compromise and the tortured woman he falls in love with. How different it was, now that I had the chance to bring its neurotic and frigid heroine to life.

When I walked into King Vidor's office, I saw Gary

Cooper's long frame settled into one of the huge leather chairs, a script open on his lap. Seeing me brought him to his feet and he greeted me with a firm handshake.

"Good afternoon, Miss Neal, I'm glad to see you again." I wondered if he had thought of me at all since our first encounter. Could he and King Vidor have spoken about me?

"I'm so glad to see you again, Mr. Cooper." What really did they think of me? Why did they choose me? But they had not yet chosen me, I reminded myself. That was the purpose of this meeting.

"Please, call me Gary."

"Of course. Please call me Patricia."

"I guess you've met Mr. Vidor!"

"Oh yes, he chased me down on his bicycle."

He laughed and I joined in, and we both gave my poor joke much more than it deserved. Was he as nervous as I?

King Vidor then guided the conversation toward the film and the way he envisioned Roark and Dominique. Gary spoke about his own interpretation of the characters. I listened and let each man, in turn, know how astute I thought he was. The meeting was low-key and friendly and concluded with everyone agreeing that I should be tested for the part.

I was on George Shdanoff's doorstep that very afternoon. We read through the short scenes that I had been asked to prepare. When we finished, he cried, "Right! Absolutely right. Just that way."

"I'm sorry, Mr. Shdanoff, but I don't know what I did," I said wretchedly. "I'm not sure I can repeat myself."

So we did it again and he responded emphatically, "That's right! No other way! No other way!" Again I pleaded that I couldn't repeat myself. We went over and over the scene for several days. Each time I felt I was a little different and each time George would approve and then firmly tell me to keep it just that way, and *no other* way.

Gradually I began to grasp what he was saying to me.

Never repeat. No formulas. No absolute rules. Perform each time with freshness of intuition. George wasn't there to teach me to act, but rather to teach me to *trust in my own instinct*.

When I walked onto the set for the test, I was Dominique.

We shot two separate tests over a period of two days. A young contract player did the Gary Cooper role. I was surprised and flattered on the first day when Gary himself appeared on the set. I wondered if it was his professional courtesy or his budding interest in a young actress. All I know is that I was told that one of the tests was a flop and the other was very good. I never knew which was better or why it was considered so, or if it was the one shot while Gary watched.

News came very soon. I would star with Gary Cooper in *The Fountainhead*. Barbara Stanwyck sent Jack Warner a telegram asking out of her contract.

I accosted every single person I met on the lot that day —"Have you heard? I got the part!"—as if each one had been personally plugging for me. I had the gift of making anyone I talked to feel as though he or she was somehow a unique part of my life. It was a great advantage—sometimes.

I sailed into the wardrobe department to see Milo Anderson, the young designer who had done my clothes for *John Loves Mary*. I spilled out my good news. He lit up and thanked me profusely. I had no idea why. But when I went for fittings, the producer, Henry Blanke, was furious with me for demanding that Milo do my costumes. I was shocked. I knew I was in no position to demand anything. I had already met the lovely woman who was doing the sketches and I adored them. "Please," I begged, "I don't want you to fire anyone." But he said it had already been done. The humiliation and hurt for that poor woman who lost her job because of me left a brand on my conscience. I never think of that incident without feeling a little sick.

But Milo's wardrobe was sensational. I went off my diet and began starving. I doubled my exercises and got massages every day. One hundred and twenty pounds was my goal. I had six weeks to work on myself, and I made up my mind I was going to be the most devastating Dominique anyone could imagine. Ayn Rand's heroine was also a horsewoman. I had to learn to ride, and how I hated it! The studio arranged lessons for me and I went faithfully. By the time we shot the first scene of the film, I could at least sit on the animal, but I wouldn't cry if I never saw another horse.

The first week of shooting was on location at a stone quarry several hours from Los Angeles. Mr. Vidor offered to take Gary and me up to the location in his chauffeured studio car. It was a pleasant drive, warmed by the anticipation of beginning what we all knew for certain was going to be the most important film of the year.

We were assigned rooms in a very modest hotel. I would be one floor above Gary for the next several days. I liked the idea very much.

The first scene shot was also the first meeting between Roark and Dominique. She stands at the top of the quarry watching him in the pit as he drills manfully into a slab of stone. She looks down at him, wanting him. He looks up at her and then casts his weight onto the drill, penetrating the rock. The sexual implications are obvious, but in case the audience doesn't get them, another scene leaves no doubt. Dominique agonizes in her bedroom while images of the drill going into the rock are superimposed. In those days explicit sex was not permitted by the Hays Office, so Hollywood found other ways to show that something sexual was going on. Frankly, I have always found that approach much more interesting.

After each day's filming Mr. Vidor would instigate a friendly supper party, after which I would go back to my room alone to study lines and nurture imagined encounters with Gary. I was desperately young and not very clever. I would telephone his room and urgently ask all sorts of silly questions about the next day's schedule. He would answer so pleasantly that I was sure he was enjoying the interruptions. Again and again I would call to confirm the time or place of the shooting, and he would be so nice I could almost hear the smile on his face. Gary was twenty-five years older than I, yet I could feel him responding to my youthful signals.

The location shooting was over too quickly and I found myself beside him in the car heading back to Hollywood. This time the signals were not from me. I felt Gary's hand on mine. It had begun.

The rest of the filming of *The Fountainhead* took place at the studio with the back lot doubling for New York City. I was learning a great deal about film acting from watching both my costars. That wonderful actor Raymond Massey played my husband. I have always held that Gary was one of the finest actors in films. He had already won his first Oscar when we met, and I dared hope his second might be for his portrayal of Howard Roark.

Gary and I did not speak of what was growing between us. But it was known in the looks we exchanged, in the occasional touch of his hand on mine or his brushing my leg as we sat watching the rushes. Our instincts warned us that the sexual tension being recorded on film might be lost if we went to bed. We knew we were sitting on a tinderbox, and there would be no leaping into a love affair while the movie was shooting. Frequently we took lunch together, which coworkers on a film often did, but we never went out after work. Gary had the reputation of sleeping in his dressing room between takes, but he began to forgo his naps in favor of rehearsing with me. And he would come to the hairdressing department and watch Gertrude do my hair. Gertrude Wheeler was classic to the breed. While quietly addressing her talents to washing, combing and curling, she caught everything with the shrewdness of an FBI agent. Gary's reflection in the glass did not elude her and she knew exactly why he was there. But I never spoke to her, or to anyone for that matter, about my feelings for Gary. I could be wrong but I don't think anyone else on the set caught on, at least not at first. We were giving ourselves completely to the making of the film, still chaste in the wonder of what was happening. Privately, I was taking practical measures to get my mother out of my apartment.

There was always a parade of visitors on the set—families, friends, publicity people and agents. I remember the day Betsy Drake appeared. Betsy had been practically set to do Regina in *Another Part of the Forest* when I got the role. I was sure she must hate me. But she didn't at all. When we met, there was an immediate rapport. Now I had two good friends in town, K. T. and Betsy.

Then I heard that Mrs. Cooper was to be our guest on the set. I was a wreck—until Gary introduced me to the gracious white-haired lady who was his mother.

Alice Brazier Cooper had braved the Montana frontier as a young girl. She had come from England to visit her brother and was marooned in Helena because of the silver crash of 1893. She met and married a young transplanted Englishman named Charles Cooper and raised two sons on a ranch called the Seven-Bar-Nine in a place once called Last Chance Gulch! I remember Gary beaming as he said, "Looking at my mother nowadays, it's hard to believe that I once saw her swinging an ax to break open bales of frozen hay at twenty degrees below zero."

I liked this lady immediately. And she liked me. I was certain of that.

The controversial Ayn Rand also made several appearances on the set, usually to protect her screenplay from any spur-of-the-moment changes we actors might try to make. No one, including Gary, was allowed to tamper with her dialogue. I rather liked her in spite of her loathing of Lillian Hellman. They were, of course, hemispheres apart politically, and Ayn lost no opportunity to run dear Lillian down. Lillian probably returned the attention in kind.

As the film progressed, my work with Gary gradually became the medium of our relationship. I looked forward to each scene we would play together with a new sense of expectation. Lines in the film became pregnant with meaning for us. Howard and Dominique said and did the things we could not yet express. In one scene, which was celebrated quite effectively as the billboard poster for the film, Dominique sits at Roark's feet with her head in his lap. We were in that position for what seemed like hours. Actors usually leap to give their places to stand-ins while endless details of adjusting hot lights and camera angles are worked out. Ann and Slim, our stand-ins, received their pay but did not work that day. We finished rehearsing and Mr. Vidor called for the crew. We didn't budge but stayed there, quite unable to leave each other's presence. I can still feel the touch of his hand on my shoulder. Later, as we sat through the rushes of that scene, I could again feel the warmth and closeness of his body. We never talked. We just looked into each other's eyes and knew.

"It would have to come, because there is nothing else that really matters" is a line from that scene. I never thought a line from a film could be so true.

That same line ends with, "I love you without dignity and without regret."

One afternoon another Mrs. Cooper appeared on the set. Her name was Veronica Balfe Cooper—Mrs. Gary Cooper—but everyone called her Rocky. She was a fabulously good-looking woman with a classic face. She had once been a professional actress called Sandra Shaw. She moved with grace, class and assurance. Clearly a cut above. Her casual but expensive California dress exposed just enough of a tan to let us know she knew how to live, and she spoke in phrases of sharpened wit that made the trashiest of words seem in vogue. I quite convinced myself that I did not like her.

She was as shrewd as any Hollywood executive, as elegant as any first lady. However, she had none of Gary's down-home charm that endeared him to the common folk on the set. She could ski, dive, ride horses, shoot a dozen firearms. She was clearly a good companion to Gary Cooper. But I reminded myself that I was younger.

Her presence that day made one thing clear to me. I had met a worthy adversary.

Mother and Pete, weeping goodbyes, finally headed for home. I looked around my empty apartment. I had to find a better place. For the time being I moved back to the Bel-Air. One night, out of the blue, I got a call from a stranger. "My name is Jean Valentino." She was not a stranger by reputation. All Hollywood knew of the first wife of the great Rudolph Valentino. I had never spoken to her before and I was surprised by her interest in my welfare. "I have a perfect place for you to live," she continued, "next to my bungalow, a mirror image of my own place. The location is perfect, a stone's throw from Twentieth Century–Fox." I protested, but she would not let me hang up until I promised to go see it.

To get to the duplex one had to walk up stairs, then more stairs and more stairs, and still more. But it was so different from the old Manhattan walk-ups. It was a series of red brick terraces built into the lush California hillside. You didn't walk up, you ascended. It was a gorgeous place with a beautiful sitting room and a lovely garden covered with ivy vines. I took it immediately.

The Fountainhead, with its grand sweep of emotions and images, had become a blockbuster in our minds. We were drunk on its dramatic gestures, and by the time we got to the wrap everyone thought we had the greatest movie Warner Brothers had ever put out. Little did we know that we were heading over the cliff like lemmings into the passionate sea.

Movie companies are plunged into ten, twelve weeks of instant intimacy. A production can seduce almost everyone involved into feeling part of something terribly important. Then suddenly the film ends, and with it the aura of being a member of a special family. The wrap party of a movie is a kind of liturgy to bury lovely pledges and fragile promises in shallow graves of sentiment.

The night we closed production on *The Fountainhead* was no different except for one thing. Gary and I were really in love with each other. By now everyone sensed it. No one spoke of it but the energy between us radiated an excitement that brought everyone at the party into its orb. I am sure most were wondering if the affair had begun or not, but at that moment our love was still innocent. Guests finally began to drift away, but Gary and I lingered. His wife was in New York. The moment had come. I knew it and so did he.

"May I drive you home?"

"No, I have my own car. But you can follow me."

We walked to our separate cars in silence. He followed me through the moonlit canyon drive. We pulled up in front and I pointed to the walk. "I'm at the top of the steps."

We climbed all those stairs without a word. I took the key from my purse and handed it to him. We stepped inside. I took him by the hand and led him to my bed.

CHAPTER SIXTEEN

After *The Fountainhead* was over, the love affair began.

Sharing a life with Gary was not complex. There was no need to steal time, for he was his own man and his presence at home was never an issue. He and Rocky had long had an agreement to give each other room. He made it clear he did not want to be run by his wife's social calendar, and took what time he needed to go hunting or fishing or just visiting friends. Rocky, too, traveled her own circuit—from Hollywood to Sun Valley to Palm Beach, New York and Paris. She went to shop for clothes or paintings, to sports or social events. They did occasionally travel together, usually to ski or to visit Rocky's mother and stepfather on Long Island.

I did not question Gary about what he did or whom he saw after he left my apartment. I knew I had no rights with him. I did not allow myself then to consider the possibility of a permanent relationship. We were not building a future together. We were seizing moments. He came into my life as he wanted, and although I never thought of *having* to keep myself free for him, I was always there.

At least a couple of times a week Gary would arrive in the early evening with flowers or wine, sometimes a small bag of groceries or little things for the apartment, once a fur rug made from a creature he shot in Africa. And once

I found a lovely surprise among the groceries, a ruby-and-sapphire pin of a Civil War woman in hoopskirt and bonnet, an homage to my Confederate roots. It was Gary's first present to me.

And there was always tons of stuff for my new neighbors, Jean Valentino and her roommate, Chloe Carter. Jean and Chloe would often cook for me when I was working, but when Gary came they adored fixing special dinners for both of us. Sometimes after dinner the four of us would sit in the garden having drinks together.

But when Gary and I were alone, I loved to do the cooking with him. He would prepare the shrimp cocktail or whip up a scrumptious guacamole dip. Our meals were simple—steaks or veal, a favorite of mine, or fish, which Gary adored any way I did it. Television was brand-new, but after supper we preferred just to sit and listen to records.

At times we ventured downtown for Mexican food. One can actually *get away from it all* by going into the obscurity of downtown Los Angeles. We'd take evening rides along the Santa Monica or Malibu beaches and park and walk along the beach hand in hand like movie lovers. We would smoke tipped Parliaments, and I loved it when he would light them together and then hand one to me, playing Paul Henreid to my Bette Davis. It was a romantic time and we gave in to all the old clichés.

I did not hide my past affairs from Gary, and he told me frankly about the women in his life—the early affairs with the Countess di Frasso, Clara Bow and Lupe Velez and, later, Ingrid Bergman. That had not been just a rumor. Theirs was not a great love, but they had been sexually attracted to each other.

These women had been very important to him. He related to each one in a special way. No matter what his biographers say about his philandering, I do not believe he ever intended to use a woman badly.

Gary was famous for his brief "yups" and "nopes," but he never stopped talking when he was with me and I never tired of listening to him. I loved his humor and the way he always made himself the brunt of a story. If someone told him he was good in a picture, he would say the boys in the cutting room pieced together his best stuff. And when people commented on his "natural talent," he would remind them of the hours he had spent with William Wyler, Frank Capra, Sam Wood and Howard Hawks and claim it was time spent with masters, learning. Whenever the subject of stage-trained actors came up, Gary would announce that he had gotten his training in hog calling and then prove it by letting go with a high-pitched "sooie-sooie," no matter where we were.

We often talked shop, and if he had a suggestion about a film that might be good for me, he offered it. He knew that, as ambitious as I was, it would never enter my head to check out any of the new properties at the studio. He seemed very secure in his own career. He loved his work and was not worried about his status. If he had any doubts about it then, he never said a word to me.

And he always looked divine. He was beautifully tailored, the most elegantly dressed man I ever knew in my life. He had fantastically long, narrow feet. I remember he wore Indian boots of the finest leather, over hand-knitted socks. Even when he came over just to sit around the yard he looked perfect, as I'm sure he did when he took hunting trips to the woods with his guns and dogs. But of course, Rocky would be with him then.

His eyes were the most fabulous shade of blue and always sparkling, and he had long eyelashes that were curled more outrageously than any girl's. His hands were long and graceful and beautiful. I think his hands are what I remember most.

One evening he appeared with his usual armload of goodies. There was a special bag for me that delighted him enormously. It contained a summer dress of red material with white polka dots, yards of skirt and a big red belt. It was just a cheap off-the-rack dress, but Gary could not wait for me to wear it. I went to my bedroom and slipped the dress on. It bunched up like a great sack and the bodice sagged. It looked like hell on me. So I made up a story that I could not present myself in it just yet. The next day I took it to a dressmaker, who fitted it

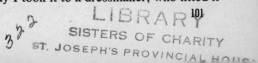

and lined the bodice with elastic to hold it tight. The dress was saved. I loved it and proudly wore it for Gary, who was none the wiser. Sometimes a woman must be clever enough to make a gift look as grand as it was meant to look.

We would also share thoughts about our lives. Gary would speak to me with real tenderness of his days growing up on the ranch with his parents and big brother, Arthur, after the turn of the century. Montana and Kentucky were not unalike, and I listened from a familiar place. Last Chance Gulch had also been a mining town in 1864. By 1910 its name had been changed to Helena, but there were still flakes of gold left in the creek. Gary and his friends would find enough to keep them in licorice money.

"And let me tell you," he would repeat, "you'd get weather!" Then he would tell about the Montana wind called the chinook. "It's a mighty warm wind that comes in early spring right after a winter of big snow." I loved how his eyes crinkled up as he recalled a chinook melting every foot of snow east of the continental divide. A wall of water came down the gorge and took the Helena dam. It also swept the Cooper ranch down to bedrock. "If we had had any hayseed left," he'd chuckle, "we'd have had to use dynamite to plant it." Then he would look at me very seriously and say, "Them warm winds are real treacherous ladies. They can do a man in for good."

Coming from gold mines and coal mines, from grandfathers who ranched and who raised tobacco, we shared a slice of the folk heritage that was deeply American.

His mother sensed this, too. I felt very comfortable going to her house with Gary. It was not difficult to get Mrs. Cooper to talk about her boy. Her eyes lit up when she reminisced about young Frank, as she had named him. She had been sure he would grow up a savage. He and Arthur apparently had no manners, and used to play wild Indian games and hunt for wolf dens. The Coopers sent their boys off to school in England to get some of their corners rounded. Mrs. Cooper was relieved when, after three years at Dunstable, young Frank Cooper could speak French, recognize Latin, wear a top hat, solve an equation and bow from the waist.

Mrs. Cooper seemed to know nothing of our affair, and if she suspected I was the chinook in her son's life, she never hinted at it.

She was not the only one who looked the other way. The studio, the press, all of Hollywood seemed totally oblivious to our relationship. We did a lot of publicity for *The Fountainhead*, and in spite of all the interviews, no one asked *the* question. Perhaps Gary's stature, like that of Spencer Tracy, put him into an untouchable range above low-flying debris. Gary's wife was also oblivious. I was sure of that. She once called to ask me to attend a formal dinner party at the Cooper home and I knew from the tone of her voice that her invitation was sincere. Of course I made up an excuse. But she thought I was snubbing her.

Jean and Chloe were the only ones who knew the truth. They never questioned our relationship, and Gary and I never questioned theirs. We quietly cheered each other's team, knowing we were all in murky waters.

I never talked about Rocky to my friends or even to Gary. He would not have respected me if I had taken potshots at her, but I was secretly glad when I heard someone else say she was cold or selfish or bitchy. Any cut could boost my chances—oh, yes, thoughts of permanence were beginning to creep in. Gary never spoke badly of her. At times he would just say it was tough at home and I knew he wasn't talking about Maria, their only child. I met Maria on the set and was taken by how much she favored Gary in looks and temperament. She was a beautiful eleven-year-old, a rare combination of vivacity and sweetness, and I could see that Gary adored her. I might even have guessed that in a showdown, he would choose her over anything—or anyone—in his life.

Gary had genuine feelings for his wife, too—a kind of devilish appreciation. One time in Sun Valley Gary and a buddy had gone off for a drive, ending up at the local whorehouse—but only to have midnight tea with the girls, who were all Cooper fans. He returned to find his room a shambles. A furious Rocky had torn everything apart—bed, dresser, closet—and then locked herself in Maria's room. Gary clearly enjoyed this episode and seemed to love the fire in Rocky's jealousy.

It must have been past twelve on one of the nights Gary stayed at my place when we were awakened by the sound of a crash. I grabbed my robe and dashed outside.

Under the streetlight I saw a mangled car wrapped around a telephone pole. The driver was sitting in the street, blood streaming from his wounds. He was dead drunk. A woman was pinned inside the wreck.

Two teenagers were already at the scene. "We better call the police," one of them said. "Got a phone at your place?" A fright went through me. Gary could not get involved.

"No," I lied. I directed them to the gas station at the corner. It was closed. "Kick in the glass!" I ordered and one of them obeyed, slamming his foot through the pane and withdrawing it with a scream. The glass had slit his ankle.

Suddenly, sirens were heard and a police car arrived on the scene. Within moments the corner was a beehive of activity. The two injured people were taken away in an ambulance and I overheard a policeman remark that the man was married but the dying woman was not his wife. Slowly, people began to slip back into the darkness. To my horror, I saw Gary standing in the middle of the road in *my* dressing gown, oblivious to the sensation he could have caused.

After we reached the refuge of the apartment, I was appalled that my first thought had not been for that poor boy with his cut ankle or for the dying woman. All I really thought of was protecting Gary. No one else mattered.

Even though Gary and I never appeared in public together, Hollywood is a small town and it was not uncommon for us to meet by chance at a party or premiere, me on the arm of a date and Gary with his wife. Once when NiNi and her husband, George, visited, darling Jack Carson took us all to dinner. We were seated right next to

Gary and Rocky. Of course, we could not speak except as professional friends, but through the entire meal I never felt his eyes leave me.

Another time, at a studio dinner, we sat next to each other. Above the table we showed no signs of intimacy, but below, his hand held mine and the warmth was as torturous as it was comforting.

CHAPTER SEVENTEEN

I n late fall of 1948 Warners alerted me to pack my bags. I was going to England to do a film called *The Hasty Heart,* again with Ronald Reagan. I had gone to the play with Hugh Marlowe in Chicago and thought it was wonderful. It was the touching story of a doomed Scottish soldier in a Burmese hospital, and how a nurse and five wounded men break down his antipathy toward mankind with liberal doses of loving-kindness. I had the only female role. I was so thrilled I didn't worry about leaving Gary. I simply announced my wonderful news at supper, certain he would love the idea, too. And he did. I never knew anyone who could take more real joy in someone else's good fortune.

We worked out a plan for communication. He could easily call me in London, but of course, I would not be able to phone him. So I would write letters, which he would pick up from Jean and Chloe.

As soon as I could get hold of a script, I called George Shdanoff. I wanted every bit of help I could store up. We had very little time to work because I still could not bring myself to travel by air. I would travel with Sue and Alan Ladd, who were going by train and boat to attend the Royal Command Performance in London.

Of course, Gary could not come to the station, so we said our goodbyes privately and I was off. Our parting was simple. There were no promises to be kept.

I learned a lot about being a movie star while crossing the country with Alan Ladd. Alan loved people. He would get off the train and walk among hundreds of fans and never lose a button off his suit or have a necktie pulled awry. I learned then that *you* set the tempo for the crowd. If you respect them and let them know it, they'll do the same with you.

The boat trip to England was straight out of a Jacques Tati comedy. We had not been at sea long when a gentleman joined me and began chatting. We huddled into our coat collars to escape the freezing wind. "What do you do, sir?" I asked, vaguely aware that I had seen him someplace. Suddenly a gust of wind lifted the hair right off his head and sent it sailing into the sea.

"I'm a comedian!" he said, bowing his bald head. "My name is Billy De Wolfe."

There were lots of celebrities on board—Joan Caulfield, Virginia Mayo and Michael O'Shea, as well as Alan and his dear wife, Sue. We were forever getting our pictures taken, and Sue Ladd, quickly noting my towering five feet eight inches, made sure that Alan and I were always at opposite ends of the line. Joan Caulfield was traveling with her mother, who was the horror of the world. This lady just took over our every waking moment. She went so far as to order all our food at every meal. For three nights and days I stayed in my stateroom so I would not have to deal with her, but that was hardly a penance, since I had one of the best staterooms on the ship.

I liked Joan, though. She was a lovely girl and we had some good talks. She, too, was in love with an older married man who was quite as famous as Gary. She confided to me that she desperately wanted to marry Bing Crosby. We were in the same boat in more ways than one, but I could not tell her so.

The wind remained so strong as we disembarked at Brighton that we could barely walk down the ship's gangplank. As I stepped on British soil for the first time, I could never have guessed that England would someday be a mother country almost as dear to me as my own.

We took a day train to London. Looking out the train window, I was immediately confronted with the devastation of the war-scarred landscape. Everywhere I looked there were heaps of rubble, and I could not bear to think of the death and agony this implied. Soon a gray haze began to blur my view and the tortured countryside was mercifully lost in the fog. By the time we reached London, I could see absolutely nothing. It was a famous English "pea-souper." I took it on faith that we had arrived at the great London Savoy. As I passed through the huge oak doors into the lobby, I got a breathtaking introduction to old-world charm.

The porter showed me to my room and swept apart the velvet drapes that covered a large picture window. "You have a lovely view, madam, right over the Thames." I looked, but all I could see were swirling clouds of gray.

Those clouds were far more ominous than I knew. Soon after our arrival we were told that the king of England was deathly ill. I was surprised to learn that I was to offer a sympathetic message from the American people at the Command Performance for the royal family. It did not seem proper to be so excited about such a grave matter, but I was, after all, going to appear on the same stage with Sir Laurence Olivier. He would introduce me.

I stood in the wings waiting for what I knew would be a magical moment between us. But a messenger interrupted Olivier's entrance with a telegram. Everything stopped.

Impetuously I left my place and rushed to Olivier's side. "What is it?" I asked.

He looked at me as if I were the most revolting thing in the world. "It has nothing to do with you, dear," he said sharply.

I got through my speech that evening, but I was so humiliated that I had blown my big moment with the idol of my life.

Before we started shooting I made a quick trip to Paris. To be in Paris for the first time in my life without my love was an exquisite kind of torture, and I could not wait to write and tell him so. I went on a shopping spree, treating myself to my first Christian Dior. I bought a divine scarf for Gary and a pretty little coat for Emily Mahan's baby.

Making a film in England in 1948 was totally different from making one in Hollywood. Elstree Studio was in the process of being reconstructed from what had been a camouflage headquarters during the war. As humble as it appeared to us Americans, the new film studio was a symbol of pride to the English because it showed that they were "getting on with it."

The studio was able to provide the bare essentials but had no money for anything deluxe. My dressing room, although new, was cramped and terribly cold as we approached Christmas. I thought I would be sitting in it forever as the shooting went on at a snail's pace. Setting up a scene took even longer than in Hollywood, and those civilized English tea breaks cut into filming several times a day. Unions were new on the scene and at the drop of a hat a meeting would be called, again holding up production. The studio had a tiny dining room, but the food was ghastly. Cardboard fish covered with soggy bread crumbs and exhausted vegetables was the regular menu. I tried not to complain because I had been trained at home never to criticize food, even in a bad restaurant, and I did feel deeply for those people, who were offering us the best they had. But it didn't make the lunches go down any easier.

We had none of the goodies we got in Hollywood. We were not spoiled, pampered or treated as royalty. The English knew the difference. We were fellow workers and given healthy professional respect. But at the same time, we were Americans—which often made the atmosphere very tense. We simply had not suffered what they had during the war.

The work went well. We had a good director, Vincent Sherman, and a marvelous cast of crazy, funny Englishmen. The key part of the dour Scottish soldier was played by a new young actor, Richard Todd. It was his big break. He ran away with the picture and was nominated for an Academy Award. I respected him immensely as an actor, and later when I lived in England, I always saw him whenever he played Oxford.

In fact, the only problem I had on the film was with the hairdresser. I played an army nurse, and when I started out I had a rather nice little pompadour tucked neatly under my cap. Every day it rose higher and higher, until I was sure it was the only thing the audience was meant to see. The hairdresser probably thought all American actresses should look like Rosalind Russell. I just patted it down and "got on with it."

When Ronnie Reagan and I were not needed on the set, we were sent anywhere that would make good copy. Fortunately, we got on well enough to choose each other's company even when we were not working. We would have dinner and even go dancing at one of the local dance halls. People may have been shabbily dressed and their food rationed, but at night they sang and danced with all their hearts. They were so happy the war was over.

Ronnie adored steak and had them flown in a dozen at a time from "21" in New York. He gave them to the Savoy kitchen and asked that they be kept refrigerated for him. I was delighted one evening when he invited me to share his precious treasure, but when he asked for the steaks he was told that they had "gone bad." Ronnie was furious. All he could do was call New York and place another order. He began inviting me to steak dinners every evening, and, sure enough, six out of every dozen "went bad." Strange things happened down in the Savoy kitchen.

Ronnie was a delightful and interesting companion. Our conversation more likely than not turned to politics, which meant it was not a conversation but a monologue. I just listened in fascination to this budding giant. I sensed that he was still carrying a torch for Jane Wyman, but whether or not this was true, we never crossed the line beyond sharing a great steak.

Gary was halfway around the world, and I longed to see him. I thought about him constantly and wrote him almost daily. I chatted about every little thing, but basically my letters carried only one message. He called several times a week and, oh, his letters! I would read them over and over, treasuring each word. He was a beautiful writer and his letters were filled with a quiet, pervasive passion. I kept all of them for many years, until they disappeared at the time of my stroke. Gary told me he would go by Jean and Chloe's every day to see if there was any mail from me. Chloe was to be our emissary for many years, and my last message to Gary before his death would go through her hands.

The long bleak winter was not without its bit of fun. The two Taylors—Elizabeth and Robert—were also making a film in England and both were at the Savoy. She was exquisite and so young, and traveling with her mother, of course. Robert delighted in teasing Elizabeth. "If you don't shave those legs, Elizabeth," he'd warn, "I'm going to shave them for you!" She would giggle with enjoyment. Ronnie and I occasionally joined them for supper. I had become his "straight man" and used to urge him to tell one or another of his amusing stories. He would always "reluctantly" bow to my request and become the hit of the evening. He may remember those days, but I wonder if he would credit me for our act.

I also met Montgomery Clift for the first time. He had been at The Actors Studio, but our paths had never crossed there. One night he asked me to go to the theater. I was dressing when he rang me up. "Patricia," he wailed. "I have the most terrible news for you. I'm so sorry, but I could get only one ticket for the play." I assured him that was all right, that we could do something else. "Oh, no, that's not what I meant," he stammered. "I can't take *you* with me tonight!" So I stayed at home and that was the last I ever saw of the gorgeous Mr. Clift.

A most rewarding part of making *The Hasty Heart* was the friendship I formed with a young dentist named Hamish Thomson. He was in love with my friend Helen Horton, and, since she was not in England, she entrusted Hamish to me. I liked Helen's young man very much and hoped they would marry, which they did, becoming one of my anchors in England for many years to come. I remember Hamish would take Ronnie and me on country drives, and on one of those jaunts, he recited a little quiz he had seen in a magazine, the kind that asks what you would like to be or do or eat, that sort of thing. Well, he asked Ronnie what he would most like to be in the whole world, and Ronnie laughed and said, "The president of the United States."

CHAPTER EIGHTEEN

he boat trip home was so quiet, I almost wished for Mrs. Caulfield. Ronnie flew back to his beloved America the minute we wrapped the picture. Everyone else seemed to prefer the air route, too. But even Gary Cooper could not tempt me to get on a plane then. I sent a wire to Jean and Chloe, telling Gary that I was returning by boat and would stay a few days in New York with Jean Hagen before coming to Los Angeles by train. My old roommate was now Mrs. Seidel, and although Hollywood was making tempting offers, she and Tom still lived in Manhattan. I was looking forward to a grand reunion of the old group.

The skyline of New York had not been visible from the dock. But blindfolded I would have felt the throb of that great city as we came nearer to midtown Manhattan. It was February 1949. I had just turned twenty-three.

"Keep the change," I told the driver, feeling very generous and terribly excited for some reason I could not understand. The Seidels' door flew open and in an instant I was engulfed by the screams and hugs of the old gang —Helen and Petey and Natalie and Nancy. I told them all about my fabulous trip and they had just gone their way when the doorbell rang. Jean said, "Patricia, why don't *you* get it?" I opened the door and felt my heart leap into my throat.

I fell into his arms, cooling my blazing face on the

February cold that clung to his overcoat. I had never seen Gary dressed for winter. "You look wonderful," was all I could seem to say. "Wonderful. Just—wonderful!"

Gary was in New York for a couple of days. With Rocky. He had arranged the surprise with Jean Hagen. Obviously she knew about us, and, knowing Jean, I sensed she would disapprove of our affair. But she and Tom gave us the use of their apartment anyway. My friends would not return that afternoon.

Once back on the Coast, Gary and I quickly slipped back to living under the rose. He continued to surprise me with gifts, and they were becoming more extravagant. I returned to find he had traded in my Buick for a brand-new Cadillac. And he presented me with a pair of beautiful diamond drop earrings from Winston's. Gary had been educated by the women in his life in how to please them. Rumor had it the Countess di Frasso had taught him everything he knew, from reading a wine list to choosing a tie. It may have been true, but I found it hard to believe after having met Gary's mother.

It was becoming very hard to contain my longings for a family of my own with a man who would love only me. I would court those fantasies sometimes, imagining us giving up our careers and going to some faraway place, starting all over again, even in a poor shack, scraping together our living. My daydreams came complete with Dominique's lines from The Fountainhead: "I'll cook, I'll wash your clothes, I'll scrub the floors . . . let me do everything with you . . . let me, please."

But there would be no taking Gary Cooper out of his environment.

He wanted the best of two worlds. He used to joke that in the old Westerns, a cowboy could kiss his horse but not his girl. He wanted both horse and girl. I was beginning to feel more and more like his horse.

About this time a very young and handsome Kirk Douglas began asking me out. Kirk had just become a huge success in Champion. He was my escort to the premiere of The Fountainhead. Jack Warner had already screened the film, and he sent me a wire stating that I was the greatest thing to hit Hollywood since Garbo.

I shall never forget that night. I had the grim feeling all through the screening that I would not emerge a champion, a feeling that was not dispelled by the crowd. When Kirk and I moved out into the bright lobby it seemed that everyone just turned their heads and looked in the other direction. One familiar face from the trip to England did not avoid me. Virginia Mayo gave my hand a squeeze and said, "My, weren't you *bad*!" I hoped she meant the character I played, but I knew my career as a second Garbo was over before it began.

The Fountainhead was a bomb.

I continued to go out with Kirk. He knew nothing about Gary and me and was an ardent pursuer. We would sometimes come back to my apartment for a drink, but there was never anything between us but goodnight kisses, until one night. I was feeling low. I had had a few drinks. And, let's face it, Kirk was very attractive. I found myself responding to his extremely persuasive kisses. But when it came right down to it—and it did—I simply couldn't.

After he left, the doorbell rang and an unexpected Gary Cooper was standing on the threshold. A strange cloud darkened his face. "I looked into your window tonight, Pat, and I saw what was happening." Nothing had really happened at all, but I was impressed by this outburst of jealousy, which was so unlike Gary. I could feel myself starting to smile.

Suddenly Gary slapped me. I felt a sting of pain shoot through my nose. My hand sprang to my face to soothe the blow. I looked into my palm and saw blood, then back into Gary's shocked eyes. Suddenly, I hated him. "You don't do that to me."

The softness in Gary's voice broke the ugly spirit between us. "Baby, I'm sorry. Let's just forget about it."

And he did. As strange as it seems, we did not speak about that incident again. It was as if he had lowered a curtain.

But he never hit me again.

CHAPTER NINETEEN

Only rarely did I ever catch a fleeting touch of regret in Gary. Once in a while he would say, "I'm too old for you, baby." That was absurd. I loved the fact that Gary was older than I was. That didn't put any distance between us. He had no problems mingling with my friends, who were all younger. We spent time with Jean and Tom, who were now in California and very pregnant. We would go down to La Jolla to visit Mimi Tellis, a close friend from Northwestern days, and her husband, Alexis. And we saw K. T. and Hugh and their little son, who utterly adored Gary. He had a wonderful way with young boys that made me so want to give him a son of his own.

How I would fit into *his* social set was not yet a problem, since I did not see his friends.

Kirk Douglas generously continued to be my public beau. I say generously because he now knew about Gary and me, and although it had cooled his ardor, it had not diminished the warmth of his friendship—which was very needed.

Warners was signaling me for "Rock Bottom," a film whose name was later changed to *Three Secrets*. It was an interesting story about three women, each of whom had borne a baby and then put the child up for adoption. A few years later, at the site of a plane crash whose sole survivor might be that child, the women meet. It had a very good director, Robert Wise. Gary thought I should grab it, and so did I.

Even though Eleanor Parker got top billing and Ruth Roman had the most sympathetic part, *Three Secrets* had a great role for me and I think I gave the strongest performance in my young screen career. I loved my character. She made her own way in a man's world, only to lose her husband because he thinks she's too ballsy. It was an early bow to the unrest that would emerge as women's lib. Eleanor detested her part. Onscreen she was another butter-wouldn't-melt-in-her-mouth type. But off, she had the most delightfully wicked sense of humor. How that lady could make me laugh.

Then came the greatest news I could have hoped for. Warner Brothers decided to team Gary and me again in a film called *Bright Leaf*. Set against the tobacco industry at the turn of the century, it was a tale of love and revenge and the rise of the cigarette, but it was neither firm nor fully packed. The part of Margaret was underlined on the script I was sent, but when I read it I knew the other female role, Sonia, was the one I wanted. Margaret was another cold, ruthless bitch. Sonia had warmth and honesty and goodness of heart. In short, Sonia was a real woman. I did everything I could to get it. I wept, I pleaded, but they wouldn't budge. I suspect they were so adamant because there were shades of Regina Hubbard in Margaret.

I even begged Gary to make the studio give me the part, but he would not fight for me. Not because he thought I should fight my own battles and not because he was unwilling to raise suspicion about our relationship. He simply did not want to get involved in any conflict. Conflict was something Gary Cooper was a master at avoiding. I was so furious with him. Lauren Bacall got the role. The first minute I saw Lauren in costume, beautifully dressed but bareheaded, I felt another flush of rage go through me. Sonia would wear a hat, I said to myself. That kind of woman would wear a hat!

The director was Michael Curtiz and the chemistry between us was ghastly. But except for my stormy bouts with Mike, I had a smooth relationship with all the cast and crew on *Bright Leaf*. We had the great Donald Crisp and an old friend, Jack Carson.

The wardrobe was one of the best things about the picture. My dresses were beautifully done in expensive silks, velvets and brocades, every detail authentic to the period. One of the necklaces I wore was made of baroque pearls. I let everyone know how fabulous I thought it was, but my hint was ignored. The studio was not about to part with it.

One scene in the film moved me very deeply. Not when we shot it, but a long time afterward. Donald Crisp, who played my father, commits suicide with a dueling pistol. Many years later, my father's brother Eben took himself to the woods and blew his head off with a rifle. Even when I watch *Bright Leaf* today on television that scene brings tears to my eyes.

As much as Gary and I liked the movie, it was not successful then and, I'm sorry to say, doesn't stand up now. But I had a lovely remembrance from *Bright Leaf*. During production Gary had an exact copy of the pearl necklace I loved so much made as a gift for me.

I wish I could say that I still wear it, but the lovely pearls disappeared a few years later, along with other pieces of jewelry that meant a great deal to me.

Once on a trip to New York I had a reunion with a college chum, and after she left, I discovered that several good pieces were missing from my jewel case, including the Civil War pin from Gary. The investigating detective had no doubt that the thief had to have been my guest that evening. The same anger I felt as a child consumed me. When the theft was reported in the papers, my "friend" called to offer sympathy, but I could not bring myself to speak to her. Why, why, why do some people think that they have the right to take what is yours?

Surprising as it seems, Gary shared my enthusiasm for acting classes, and he came with me to sessions with George Shdanoff to work on scenes for *Bright Leaf*. Occasionally he studied with Jeff Corey, who was also in the film.

Michael Chekhov lived in Hollywood and had agreed to conduct a limited number of teaching sessions. Both Gary and I got into his class. So did Anthony Quinn, Shelley Winters, Robert Stack and Arthur Kennedy.

Chekhov worked through short improvisations. He called Gary up to the stage and gave him a problem. Gary thought for a moment and then began. He captured us with his ability to create an entire character with only the simplest suggestions. When he finished, his audience burst into cheers. No one anticipated the raw talent in the movie star who was usually accused of playing only himself. But I was not surprised at the subtlety of his work. It was the same subtlety he brought to his movie roles, a masterful ability to create "real" people through the most careful modulation of voice, gesture and expression that is usually associated with modern post-Method actors.

As soon as I completed *Bright Leaf,* I was happily assigned to *The Breaking Point*. It was based on the Ernest Hemingway novel *To Have and Have Not.* A movie with that title, made in 1944, was generally thought to be the film version of the book, but William Faulkner—who disliked Hemingway—wrote an original script, keeping only the title and the name of the lead character. It was the movie that introduced Lauren Bacall to both the screen and Humphrey Bogart.

Our film was, in fact, a very faithful version of the novel. I played a loose woman who gets mixed up with gun runners and John Garfield, whom I lure away from his wife, played by the delicious Phyllis Thaxter. In the end, John goes back to Phyllis and I get what I deserve. My last lines in the film still give me a kick. "I guess I should have swam back to port. Or is it swum?"

John Garfield always projected a strong male animal quality in his films. It was not an act. John had an eye for the ladies and did not waste time. "I want to talk to you," he commanded when we met. "You know, you're a whore?" I looked at him aghast. "In the picture, I mean. You are *all whore*." He took my hand and smiled ever so slightly. "You know what I mean? You understand me?"

I understood exactly what he meant, but I did not explore the subject with him. I was Gary's woman.

Yes I was, and my double life was becoming hellish. I wanted to be with Gary always. Always. Never parted, not even briefly. I began to allow myself to feel it was only a matter of time before the truth of our love would have to be known and accepted.

CHAPTER TWENTY

here were two other important men in my life at this time. One was Dashiell Hammett. I had heard from Lillian Hellman soon after I came to Hollywood. She had reacted angrily to an interview I gave about *Another Part of the Forest* in which I simply said that I had thought it was going to be the greatest success ever on Broadway, but that it had not turned out that way. "If you bad-mouth me," she threatened, "I'll bad-mouth you." I wrote immediately and apologized, but got no reply, not even a warning that Dash was on his way to the Coast. So when he called, it was a wonderful surprise.

Dash began to take me out. He chose the most expensive restaurants in town. We didn't talk, or at least he didn't. I would have to keep the conversation going and all he would interject was an occasional "Ehh?" or "Hmm?" Then everything would go silent and we would just sit. Dash was not drinking or writing now. He just ruminated on his own thoughts. But I so enjoyed simply being with him. After dinner we would go back to my place and he would hold me in his arms very contentedly. That was our ritual. I began to feel a bit like the Shulamite in the Bible story of King David. She was put into the old king's bed just to keep his bones warm.

The other man was Harvey Orkin. I met Harvey at

121

Gene Kelly's house one Sunday afternoon. The Kellys' was home base for the whole Hollywood scene on weekends. You did not need an invitation, you just stopped in for a drink or a swim or a game of volleyball. Harvey was a totally appealing, warm and joyful human being. I responded to him immediately and the mold for a lifetime of love was set. Ours was never a romantic love. Thinking back on Harvey leaves me frustrated by the English language. There should be as many words for love as there are people we love.

As fate would have it, Harvey was also Gary's good friend and publicist. But even though he worked closely with Gary, he did not know about us. So it was Harvey, in all his innocent good humor, who opened the Pandora's box of our secret life.

One Sunday morning Harvey and his girlfriend Helen and I were brunching at the beach, when he was struck with inspiration. The great Albert Schweitzer was going to give a speech in Aspen, Colorado. Coincidentally, Aspen was the site of the new Cooper family home, which was under construction. Harvey thought it would be a wonderful idea if we all drove up there together. We could see Schweitzer and the house at the same time. We "all" would include my mother, who was visiting me at the time. I knew she would be delighted to join us because she loved being part of my Hollywood life. She had met Gary and adored him, never entertaining the slightest notion that anything was going on between us. Still, I had my doubts. "Come on, the more the merrier," Harvey insisted. I didn't want a weekend with Rocky, but damn it all, it would be the only chance in my life to see Schweitzer.

Harvey went to call Gary. I couldn't imagine what he would say. Would he want to risk throwing us all together? He couldn't possibly say yes. Harvey returned to the table. "Gary was pleased as punch! He said for us to come right over to talk about it."

I had never been in Gary's house before. I turned off my brain and gave way to female curiosity.

Gary met us at the door. I could tell that he was very

excited to have me in his house. He tripped over the carpet like a gangly boy.

"What *are* you doing, Gary? Will you pick up your feet?" The minute I heard Rocky's voice I remembered I was in her territory.

The Cooper home was a study in casual elegance. Graceful rooms joined in a circle of comfort around a central garden and pool. There seemed to be flowers everywhere. Flowered prints on chairs, flowers in paintings, yellows, pinks and oranges. I felt embraced by flowers. Standing in the living room and looking out the great bay window gave me the impression of being inside a garden. I looked with considerable interest at the yard. I knew Gary was a fine gardener and wondered what of this lovely Eden was his creation.

Rocky showed us through their house, and I noted with some small pleasure that Gary had a bedroom of his own. Afterward we had coffee on the patio and talked about Aspen. Rocky thought it was a great idea and took over. She and Maria would be flying up early. Gary would drive up with us and join them at the Jerome Hotel, and she would see that all of us had reservations elsewhere. Two cars would be needed. I was already plotting how to get Mother to ride with Harvey and Helen.

As we left I could not help but notice a family portrait of Gary, Rocky and Maria on the mantel. It was glowing with love. The thought crossed my mind, If I was a good woman, I would call this whole thing off.

The route to Aspen went through the Mojave desert—which is fiercely hot in July—so Gary and I agreed to leave in the late afternoon and hit the desert at night. The road ribboned ahead into miles of sandy slopes, and for a long stretch we drove in silence. My hand in his said simply, It continues. My eyes traced his profile. Behind it a red sun began to slide into the parched hills, and soon the stage gave over to hundreds of small prickly silhouettes. We had agreed upon a rendezvous point with our companion car; shortly the motel came into view. I hated turning into the glare of neon and I hated returning to the company of the others. But supper was short. Harvey and Helen wanted to be alone. Mother was tired and wanted to go to bed. Gary and I seized the opportunity to return to the night desert.

As if we had agreed upon the moment, Gary brought the car to a gentle stop. We sat for a while in the hush of the desert. "Let's walk," he said and opened his door. I waited, as I always did, for him to let me out. We removed our shoes and walked out onto the sand until we escaped into the illusion that we were as free as the desert around us. The sand was warm and soft as we lay down together.

The next day we all arrived on schedule and went right to the construction site. Maria ran to greet us. Soon we were moving through the wooden skeleton with Gary pointing the way. I don't know when it was that I became aware that Gary's manner was strained. I felt uneasy myself. But no one else seemed to notice, not even Rocky, who was totally taken up with showing everything off to us. The afternoon went smoothly; then we all parted for an early dinner and a needed rest at our respective hotels. Wishful thinking. I did not rest well at all. I wanted to be with Gary. I couldn't shake the feeling that something was going wrong.

The next morning Harvey drove me to the Jerome Hotel. Gary was waiting for me in their work truck. He did not jump out as he normally did to open the door. I got in beside him. When I saw his face, my blood turned to ice. Before I could say anything I heard someone approach, and as I looked out the window Rocky and Maria passed into my view. Rocky's face was like stone. Maria's was stained with tears. The child looked at me and spat on the ground. Such a little girl, and she spat with so much hate.

Gary and I drove out into the countryside and were quiet for a long time.

"Last night Rocky asked me if I was having an affair with you. I said yes. She wanted to know if I was in love with you. I said yes."

There was another silence and he continued. "Maria came in just about then and Rocky told her everything."

I was absolutely dumbfounded. It was beyond my understanding that Rocky could have done that to her own daughter. I never understood until I heard myself blurt out the same wounding message to a daughter of my own, twenty-five years later.

Mother, who knew she was having a terrible time but could not imagine why, asked to go home by train. I went to hear Schweitzer with Harvey and Helen, and then the three of us drove back to L.A. By the time we reached the desert I was almost convinced the whole thing had been a terrible dream. Suddenly the car began to sputter and came to a halt. Harvey jumped out and I followed him, as if I could possibly know one thing to do. There was nothing for miles but sand dunes and not a car was in sight. Harvey began fooling with the engine, removing bolts and screws and handing them to me with globs of grease and dirt. Helen followed his instructions to pump the accelerator. All at once the motor turned over and began to race. Harvey shot a grin at me and called to Helen to take her foot off the gas.

"But I haven't got it on the gas!" came her frantic reply.

The engine was showering us with dirt. We looked at each other, our faces streaked with oil and sand, and began to laugh. We fell on the ground, hooting until tears streamed down our faces. The pain in me exploded into shrieks of laughter.

CHAPTER
TWENTY-ONE

What gives a woman the right to heaven in the arms of another woman's husband? What gives her the right to say, I have something to give that she cannot? If you believe in the institution of marriage, how can you insert yourself into that bond between a man and the woman he has chosen first?

I never tried to compete with Rocky. She gave her husband more than a life style with a classic profile. It would be many years and a marriage of my own before I would value her gift—a quality of caring. But there was no doubt in my mind that I was unique and special to Gary. I knew I gave him something she did not.

We had reached a depth of real appreciation that all people desire but few realize. He truly loved my body and I loved his, and he knew it. When he reached out to love me it was first with those penetrating eyes, which stripped away all barriers between us, and then with those godlike hands, which seemed to create me. In his arms I thought, *I am, at last I am.*

When the young doctor took my virginity and made me a bad woman, I made up my mind I would never get hurt like that again. Sex was an indoor sport and I did not confuse it with commitment. I had lost my belief in marriage. That is why I so easily became involved with Victor and Peter.

But Gary touched my heart as no one else had done before. I was really in love, and it was like I was innocent again.

Dared I hope this time I would be anything but the other woman?

I began to allow myself to believe the impossible. Gary would leave his family and marry me. It would be just a matter of time. But there were mornings after Gary left when I would lie thinking. I felt hurt that I was so very much alone and, yes, annoyed that he could go home to a life with his family. That I did not have. I wanted a family of my own so desperately. And I felt ashamed. My life tasted beautiful in my mouth, but digestion was bitter.

I waited for him to say something about Aspen. Yet what happened and the implications it might have for our future were not discussed. He never said anything that might give me reason to think he would get a divorce. But I simply could not accept the possibility that he was *not* thinking of marrying me. I was twenty-four, and more naive than I knew.

When Gary finally mentioned Aspen, it was only to say that Rocky had passed off the whole thing as something belonging to his trinket box. She even wisecracked about his "southern cow who eats corn bread and black-eyed peas." Maria thought that was the funniest thing she had ever heard. Gary chuckled now, too, as if her remarks were too silly to hurt. Then he grew sober. "I'm worried about Maria," he confessed. "I never talk to her about us, but it's bothering her quite a lot. She's started walking in her sleep. We found her the other night near the edge of the pool." Some deep intuition told me that if I had only Rocky to contend with, it was fair play. In Maria I was fighting the angels.

Before I met Gary Cooper I had been attracted to other women's husbands, but I had not been in love with them. I played my cards straight. It was pure competition, and if a woman wasn't strong enough to hold her man, it wasn't my problem. But love stripped away the old attitudes.

I was totally taken off guard one night at Jack Warner's house. I was seated across the dinner table from Rocky. It was a large party and the din would protect me from any direct communication. But Rocky did not need words. Her look was a laser beam that went right to the pit of my stomach: You really are a slut. You really are.

I did not dismiss the terrible guilt I felt, but now I could not look down in shame. I looked back at her because for the first time in my life I was really in love, and I knew it. Our eyes stayed riveted, and in that moment, our souls locked horns in a combat that would become the coldest of wars for the next thirty years.

I began to emerge from the woodwork into Gary's social life. He had laughed about my devastating encounter with Laurence Olivier, and when my idol and his wife, Vivien Leigh, came to Hollywood, Gary decided to bring us together again. He hosted a small dinner at a swanky Chinese restaurant to give me a second chance at that magical moment.

The other guests were Elia Kazan and the divine Ethel Barrymore. Vivien Leigh had just made a great success in London in *A Streetcar Named Desire* and Helen Horton had taken over her role on the road. When we were introduced I said, "We have someone in common. My good friend Helen Horton took over for you in *Streetcar.*"

Vivien looked at me coolly. "No one takes over for me, dear. When I leave a play, it's over."

I thought to myself, Oh God, this is not getting off to a good start at all.

Things did not improve. Gary and Ethel and Laurence shared at least a century's worth of career stories and Vivien was locked in conversation with Gadge, who would soon direct her in the film version of *Streetcar*. I sat and listened and sipped wine. And more wine.

"Say, Larry," Gary suddenly said, his eyes twinkling, "how would you like to make a fortune?"

"Very much," replied Sir Laurence.

Gary presented his absolutely surefire idea: "Why not host a TV show?" This was, mind you, in the very early days of the new medium and well-known actors weren't caught dead on the tube. But Gary wasn't joking. He carefully proceeded to outline the future advantages of owning one's own television show, unaware of how affronted Laurence was. The Oliviers just stared, open-mouthed. The room fell silent.

I thought Gary was kidding, but I found out a fit of giggles was the wrong way to express it. Gary scowled at me angrily. "What the hell are *you* laughing at?" This did not improve the situation. Our guests soon excused themselves. So much for my second chance with Olivier.

At home I didn't feel like laughing at all. How could I have been so foolish? "I'm so young and stupid," I apologized, "I want to be old. Old. Old."

His embarrassment and anger gone, Gary said softly, "I love you just the way you are." And he stroked my cheek until I fell asleep.

One of Gary's best friends was Ernest Hemingway. He was a special part of Gary's life and I was thrilled when Gary promised to take me to meet the great man. I sensed a crucial audition in my future.

In January 1950 Warner Brothers invited me to go on a publicity junket. When you were under contract you were "invited" to do what the studio wanted done. I was to attend a film festival in Uruguay. I told Gary I would not be returning home directly from the festival. I planned to stop over in Florida, where my Aunt Ima now lived and where my brother was happily attending military school. Mother would come down to meet me.

The Hollywood contingent included June Haver, Lizabeth Scott, Joan Fontaine and Wendell Corey, who was a terrific dancer. France sent the handsome Gérard Philipe. Of course, we would have to travel by air. So I simply decided the time had come to stop all the fuss about flying.

The junket took us to several countries. We even met

Evita Perón, a charming horror, I thought, but I kept this opinion to myself. Mr. Philipe, however, despised her and made no secret about it. He was appalled at the splendor she lived in while there was such poverty right outside her door. At our audience, he said something curt in French that I of course did not understand, but that visibly shook the lady. June Haver transcended the tense moment. She immediately stepped forward and presented Evita with a crucifix.

The week was one big orgy of luxury hotels, scrumptious meals and parties. At one of these a woman approached me. "I understand you know Gary Cooper very well. I did, too, my dear." The Countess Dorothy di Frasso was now much older than when she and Gary had spent their days together at the Villa Madama. But the fascinating face artfully defied time by graciously accepting it.

She spoke with a still-lingering love for the young man she had taken under her wing. I couldn't keep from asking if it was true that she had taught him how to dress. "Well, maybe a little, but not much. It was in his blood to 'dude himself up,' as he would say. I just told him how wonderful he looked."

We met three times while I was in South America. The last time was at a magnificent villa outside Montevideo. Our host was a very old man who I was told was one of the richest people in the world. I shall never forget that party, because the aged white-haired gent came downstairs to greet us all and see to it we had everything we wanted, and then went back upstairs and died. I remember the Countess thought that was "spunky."

I never asked her how she knew about Gary and me or why she seemed so sure he loved me. But when we parted she said, "Fight for him, he's worth it."

"But I've met Rocky," I said, "and she's tough."

"I met her, too," the Countess smiled. "She had me for tea with two other of Gary's ladies. She took the occasion to return the gifts each of us had given him. You're going to need all the spunk you've got, my dear."

I can't remember one film I saw at the festival, but I

certainly remember June Haver. She would go off on her own a lot. June's fiancé had recently died, and she was courting the Catholic Church with intentions of leaving her career and becoming a nun. Of course, I didn't know that then, but I was drawn to her and began to follow her around like a lamb. She took me to masses in the big cathedrals—territory forbidden me as a child—and even to a nunnery, where we ate a meal with the sisters. We met priests and they were not somber at all. In fact, they were a lot of fun. And quite handsome. During those times with June, I was aware of the great comfort she seemed to find in her religion. I had never been devoutly religious, but there was something that seemed to be speaking to me, too. I felt wholesome. I forgot I was sleeping with a married man.

Mother was waiting for me at the airport. She was bursting with excitement, but not only from seeing me. There was a limousine waiting and in the back was my Gary. "He called me at the hotel. Imagine that? I was shocked," whispered Mother as we hurried toward the car. "He was downstairs and said, Would I mind riding out to the airport with him? He wanted to talk to me."

At that moment I did not want to see Gary Cooper. He reminded me of what I had forgotten. I was a bad woman.

It was years before Mother told me what she and Gary had talked about on that astonishing drive. Gary had actually spoken quite freely. "He told me he had never known a love for anyone the way he did for you, Patsy. There was no reason for him to fib to me. Still. . . ." And then she paused. "Still, I told him that my family was not accustomed to anything like that." She never defined what she meant by "that."

Mother had not been as blind as I thought.

Gary had a surprise for me. He had not forgotten his promise to take me to meet Ernest Hemingway. We would fly to Cuba by chartered plane and spend the weekend with Ernest and his wife, Mary.

The Hemingway cottage was hidden away in the still-virginal wilds of the tropical island, which was almost overdone with lush trees heavy with their burden of ripe fruit. Dogs and cats scampered away from the wheels of our car as we turned into the driveway. Hemingway shot out of the house, his arms outstretched. This huge bear of a man grabbed Gary and began to pummel him. It was a great masculine show, complete with hoots of joy. It could have been just another of their reunions to join up for a pigeon shoot and some fireside chats. But there was more to it than that. Gary wanted something from his old friend. He wanted an opinion.

We arrived at about five in the evening, just in time for a drink before supper. A housekeeper and manservant attended our very simple meal. I remember only two exchanges during dinner. I asked Mary Hemingway if she liked to play bridge and she replied, with a twinge of disdain, "I have so many books to read, I don't have time to play trivial games."

Hemingway glanced up and winked at me. "I write goddamned good books, you know!" I knew he liked me. He told me he thought *The Breaking Point* was the best film made from any of his books.

During our time there I was very much aware that Gary was seriously confiding in Hemingway. I did not hear their conversations, but I just knew Gary was telling him that he wanted to marry me. He was asking for Papa's blessing, and I was sure he was getting it. And as sure as I was that Papa liked me, I was just as certain Mary Hemingway did not. As time passed I realized her antagonism toward me was not personal. When we met again, in an entirely different context, she could not have been kinder. But in 1950 I spelled crisis for the Cooper family, and most of their circle resented being challenged into separate camps. Mary was a loyal friend to Rocky Cooper.

So I should have been more than surprised when Gary and I were escorted to the little guest house and found it had one double bed, which had been turned down for us to share.

Years later I read that Ernest Hemingway disapproved of our affair. He did not then. No matter how brief the candle, it was lit for me that weekend.

At its end Gary put me on a plane back to Hollywood. He remained with Hemingway for another day and then flew to New York to make a rare radio appearance. He and Shirley Booth were to do *Come Back Little Sheba* on the air for the Theatre Guild.

On the way home, my mind all but exploded with questions. Had Papa liked me well enough to encourage Gary to get a divorce? How many other friends would have to approve? Why couldn't Gary decide for himself? Maybe he wasn't trying to decide, after all.

To this day whenever I see Gary on the screen, I fall in love with him all over again. Even the sound of his voice is enough to renew my passion. So it was when Jean and Chloe invited me to listen to *Come Back Little Sheba* at their house. I thought the play was beautifully done and Gary was a wonderful Doc. I couldn't wait to let him know. I sent a wire to his hotel telling him how fabulous I thought he was.

The next day *I* got a wire. I could not wait to see his answer. I excitedly tore open the envelope. I HAVE HAD JUST ABOUT ENOUGH OF YOU. YOU HAD BETTER STOP NOW OR YOU WILL BE SORRY. It was signed MRS. GARY COOPER.

I dropped the telegram and stood for a long, paralyzed moment staring at it on the floor. *Jesus Christ, what am I doing? I should be more careful.* I saw the strained face of a very frightened woman looking back at me from the hallway mirror. *I shouldn't be doing this at all.*

CHAPTER TWENTY-TWO

am not certain when it was that I began to see a psychiatrist. I remember there came a point when I would be driving down the street or shopping at the grocery and suddenly my eyes would be blurred with tears. I would cry and cry all the time. I was seeing Harry Kurnitz quite often and he became clearly concerned about my behavior. It was Harry who set up the appointment with the analyst.

The first day I went to my new doctor's office, I recall seeing Peter Lindstrom, the husband Ingrid Bergman had abandoned. He was a colleague and not there for treatment, but I could not help wondering what he might say on an analyst's couch.

I knew from the first session that I was not going to like the psychiatrist. He had an insinuating smile that said *there's something you're not telling me*. But I was so convinced I needed to talk to somebody that I went back.

It would not have taken a genius to figure out why I was a wreck. I loved Gary, but he would not commit himself. No amount of probing my psyche was going to help. I told the doctor I wanted a family of my own, I wanted a home of my own, I wanted a husband of my own. And I wanted to stop the sessions. He smiled that smile and said, "But you haven't mentioned masturbation." I leapt to my feet and ran to the door.

* * *

Warner Brothers decided to put me in a film with John Wayne. It was a typical war movie called *Operation Pacific*. John Wayne had enormous appeal for the public, but I did not find him appealing in the least. I think my charms were lost on him, too. He was going through marital problems, which kept him in a bad humor all the time. Duke was at odds with the director and could be a bully, particularly with a gay publicity man who seemed to draw his wrath at every turn.

But whatever anxiety I felt, I was soon to be shaken by something more serious than squabbles on the set.

I was usually very good about remembering my period. I don't know why I didn't advert to the fact that it had not come for two months. Perhaps somewhere in my heart I wanted to be pregnant. Jean Valentino made an appointment with her doctor. He called a few days later and told me I was pregnant.

I was so thrilled to hear his words that for a short while I forgot completely that there would be any question of whether or not this baby would be born.

I could see it in Gary's eyes, too, when I told him. He wanted me to have the baby. He held my hands and pressed them to his cheeks. The new life between us was our love. It was a night of wonder.

But the next morning my joy, my strength drained out of me as rational terrors whipped my brain. Career. Family. Oh, God—my mother! She would kill herself if I had a baby out of wedlock.

And what about Gary? If I pressed him, what would he do?

Suddenly everything was so damned dispassionate and reasonable. Gary and I stood like puppets. *Please God, don't let him drop that curtain,* I silently prayed.

"I don't know what to do in this kind of situation," he said weakly, "but I know someone I can ask."

"Good," I answered blankly.

For the next several days we went to work, we saw each other, we had dinner, we made love. We did not talk about the baby.

Then one evening Gary called. "There's a doctor in downtown Los Angeles," he said. "I suppose we have to, Pat. Our appointment is tomorrow afternoon."

Our appointment? I told him he couldn't possibly go with me. I felt it was too risky for him to be known as the father of this baby. But Gary wasn't listening.

"Shall I bring Chloe with us?" he asked. "She could wait with me in the car."

I remember it was a beautiful blue October day. We drove to a shabby office building, more like a small house, in an area I had never seen. We parked and I got out.

I walked alone to the entrance and knocked. If I had let myself think about it, perhaps I might have been disappointed that Gary did not insist upon coming inside with me. The door opened and a young, disinterested face acknowledged my presence. I stepped inside. The room was painted a drab gray, or else the white walls had become dirty. There was no furniture to speak of, just a big examining table, and no one else in the room. The young man was the doctor. I handed him Gary's envelope of cash.

He did not say anything more than was absolutely necessary. I followed his instructions without a word. I remember he held a needle at bay while he filled the syringe. It was the longest needle I had ever seen in my life. I closed my eyes. The needle's impaling gift was supposed to relieve pain. I thought I would die. My body began to sweat from every pore. The most agonizing hour of my life commenced. All I could hear was the sound of scraping.

I could not believe it was still daytime when I stumbled back into the shocking light. Gary sat rigid in the car. He was also soaked with sweat.

We wept together that afternoon. I lay in his arms on the floor and we wept. After a while, Jean and Chloe brought a blanket and pillow to put under us.

The bleeding went on for five weeks. I called in sick to the set for only two days and then continued my work without anyone realizing what had happened. Life went on as usual.

But for over thirty years, alone, in the night, I cried. For years and years I cried over that baby. And whenever I had too much to drink, I would remember that I had not allowed him to exist.

I admired Ingrid Bergman for having her son. She had guts. I did not. And I regret it with all my heart. If I had only one thing to do over in my life, I would have that baby.

Gary told his wife about the abortion. I was both astonished and hurt. Whatever else transpired between them I will never know. But in the wake of his disclosure, he moved out of their Brentwood home and went to the Bel-Air.

At last, I told myself, at last.

If I had been older and wiser, I would have realized that Gary had no reason to tell Rocky about the abortion unless he was going to stay with her. He was not going to pick up my option.

CHAPTER
TWENTY-THREE

Neither was Warner Brothers. I was becoming an expensive commodity for the studio now. Their investment in me had not paid off. The critics had been kind, but I had not hit the jackpot at the box office. I certainly had not become the new Garbo.

The entire time I was with the studio, I never refused any part or any request to do publicity, no matter how silly. I marched with the Junior Rose Bowl Queen and posed at Pacific Ocean Park with a rifle in one hand and a Kewpie doll in the other. I even drove a bulldozer in ground-breaking ceremonies for a Salvation Army boys' club. I accepted all the arranged-for citations. I was honorary nurse at the Huntington Memorial Hospital and Burbank's lady mayor for a day.

The first and only time I ever said no was to a cheap little Western the studio wanted to put me in, the title of which I've blocked. They promptly took me off salary, where I remained until I was chastened enough to accept a gem with the inspired title "Along the Santa Fe Trail." Changing that to *Raton Pass* and my hair back to brown did not help in the least. The golden age of Patricia Neal was over in more ways than one.

It was my last film under the contract, which had begun with so much fanfare. The day I left the Warner lot for the last time I was alone. I said goodbye to the cop and drove out the gate. I didn't leave completely empty-handed. My agents had gotten me a three-picture deal at Fox. Still, 1951 promised to be a very hard new year.

I always reached for friends when I sensed trouble was coming. I didn't think I had too many left in Hollywood. Gossip about Gary and me was being whispered all over town. No official Cooper separation had been declared, and no one wanted to be on the wrong side when the lines were finally drawn. I was no longer the young darling of Hollywood. I was the unsympathetic side of a triangle. Gary sensed my increasing anxiety and grew more tender toward me.

Actually, he was under as much tension as I was. I could see it in his face, feel it in his body. But of course, he did not talk about it. I did not know he was becoming very ill.

My first film of the new Fox contract was going to be a science fiction thriller called *The Day the Earth Stood Still*. I was not encouraged in the least, but I did not want to begin my career at Fox by going on suspension. The director was Robert Wise, who had been good to me in the past. He believed in the project and wanted me to do it. I am very glad I said yes. I worked with an old friend, Hugh Marlowe, and a new one, Michael Rennie. I do think it's the best science fiction film ever made, although I admit that I sometimes had a difficult time keeping a straight face. Michael would patiently watch me bite my lips to avoid giggling and ask, with true British reserve, "Is that the way you intend to play it?"

The press was relentless now. They followed me everywhere, even onto the set, but I would not speak to them. The publicity department made up responses for me to their questions about Gary. So in print, I could be vague ("We're just good friends") or cute ("If I were in love with him I'd be silly to advertise it. After all, he *is* a married man") or even haughty ("I *do* wish people would find something else to talk about").

Dear Michael, who was as exasperated as I was, thought I should honor their rude questions with my favorite line from the film.

"Miss Neal, did you break up Gary Cooper's marriage?"

"Klaatu barada nikto!"

For Gary it was nothing to joke about. I could tell by looking at him that he was fed up with all the fuss. It didn't help matters that his career, too, had been in a slump for the last few years. That was about to change.

Stanley Kramer sent him a Western called "The Tin Star." Gary didn't think it was a blockbuster, but he liked the part of the town marshal, a man a lot like his own father, who had been a trial lawyer and a judge in Montana. The writer was Carl Foreman. The director was Fred Zinnemann. The movie would be called *High Noon*.

I went up to the location for a couple of nights and had dinner with Gary, Fred and a new young actress named Grace Kelly. Grace was very pretty, as I had heard, but after a cordial exchange of greetings I realized she was neither looking at me nor talking to me. I was used to being snubbed in public, but this I couldn't figure. Unless she felt I was competition.

When I was alone with Gary, I asked a question I never had before. But I did it in a roundabout way. "Is Grace interested in you?"

He wasn't totally convincing. "Nope. I think she's set her cap for Freddie."

Whatever I may have thought, I did not ask him about Grace again.

Fox loaned me to Universal for a lightweight comedy called *Weekend With Father*. It's a forgettable little movie but it was such a pleasant experience working with Van Heflin, whom I adored. It was Gary's turn to be camp follower and he was, indeed, a frequent visitor on the set. He even came to our Lone Pine location.

I was more than happy when Helen Horton accepted my invitation to come for a visit. From the moment Helen got off the plane, Gary responded to her with unabashed joy, which totally charmed both Helen and myself. I quickly prepared her for our living arrangements and asked if she'd mind if Gary came to the apartment while she was there. "It's your life, Pat," she smiled. If I sensed a hesitation in her voice, it was not because of any moral objection. It was simply because she was my friend and could feel my struggle.

Gary and I, separately of course, had received invitations to a big party at the home of David Selznick and Jennifer Jones. A Selznick party could fill every footprint in Grauman's Chinese Theater with its living counterpart. It would be the thrill of a lifetime for Helen.

Helen went into a panic. She had nothing to wear. So Jean took her shopping in the Hagen closet. Years later, she shared her conversation of that day. Jean had told her, "Pat thinks Gary is going to marry her. But he is not. Everybody in town knows it but her. And Pat is not going to accept it."

From the moment Gary and I walked in together, I could almost smell the hypocrisy in the air as the women in the room quickly looked away. Most of them were also sleeping with lovers, with married men, but I seemed to make their guilt visible. The only friendly face I remember that night belonged to the lovely French actress Annabella, who was once married to Tyrone Power. I recall that she was wearing a fantastic dress covered with butterflies, and she had a special fragrance. She was the only one who was decent to me.

I wanted Helen to see *Saratoga Trunk,* which Gary had made with Ingrid Bergman. Gary was delighted. It was a favorite film of his. He had a 16mm print and all the equipment to run it at his house, and Rocky was out of town.

"Fine," I said. "You and Helen can meet me back here for tea afterward."

Gary looked at me with surprise. "You're not coming?"

"Rocky would not tolerate me inside her house if she was home, and I will not take that liberty behind her back."

Gary was so disappointed that I almost weakened. Then it hit me. There was a way.

The three of us did watch *Saratoga Trunk* in Brentwood that day. Helen and Gary from the Cooper living room, and me from the patio, peering through the glass doors.

After Helen left, I was at Jean Hagen's house all the time. She and Tom had had their baby, a darling little girl they named Christine Patricia, after me. Jean didn't know a thing about my abortion. I never told anyone. So she never knew what a healing her baby was for me.

The Theatre Guild wanted me to return to New York to do a play by Eugene O'Neill. He had not forgotten me. I felt that getting back into my own element, the stage, would be a needed shot in the arm, and I wanted Gary to see me do something good. My bags were packed when word came from the Theatre Guild that Carlotta O'Neill did not want me. And if Carlotta did not want it, forget it.

So I was overjoyed when I was offered a part in T. S. Eliot's *The Cocktail Party* at the La Jolla Playhouse, which was appreciated as an oasis of theatrical culture in southern California. I was captivated by the play and my part was a gem, a strange heroine who leaves bourgeois society to seek deeper truths in her life. She ends up crucified on an anthill in Africa! I had long, mystical speeches, but I was a good study then and learned very quickly. It was one of the first really solid acting challenges I'd had since Broadway.

During rehearsals, Gary would come down to La Jolla as often as he could. We'd spend our nights at the home of Alexis and Mimi Tellis, one of the few safe places we had outside the apartment. Their lovely, tiny house, with its Indian decor, was a charming hideaway for us.

Gary hated the play—he called it "The Yakkity Party" —but he thought I was wonderful. He came more than once to see it, braving scads of reporters lying in wait, eager for confirmation that Rocky was ending their seventeen-year marriage and that the home-wrecker was one wicked lady named Patricia Neal.

They got nothing for their trouble. Rocky maintained that, as a Catholic, she would never accept a divorce, and to the day he died, Gary never spoke publicly about us. Nevertheless, my own personal execution on the ant-hill of Hollywood began.

No one ever came out and criticized me to my face, but it was more than low-key snubs at parties now. People I thought were my friends were cutting me dead. Gary and I were invited to supper by Betsy Drake, who had married Cary Grant. Betsy called me in great distress and canceled the invitation. Later she explained sadly that Cary had not wanted any part of us. Hollywood was going to take sides. The only one I can remember now who let me know he was on my side was Clark Gable.

My next film was *Diplomatic Courier* with Tyrone Power, the only movie star I ever had a crush on as a child. I told Ty that Patsy Lou Neal had once written him a passionate love letter and wondered why she had never received an answer.

Diplomatic Courier was a fairly successful little drama of intrigue, and I was about to get involved in some intrigue of my own—on a national level. The House Un-American Activities Committee was going full steam during this period. Senator Joseph McCarthy had everyone in Hollywood so uptight that all perspective seemed to be lost. Carl Foreman was a target of this witch-hunt. A rumor was spread that the final scene in *High Noon* called for the marshal to grind his star into the dirt with his heel to show contempt for the law. John Wayne, for one, had his honorable blood boiling, and a huge clamor rose up to have this terrible scene taken out of the film. The scene never appeared in the final cut for the simple reason that it had never been written in the first place. But stones from the slings of ignorance hit their mark. Carl Foreman was branded a Communist.

Gary accepted an invitation to appear at the McCarthy hearings. The Senate Committee had gone Hollywood in a big way. This was their show, and they loved meeting all the stars. Gary was under great pressure, especially from Hedda Hopper, to renounce his professional association with Carl. I was getting a taste of what it was like to be branded, and I implored Gary to stand up for him.

I had never been so insistent with him about anything before.

The Committee members just loved him. He agreed with them that writers could get away with a lot of propaganda. But he stood by Carl.

Hedda was furious. She really let loose on Gary in print.

But Gary was glad he had defended Carl. I remember telling people how proud I was that I had talked him into it, until Jean Hagen told me to keep my trap shut before I got branded a "Commie" along with everything else.

Gary and I attended a party given by Charles Feldman. I had thrown myself together that night and looked as wretched as I felt. I was wearing the most awful dress, and some madness had possessed me to put flowers in my hair.

I don't know who made up the guest list, but it was the cheapest stunt of the year.

I didn't see Rocky come in on the arm of Peter Lawford, but suddenly there she was, looking like a million dollars. Her dress was gorgeous, her hair and makeup impeccable. If there had been tears shed, there was no sign of them now. Every eye in the room gravitated toward her. Including Gary's.

Someone asked me to dance. Gary got up and walked over to Rocky. I thought that dance would never end. My partner brought me back to my table and just left me. I sat there alone, waiting for Gary to come back. Why was I always alone? I was the one getting the knocks. I was the one who had walked into that doctor's office. When Gary returned to our table, we sat quietly, avoiding the curious eyes that followed him back. He finally turned to me and said, "Let's go, Pat. I don't feel so good."

He took me right home. I hoped he would spend the night. I needed to be close to him. But again he said he didn't feel well and needed some rest. He had an early morning flight. He kissed me goodnight and said he would call from New York.

I waited for that call from New York, but when it

came, it was Harvey Orkin on the other end. I was so happy to hear his voice, but this was no social call.

"Coop's in the hospital."

Oh God, no, I thought, there must have been an accident.

"Now don't get excited, it's not all that serious. They think it's ulcers."

Harvey gave me the number at the hospital and I called immediately. Ulcers! All those years of keeping everything inside, of not facing things, of his maddening indecisiveness.

"Mr. Cooper? Just one moment." The long-distance operator kept me at bay. "Is your call collect or paid for?"

"It's paid for," I said. "Believe me, this one is paid for."

"Hello, baby, is that you?" The minute I heard his voice I wanted to be with him. I told him I would fly to New York right away. But he didn't want me to. I argued and argued, but finally agreed to stay put.

I must have walked for hours that day. I walked and cried and sat on the sand at Malibu, where we had spent so many hours together. Why hadn't he told me he was really ill? My fright gave way to anger that he was still keeping me on the outside of *where I should be*. Someone had to help me get through to him once and for all.

I called Gary's mother. She would help. She would know what was in my heart. I was that little girl again, crying into the phone that I was ready to go to the dance and she had to make him take me. "Mrs. Cooper, I desperately need to see you."

"See you? Why should I see you after what you have done to my son? He is sick because of you. Do you know what you are?"

The ax of Alice Brazier Cooper went through my heart. She called it, all right. I have made him sick. But why can't he see that I am sick, too? I am sick and hurt and humiliated that he will not commit to me. Was I always going to be the other one? The one who did not have a husband of her own. Or a family. Oh God, my poor baby.

I picked up the phone and dialed again. If his love for me is not strong enough for commitment, why go on? I could no longer keep from facing the truth. I was a *bad* woman.

He was on the line. "Gary," I cried, "it is over. I really mean it, Gary, I can never see you again. Your mother—I called her. She insulted me. No, she told me the truth. It is all over."

Silence.

"Do you hear me? Are you there?" I felt that curtain.

"You want it that way?" he asked. "All right . . . if that's what you want."

"Yes," I said quietly into the receiver. "Yes, that is what I want." And I hung up on him.

I looked at the telephone and waited for it to ring. He would call me back. But it did not ring. That silence was the most terrible void I had ever known in my life. I prayed for it to ring. Gary, you are my love. I cannot live without you.

The void stretched into endless minutes, then hours and days and the lifetime that lay before us.

My beloved Gary.

CHAPTER
TWENTY-FOUR

n those weeks after Gary and I parted, I felt as if my life had burst apart from the inside. Everything that had given life any meaning for me was torn into shreds. To this day I cannot remember specific things about that period. I do remember being saturated by a constant, undiluted pain that blocked me from reality.

I relived those last moments on the telephone, trying to piece it together. We were finished. I knew all along it could not work. Yet it was the only thing that had ever worked.

I had purposely not touched one drop of alcohol. Not since the phone call. Some deep instinct warned me that if I did take a drink, I would not stop.

There was no staying in the Fox Hills house. I wanted out of every small suffocating corner. I found a place in Westwood, a module in a series of new modern round buildings. It had a round fireplace in a round living room. Everything was round and made of brick. There was no place to hide anything. It was cold. I moved from a trap into a tomb.

Just before Christmas the studio "invited" me to go to Mexico on another publicity junket. One week in Mexico! I grabbed it, sure that the time out of town would help.

I boarded the southbound plane with celebrities like

Groucho Marx—who was a merciful tease all the way—Alexis Smith and her husband, Craig Stevens, and Lex Barker. Lex was a good friend and had taken over my Fox Hills place. He told me that Rocky, whom he knew, had asked to see it. "I invited her over," he said, "I hope you don't mind." I had fixed that place up beautifully. I hoped she had noticed.

Crazy Katy Jurado, who had made such a fiery impression opposite Gary in *High Noon,* was our unofficial hostess in Mexico. I remember there was a small earthquake the night we arrived in Mexico City, which scared us Californians. Katy laughed it off as a welcome from the gods.

We spent a few days in Acapulco at a gorgeous new hotel and watched young boys dive from that high cliff into the sea. I fell quickly into the spirit of the trip. My heart grew lighter and that shoot of hope in me took fragile root again. I began to shop for Christmas, something I had not even thought of in Los Angeles. I purchased gifts for family and friends and, before I was aware of it, began shopping for Gary. I had sweaters and socks knitted for him and found some beautiful handmade silk shirts. In one tiny shop, I found a set of miniature antique guns that had moving parts. I was ecstatic. He would simply adore them. I couldn't wait to take them home. To him.

I almost didn't get to take them home at all. When asked at customs what I had purchased, I listed everything, including the guns. "Jeezus, kid," came the cryptic voice of Alexis Smith over my shoulder, "do you have a brain in your head? They'll take them away from you." And they did. Almost before she finished her sentence, the customs official was opening my luggage and removing my beautiful presents. I stood there feeling so stupid, and suddenly very empty again.

But within a week I got a message from the customs department that I could pick up the presents.

It was strangely consoling, just handling those gifts for my Gary. I wrapped each one, carefully choosing the right paper, and sent them off to the Bel-Air. I felt better after I sent those packages.

On the Sunday before Christmas, Harvey Orkin's partner stopped by with his girl. I wished it had been Harvey, but he had decided to stay on in New York. Christmas without Harvey was like a decorated tree with no lights. I was not socializing much except with a handful of close friends who didn't expect me to talk, so I was glad when my chattering guests finally stood up to leave. I saw them out and noticed a huge box on the doorstep. It must have been at least three feet long and was beautifully wrapped. *He was here, right here, and I didn't get to see him.*

I raced inside and tore the wrapping from the box and then felt a twinge of fear. *What if it was not from him?* I opened the lid and pulled back the delicate tissue. Inside was a soft mink jacket with a small white card tucked into the lapel. It was the last time I would see the beautiful, familiar hand. "I love you, my baby. Gary."

Once again I was certain he would call. His gift was the sign I had been praying for. Each time the phone rang a conversation would race through my mind. "Hi, baby, did you like the fur?" "I love it. How are you?" "I'm terrible. . . ." "I can't bear it either. Let's talk." "I'll be right there." And then the voice on the telephone would not be his and I would die again and feel so stupid for my fantasy.

Just before the New Year I heard that Gary was in Sun Valley with his family. I couldn't stand it any longer. I picked up the receiver and dialed the operator for the number of the Sun Valley Lodge in Idaho. To this day I don't know how I got through that hotel switchboard to Gary Cooper, but I did.

The conversation did not follow my imagined script.

"I love your present," I began, "have you received mine?"

His voice seemed strained and hollow. No, he had not received my gifts. He was not coming to California. I heard myself asking if he was going back to Rocky, if he was seeing other women. I was shaming myself and I knew it.

"Gary, I love you," I pleaded, "I can't bear this. What are you doing to me? Are you leaving me? What are you going to do now?"

"I don't know," he said, "maybe I'll go to Paris."

I slammed the phone down on him for the second time. This time the silence was very different. It was not the silence of pain. It was the stillness of fury. I sent the telephone crashing to the floor. "I hate you!" I screamed. "I hate you!"

I wept and wept. All I could do for days was cry. I moved through my four round rooms like a prowling zombie. I had no appetite but forced myself to prepare meals, which I just stared at until the food was cold and had to be thrown out. The nights were the hardest. I lay staring at the ceiling until my eyes burned, praying for the sick ache in my throat to pass. I must have slept sometimes. I don't remember. Morning always brought another meaningless day.

Jean and Chloe rallied to me and did what they could, but I was beyond their help. My darling George Shdanoff tried his best to talk to me. Mimi Tellis did coax me into taking a trip with her to Palm Springs, but the prattle of her children made me all the more frantic. Jean Hagen was relieved that I was out of that mess and made no bones about it. Mother, who had been living in Atlanta with NiNi and George, knew something awful was happening to me and came to California.

She took one look at me—I was down to one hundred eleven pounds, so skinny the flesh on my face looked glued to the skull and my eyes as if they would pop out of my head—and got two train tickets back to Atlanta.

The train made a brief stopover in New Orleans. I did not know then that at that very moment, Gary Cooper was in a hospital in that same city. He had not gone to Paris, but to seek further medical advice on his poor health.

When we arrived in Atlanta NiNi called her family doctor immediately. His name was Henry Stelling and I am convinced that without his help I would not be alive today.

When he first saw me I could not even talk. He took one look and said that there was nothing he could do until I got a night's sleep. Then he gave me a shot that put me out cold for twenty-four hours. My exhausted body collapsed into the wellspring of his care.

Henry, as I quickly came to call the doctor, returned three nights a week to see me at NiNi's apartment. I adored him. He was a stout, barrel-chested man with a laugh that bubbled like a brook. He would throw his arms around me and pick me up like a child. Darling Henry made me feel as if I had come home to Daddy, and I began to talk.

I did not stop talking for twelve weeks. I talked about my career and the shattering disappointment I felt. I told him everything that happened between Gary and me, even about the abortion. Henry just sat and heard me out. Sometimes he shared himself, his love for fishing, his beautiful wife and family. He never treated me with a drug after that first night or prescribed any medication. He was not a psychiatrist. He was just a family physician who took a deep personal interest in me. He listened to me and absorbed my pain as a dear friend.

I had been on NiNi and George's very generous doorstep since Christmas, and now it was mid-March. MGM had a comedy for me called *Washington Story*. It was a piece of fluff and I didn't know if I was up to doing it. Besides, the leading man, Van Johnson, was a close friend of Rocky's. But Henry said flatly, "It will get you up in the morning and back onto a film set where you belong. There is nothing wrong with you that living won't cure." I decided to follow his advice. *Washington Story* was another minor film, but Van was a surprising delight to work with.

When we said our goodbyes, Henry refused to accept any payment from me. The only thing I could do to show my profound gratitude was to surprise him with a gift that I knew would please him. It was a small white speedboat, certainly a symbol of the saving gift he had given to me. He not only pulled me out of the wreckage, he gave me back my desire to live. And all he did was care.

CHAPTER
TWENTY-FIVE

Like so much graffiti, dozens of important phone numbers adorned the wall behind the battered phone on the soundstage. The jolly voice identified itself as Johnny Grant. Would I like to come with his troupe to entertain the boys in Korea? I protested that I didn't sing or dance. What could I do on such a trip? Johnny assured me that whatever I had the boys would appreciate, so I gave a tentative yes and we made plans to talk again when the film finished.

The soundstage was buzzing with guests that afternoon. One of them, Lewis William Douglas III, was tall, handsome and young, the son of the United States ambassador to England and brother of Sharman Douglas, a formidable social figure. The minute I saw him, something happened to me that had not happened for many months. I found myself attracted to a man. He did not wait for introductions, but came over and cheerfully greeted me. I remember he took my hand and made certain he had my phone number before he left the set that day.

Peter, as he was known, lost no time getting to a phone. He called that same evening and arranged a double date for supper the following night. We went to a Hawaiian restaurant and I had a good time. Peter was just what I needed. When he asked me out again I had no trouble saying yes.

Thus I began going with Peter Douglas, who was, I learned, a rising star in the oil business, determined to become what a fortune-teller had predicted—the richest man in the world. I had gained back enough weight to cross the line from walking cadaver to skinny chic. I was back on the town's social calendar, on the arm of an ambassador's son, and it felt good. Peter was making me feel special at a time when I badly needed it.

I had given up my round apartment when Mother took me to Atlanta. Home was once again the Hotel Bel-Air. Whenever Peter was in Los Angeles, which was more and more frequently now, he would come by the hotel and we would sit around the pool. He was thin, almost boyishly gawky in his trunks, and had the most fantastically long neck. He always seemed younger than I, even though we were both on the dark side of twenty-five. He was like a cool balm on a terrible burn. Unspoiled and fun and fresh. And rich. But I did not choose to be with Peter because he had money. I was sexually attracted to him. I felt I could sleep with him, that it would be possible after Gary. I so needed to be touched. There was no ulterior motive.

I never chose a man for an ulterior motive, except the one I married.

Peter invited me to come to Arizona to meet his brother. The minute we boarded the plane, he became terribly nervous. Even before takeoff he was in a cold sweat. I realized he was more terrified of flying than I had ever been. I played the brave and comforting air veteran, aware that my new young man was really very much a rookie.

The Douglas ranch was grand. His brother's family embraced me warmly and made me feel a part of them from the first moment. I was even invited into the children's room to hear their nightly prayers. It was very touching. It occurred to me then that I might want to marry Peter, but I kept my thoughts to myself. It was far too soon to suggest anything permanent. But that night, he did come to my room secretly and we stayed together for the first time.

* * *

My old friend Robert Wise cast me opposite Victor Mature in a comedy appropriately titled *Something for the Birds*. I probably would have been depressed if it hadn't been for Peter.

We were constantly out on the town together. At one of the many parties we attended, we were chatting with people when I glanced up at the door.

I couldn't see his face, but I knew every line of that body. Gary looked over and our eyes met for the briefest of moments before we fled each other's gaze. I watched as he disappeared into the bar. I vaguely remember there was a girl with him, but I did not want to know who she was.

My first thought was to damn the hostess for this setup. But I could not deny that I wanted desperately to see him. It seemed ages before Gary came back into the room. He was alone. I felt a slight hush fall, but could not bring myself to look up to see if everyone was watching. Then Gary was beside me. I introduced Peter, who discreetly excused himself to freshen his drink.

"Baby, how are you? You look good."

"I'm perfect!" I loathed the phony ring in my voice.

I was shocked at his appearance. He looked as if he'd been drinking for a long time. He was very thin and he needed a shave. I never knew Gary to go without shaving except when he was out with his dogs in the country. His tie was spotted and his coat rumpled. I spoke into the saddest face I'd ever seen. "How are you?"

"Great! What are you doing with yourself?"

"I'm working at Fox," I answered. "Everything is sensational." We both were going to pieces and stupidly trying to hide it from each other.

He just kept saying, "Are you all right, baby?" and I kept lying.

There was a silence that the hushed chatter in the room barely covered. I looked at him searchingly. There were tears in his eyes. I thought my heart would break.

Gary excused himself, and as he left, I could feel half of me being ripped away. Peter was back at my side. I was so glad Peter was there. We left without thanking our hostess.

The days that followed were like reliving an old nightmare. Gary was part of my soul. I had to see him again. The phone became, once more, an instrument of torture. Again I began waiting—jumping on its every ring.

"Hi, Pat, remember me? It's Johnny Grant." I had forgotten about going to Korea. And at that moment, I didn't want to go. I didn't want to leave Peter. But I had given a promise to be a part of Johnny Grant's Galaxy and I knew I had to get away from the pain of wanting Gary.

I said goodbye to Peter. He would be waiting when I returned in three weeks.

We were a fearless little troupe: Ginny Jackson, Joy Windsor, an acrobat named Pat Moran, the accordionist Tony Lovello and me. Flying over, a strange thing happened. I was in the seat behind Tony, who had fallen asleep. Johnny nudged him for something. Suddenly, Tony rose to his feet and froze. I mean he just froze, like a statue. He did not respond to hearing his name called or to being touched. Three uniformed men came immediately to his side. They checked his pulse and then his pockets for any medical alert data, then talked to him, asked him questions. The rest of us sat in stunned silence, watching them try to snap Tony back to reality. Nothing worked.

"Why not ask him to smile?" I suggested, half jokingly.

One of the men started urging him to do just that. "Can you give us a little smile? Come on, boy, smile." The muscles in Tony's face relaxed a little and I saw the corners of his mouth curve up ever so slightly. Then he did. He smiled. His body seemed to thaw and he came back to us.

After the excitement passed, I sat down next to him and asked what had happened. I remember Tony grinning as he explained, "It's happened before and I love it when it does. It takes me right out of this world. I feel such peace."

You're a lucky boy, I thought.

Korea was hardly an escape for me. I walked smack into the front lines of my own personal battleground. In the three weeks that followed, we did twenty-six shows, with me playing straight man for Johnny, sometimes performing as close as four miles from the front. We could hear gunfire and shells exploding. The heat and humidity were appalling. I could never keep my hair rolled. It always looked like a used mop. Ginny, Joy and I were tired and dirty all the time, hardly what you would call glamorous, but those boys had not seen an American woman for months and we must have looked like Thanksgiving dinner on a platter.

I'll never forget the first night we arrived in Seoul, when I was awakened by GIs trying to get into my room. Eventually one slipped through the window and crawled into my bed. I ran screaming for help. I had no sense of humor about the matter.

During our shows, it was a common thing to hear a GI shout, "Hey, Pat, how about Gary Cooper?" I couldn't quip back. I know they thought it was funny, but it hurt. I had come hoping to forget my troubles and instead found them thrown back in my face.

In fact, I remained deeply alarmed. I was someone I did not respect at all.

Peter and I went out as soon as I got home. He had done a stint in the army himself and laughed his head off at my war stories. I really did like him. But when I spoke about us, he must have sensed I was taking myself—and him—very seriously. It was true—I thought he would make a good husband. I thought we would really get on. We made a date for the following weekend.

We had not set an exact time, so I did not start to wonder what might be delaying Peter until about seven-thirty. I had been dressed and waiting since six. By eight o'clock, I began to be concerned. And by nine I was imagining all kinds of things. By eleven I had decided that Peter damned well better be dead or I would kill him myself. Around midnight I undressed and got ready for bed. I quite knew Peter wasn't going to show. It was the last straw.

I looked down on those swans and the perfectly groomed gardens. There was no real life for me here now.

I was finished with Hollywood and its disappointments and its heartaches. I wanted a career I could be proud of. I wanted a home and family. I wanted my self-respect.

As I slipped between the sheets, I felt the moorings being cut. I remember telling myself, just before I went to sleep, *I'm going back to New York.*

CHAPTER
TWENTY-SIX

had little in my bank account to show for being a movie star. I made a quick transfer of what funds there were to a New York branch, arranged to have my furniture shipped, stopped at the hospital to see Jean Hagen's newborn boy, called George Shdanoff and Mimi Tellis to say goodbye and left town.

I stopped briefly in Atlanta to see my family and check in with Dr. Stelling, who was very happy with my progress. He gave me the name of a doctor in Philadelphia in case I might need someone to talk to again.

I took an apartment on Park Avenue that was more than I could afford, and wasted no time letting everyone I could think of know I was back in town. The first people I saw were Harvey and his new wife, Gisella. And I contacted Peter's friends Marian and Ed Goodman, who kindly invited me to dinner. I hoped they might give me some clue about Peter. I was no longer angry, but very curious to know what had happened to him. At every turn I was reaching out to New York to say, "Here I am!" and New York took my hand in the most amazing way.

I had forgotten how exciting the city was in September. The windows were all dressed with the new fall fashions and *The Times* was full of a new season of theater. One item caught my eye. Lillian Hellman and Kermit Bloomgarden were mounting a revival of Lillian's 1934 success, *The Children's Hour*. I took a chance and called Kermit.

I asked him if I could read for the play and he set a time then and there.

Just walking down Madison Avenue on my way to an audition made me feel like an actress again. Friends had thought it demeaning that I would be willing to audition. After all, they clucked, Broadway knows you and what you can do—and you *are* a star! But star billing in Hollywood did not put me out of the range of a New York audition and I did not care in the least. I loved the thrill of the chase, something that the Hollywood studio system had denied me for a long time. The studio's refusal to let me read for the role I wanted in *Bright Leaf* was ever in my craw.

I did not blame Hollywood for my career problems. If things go well, they do. If they don't, they don't. I think I said that to the psychiatrist in Hollywood and he said I wasn't facing something. Maybe he was right. But if I harbored any hostility for not getting the breaks I thought I deserved, it didn't matter now. I was free of all that. I knew *The Children's Hour* and I knew I could play either of the two women in the play—teachers who are suspected of being lesbian lovers. And, damn it, I wanted a job.

When I walked out onto the bare stage I had the distinct feeling that I was the first audition that day. "Hello, Patsy Neal! Glad you're back in New York where you belong!" The hearty familiar voice of Lillian Hellman boomed out of the darkness. "Now I want you to know this is not a play about lesbians," she called out, "it is about a lie." I glanced over my pages. It was the key scene between Martha and Karen.

"Which shall I read?" I asked.

"You can read either one," she answered.

Five years of frustration and a broken heart exploded on the stage. Then Lillian asked me to reverse the roles and read through the scene a second time. When we were finished, Kermit was on the stage. He said something about my being the first actress they had seen and a lot of nice things about the reading, but all I heard at that moment were the welcome words, "We want you!" I could have either role, he told me. I knew immediately which one I wanted. I chose Martha. I was still ragged from the bitterness I had endured from personal rejection and public censure. I could really get my teeth into her problems.

Just before rehearsals started, Lillian invited me to a supper party at her Manhattan house. I put on a nice little dress—I always felt informal with Lillian—and showed up at her door. Lillian was dressed to the teeth. And so was the roomful of people behind her. She saw my look of dismay and said, "Oh hell, it's all right, Patsy," and pulled me into the room.

I recognized all of the guests except one. I had never seen the lean, handsome, very tall man who towered over the others. I discreetly whispered in Lillian's ear, "Who is that tall man?"

"*Roald Dahl!*" she answered in the same whisper she had used backstage in Chicago. I was sure he heard her, along with everyone else in the room.

At supper Lillian seated us together. I always meant to ask her if she had arranged the name cards before or after I asked who he was. I was absolutely sure that Mr. Dahl would spend the whole supper trying to charm me. I sat down and waited. But he began a conversation with Leonard Bernstein, seated across the table, that continued throughout the meal. Never once during the entire evening did he look my way. I tried to join the conversation but he totally ignored me. I was infuriated and tried to pretend his rudeness did not bother me in the least, but by the end of the evening, I had quite made up my mind that I loathed Roald Dahl.

"Jolly glad to find you home." The English accent on the phone caught me off guard. "How about some supper with me?"

It was my horrible dinner companion. He had gotten my number from Lillian.

"How about tomorrow night?"

I declined quite firmly. I felt a little pleasure in refusing him, but I made the mistake of thanking him for calling. He took that as an invitation to call again.

And he did, two days later. "There's this little restaurant I've never been to. I'm told it's good." I weakened, and we made a date.

He made sure I was aware that he was taking me to one of the finest Italian restaurants in New York. He knew the owner, who was John Huston's father-in-law. He was acquainted with just about everybody. And he was interested in everything. He spoke of paintings and antique furniture and the joys of the English countryside. He was as charming that evening as he had been rude the first time we met. I was fascinated. I remember his taking a sip of wine and looking at me for a long moment through the candlelight.

"I would rather be dead than fat," he said.

"So would I," I answered.

That night I had another audition. "I want you to meet a very good friend," Roald announced. "You will like Charles. He has been very good to me." He took me to a penthouse at the top of one of the big hotels where I met Charles Marsh, an old man with a strange face who owned a chain of newspapers and one of the finest resorts in Jamaica. With him was a lovely woman named Claudia. While we were there she didn't say a word, but heeded his every beck and call with the trained eye of a geisha, then quietly returned to her needlework. Charles knew what pleased him in a woman, and before we left, he told Roald, "Drop the other baggage. I like this one!"

I took the train to Philadelphia to see the doctor recommended by Henry Stelling. She told me she didn't think I needed a psychiatrist. "You need a friend," she said simply, "and if it makes you feel better to come and talk to me, please do." I was still having terrible bouts of sadness, and it certainly did make me feel better. Talking always helped me, but the last people I wanted to talk to about Gary were my friends. I could never discuss him with anyone except Henry and the lovely lady in Philadelphia.

Rehearsals started with Lillian's usual bark-and-bite direction, which I understood very well. Lillian could tell an actor where to go, how to stand and, God knows, how loud to speak, but if the actor did not know from the inside what he wanted to do, she could not help him. Kim Hunter, who played Karen, adjusted to Lillian with no problem, and little Iris Mann also got along fine. Poor Robert Pastene, who played Karen's fiancé, fell victim to Lillian's blunt and sometimes brutal method. It was frightening to watch her paralyze him, and to feel his hatred of her for doing it.

Roald often came for me after rehearsals and we would have supper together. One of his interests was the theater. But then, so was gardening. And art. And chess. He was fascinated by medicine and could have taken it up. There seemed to be nothing that he didn't know something about.

I was learning things about him, too. He was born in Llandaff, South Wales, in 1916 to Norwegian parents. His mother and sisters lived in England and he was terribly fond of them. He was obviously a real family man. During the war he had flown in the RAF and been shot down in Libya, crash-landing behind enemy lines. Quick presence of mind enabled him to save himself scant minutes before the biplane exploded, but he sustained an injury to his back that would plague him the rest of his life.

Roald Dahl had come to this country in 1942 as an assistant air attaché at the British Embassy in Washington, D.C. *The Saturday Evening Post* had arranged for a most important writer, C.S. Forester, to interview the young combat pilot. The two met for lunch and diddled away the time in stories and wine. Forester never got his interview. But Roald offered to send some notes to the magazine to help with the feature. They were so brilliant that Forester convinced the *Post* to forgo his interview, give him the agent's commission, and publish Roald's notes. Roald was paid a thousand dollars, which, he told me, he promptly lost in a poker game to then Senator Harry Truman. He was roundly applauded for the feature and began writing for all the big magazines, including *The New Yorker*. Even Eleanor Roosevelt became a fan of this new young writer. She invited him to the White House and Hyde Park.

Roald was an individualist, very cultured and caustically witty. He stood six feet six and looked down on the world with deft authority. When he said "Well done!" it was as if God Himself were bestowing the credit. I was beginning to like him in spite of myself. Whatever was good enough for Eleanor Roosevelt was good enough for me.

I wanted Roald to meet my friends. Ed and Marian Goodman, Peter Douglas's good friends and now mine, had us to supper with another couple, Edla and Peter Cusick. Edla's mother was a costume designer who did a number of Lillian's plays, and her father was in the stock market. Ed Goodman was a surgeon. I was so proud of Roald that evening. He was such a good conversationalist, relating to each of the guests in a special, personal way; he talked medicine with Ed, theater with Edla, stocks with Peter.

I was pleased to find that Lillian still invited the cast to her country home. This time she provided lovely Sunday brunches for us. There I renewed my friendship with her Dashiell. Much had changed with Dash in the months since I had last seen him in Hollywood.

Since his release from prison, where he had been sent for refusing to cooperate with the McCarthy witch-hunters, he spent most of his time at the farm or at Lillian's New York town house. I again began to keep gentle company with him. Lillian knew where it was with Dash and me and was not in the least threatened. I remember well the evening he and I went to some fancy restaurant on the East Side for an early dinner. There was no one in the place at all, but as we approached, the maître d' curtly asked Dash if he had reservations. Dash admitted he did not. The man would not allow us in. "Really, you can't be serious," I objected, "there's no one here!" But that bastard turned us away. I was so angry that I was speechless at first, and then Dash started laughing. In a moment I was laughing, too, and we left in hysterics.

"They still think I'm Red, Patsy," he explained.

"Well, are you?" I asked.

Through his laughter Dash replied, "I decline to answer that, on the grounds that it might incriminate me."

I was still dating men other than Roald, but with no

great interest. I did see a French jeweler from Tiffany's a few times. One evening after supper we went to my apartment. I had this foam rubber thing that passed for a sofa and we sat down on it to have a drink. Suddenly, the Frenchman leaped into the air and began jumping on the sofa like a monkey. I thought he had lost his mind completely until, in midleap, he pounced on me. He had obviously not lost his mind. He had suddenly found his id. I was exasperated and, at nearly twenty-seven, too old for this kind of nonsense. Needless to say, that was the last time I saw the jumping jeweler.

Roald took me to the home of the distinguished Charles Marsh for another meeting. This time, his good sponsor lost no time in getting to the point. "Just how much money do you have in the bank, Patricia?" he asked.

I was intrigued by Charles's directness, but I did not want to confess the truth. "Actresses are not always rich, some of us are poor," I replied.

"What do you consider poor, Patricia?"

"Well, I spent a lot of money while I was in Hollywood," I said, trying to put him off, but Charles would not give up until I admitted that I had twenty thousand in the bank.

"Ah yes," sighed Charles, "that *is* poor."

Roald was not making much money and had lost an inheritance on the English stock market. Charles was more than just a friend. He had provided Roald with an apartment and picked up most of his tabs. I don't know what Charles expected to find in me, but it seemed that he was hoping Roald would find a rich girl. Rich or not, Charles liked me. "I'm sure we shall be seeing you again," he promised, his eyes twinkling. I liked him, too.

December 18 finally came, the opening night of *The Children's Hour*. Kim Hunter took the first curtain call and was greeted with enthusiastic applause. Then I took mine. The personal acclamation was overwhelming. I was cheered. I knew I had been good, but the audience just would not stop. They actually screamed their approval. Oh my God, *what about Kim*? I kept thinking to myself. As we pushed our way out of the stage door and down the alley to the cars, people were still cheering. Lillian had taken an entire restaurant on Eighth Avenue, where we all went excitedly to await the reviews. If they were anything like the reception at the theater, nothing short of my coronation could possibly follow. I kept worrying how Kim would take it.

Walter Kerr's was the first review read. He praised Kim Hunter to the skies, but did not like my performance at all. I felt as if I had been shot in midair. Brooks Atkinson gave us both raves, but nothing would help. I could not hear one other review that was read that night. I was already soundly in the pits, convinced that Kerr's was the true word because he was so hideous to me. "Your performance was gorgeous," consoled Kim. She was utterly divine to me. Here I thought I was so concerned about her, but when it came down to it, I was very concerned about me, too. I wanted to be good. I felt I had been. But I reacted much the way Martha did in the play. The only opinion I trusted was the one that rejected me.

Roald began to call for me every night after the performance with a consistent but dispassionate interest that I found very intriguing. He had been with many women and had long since curbed his boyish appetites. The manly ones that replaced them he controlled with cool deliberation. Deliberate is a good word for Roald Dahl. He knew exactly what he wanted and he quietly went about getting it. I did not yet realize, however, that he wanted me.

He began to introduce me to his circle of friends, a small but carefully selected group of intimates who complied with his expectations. In spite of a propensity for the rich and famous, Roald was not so bourgeois as to limit his scope to the filthy rich. There was Josephine Hartford Bryce, who owned the A&P store chain. Her husband, Ivar, had been Roald's buddy in Washington. There was David Ogilvy, who had shared a house with Roald during the war. He was now an advertising giant. There were Bunny and Gena Phillips, who had connections with the Russian royal family and the queen of England. And then there was darling Charles Marsh, who was beginning to treat me like a daughter-in-law.

One day Roald decided to show me his flat, two floors above Charles's home. But Roald's place was very simple, not at all grand. A writer's apartment, except it had no desk. Roald had invented his own writing board covered with green felt, which he put on his lap as a work surface. I looked around the room to see if it had been tidied up for my visit. It had not. My glance went to a framed photograph of three children, the most beautiful children I had ever seen. They were Roald's twin nieces, Louise and Anna, and their brother Nicky. "My God, you make beautiful babies," I blurted out. "I mean, your family does!"

We stood for a long moment appreciating those lovely little faces. Then Roald kissed me for the first time. I wish I could say I remember feeling a thrill. But my interest was elsewhere. I simply could not get those beautiful children out of my mind.

My brother-in-law, George, had planned a visit to New York and called me with the time of his arrival. I totally forgot about it and poor George was left sitting on my doorstep for three hours before Roald rescued him. Roald was horrified that I could forget George's arrival and made such a case of it that he won George over immediately. Mother soon followed. Her first impressions of Roald were more reserved than George's, but she did admit, "He knows how to behave." The truth was, Roald and I had just begun sleeping together.

One of Roald Dahl's great assets was his desire never to leave a female unfulfilled. I learned that in the art of making love, Roald was also a master, and believe me, at this point in my life I was not easy to reach.

I hadn't told Roald of my occasional meetings with the doctor in Philadelphia, so I was taken off guard when he asked me to dinner at David Ogilvy's on a day I was scheduled to see her. I tried to decline as vaguely as possible, but excuses of "being busy" and "having an appointment" just met with more intense interrogation. I finally admitted I was going to Philadelphia, and then, after more badgering, that I was going to see a doctor.

Roald was frantic, thinking something was physically wrong with me. I told him the truth.

"A psychiatrist? You will not go to a psychiatrist! If you do, I will never see you again."

Something happened to me when Roald spoke that way. I promptly canceled my appointment and we went to David Ogilvy's. We took an overnight bag, since we would be spending the night. And Roald took his writing pad. He was working on a collection of short stories called *Someone Like You*. That evening he told me he wanted to dedicate it to me. I wouldn't hear of it. I told him he must dedicate it to Charles Marsh. I was not ready for such a gesture. Besides, I really did think he owed that book to Charles.

David designed a dinner as well as he did an advertising campaign. He was a gifted cook, and all the while he tried out advertising slogans on us.

That night his eight-year-old son accidentally burst into the room where Roald and I were in bed together. He ran to tell his parents what he had seen. So they had to sit down and tell him the facts of life then and there. He took it all in with serious consideration and then asked, "But how come they're not married?"

David's answer was shrewd indeed. "Love and sex are not necessarily the same thing."

Roald was really outdoing himself. He came to see my performances often. And each night he would come backstage, sit on the chaise and watch me remove my makeup. One evening he put a kettle on the hot plate and asked if he could make some tea. Fine, I said, I'd have some too. He didn't return to the chaise, but came to my side. He made some small talk about the dressing room being rather better than most and I told him about the broom closets Jean Hagen and I had had to use on the road. And then I told him how she and Tommy used to talk on the phone long-distance, cooing "Kiss-kiss, kiss-kiss" over and over.

"At three eighty-five a minute!" he laughed and then mused, " 'Kiss-kiss.' It's a good title, don't you think?"

There was a long silence before he spoke again.

"I have another question to ask you," he ventured

167

slowly. "I would like to know how you think it would work if we got married."

"Oh no!" I suddenly said without thinking. He looked at me as if I had thrown cold water in his face.

"Roald, let's just continue the way we are. I mean, let's not talk about that now. All right?"

He looked horrified that I had turned him down. It's simple, I thought to myself. I really don't love him and I don't want to get married. But then, that was not entirely true. I did want marriage. And a family. Roald would have beautiful children. What was I holding out for? A great love? That would never come again. When was I going to face reality?

Roald did not bring up the subject again and never gave the slightest indication that I had said no. In fact, his attitude was as decisive and positive as if I had accepted his proposal.

My phone rang. At the other end a familiar voice said, "Hi, Patrish! Can I pick you up after the performance?" It was Peter Douglas.

"Of course," I said. I certainly wanted to see him. But I did not want to pick up our affair. I would never sleep with him and with Roald at the same time. Still, I was terribly curious and wanted to know why he had stood me up that night in California.

After Roald, my Peter seemed even more boyish than ever. But I totally enjoyed him. We had a lovely dinner. On that fateful night, he told me, he had gotten smashed with some buddies in Texas and never made the plane. We laughed about it and Peter said perhaps there was something he had not wanted to face then. We came back to my apartment and lay down on the sofa, and he put his arms around me and said, "Pat, I would love to marry you."

I thought back to the time I wanted so much to hear those words. I took his hand and said, very quietly, "Too late, dear Peter, too late."

Then the most surprising thing happened. I heard myself say, "I'm going to marry Roald Dahl."

3

IN HARM'S WAY
1953–1967

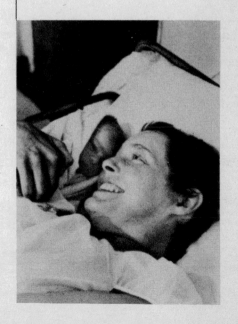

CHAPTER TWENTY-SEVEN

don't remember ever coming right out and telling Roald that I would marry him. It just sort of evolved. He did not depend upon my yes, either. He just quietly took possession of me and I let it happen.

In my apartment he suspended a wooden pole from a great hook in the ceiling and wired it to a board with paper on it. On a stool next to this he placed a kind of writing tool that created designs and patterns on the paper depending on the movement of the pole. I have no idea what it was and it obviously defies description, but all my friends came to see it and were fascinated.

One afternoon Fielder Cook came to ask me to do a play with him. We stood looking at Roald's invention as Fielder described the play, and unexpectedly I said, "I can't take a job right now. Roald and I are getting married." There was no comment at all from Roald. We three went back to admiring his amazing pole.

The complex Roald Dahl had as many facets as his incredible creation. His intelligence and dependability made him very attractive. He was not the kind to stand me up. He had a charming and elegant side that I found captivating. And an absoluteness of judgment that was as fascinating as it was, at times, frightening. There was something very freeing about feeling someone strong at my side. Although I did not love him, I admired him deeply, and at that time in my life, admiration was more important than love. Fortunate, too, because Roald had a way of demanding admiration.

Soon after my surprise announcement we were with Charles and Claudia, when the old gentleman suddenly produced a large marquise diamond ring and offered it to us. It was not a gift, as I later found out. Charles expected Roald to pay for it eventually, but he was obviously anxious for his favorite couple to get moving. Roald accepted it and gave it to me. I put it on. We were engaged.

I soon came to know, however, that Roald Dahl was not everyone's cup of tea and certainly not what my friends had in mind for me. Dash was the first in a line of noteworthy prophets of doom where our forthcoming marriage was concerned.

Dash and Roald did not get along well. The two men had squared off at Lillian's one night and had not spoken since. I tried to insist that he had seen Roald only at his worst, but still Dash warned, "Don't marry him, Patsy, he's a horror. I can't understand why you're doing this."

I told him plainly that I wanted children, a family. I was sure I could never find a man Dash would approve of anyway, so I changed the subject by promising to name my firstborn Neal Dashiell.

"God help it," he smiled, "if it's a girl."

Even Leonard Bernstein, who had been quite friendly to Roald, pulled me aside one evening at Lillian's and whispered in my ear, "I really think you are making the biggest mistake of your life."

But most of my friends were not quite so outspoken, even though many had come in for some rude Dahl behavior. Roald could be like sand in an oyster shell. He seemed to feel he had the right to be awful and no one should dare counter him. Few did.

One evening at Millie Dunnock's, I heard Roald turn on her. I couldn't believe my ears. What about darling Millie could have displeased him so? I must say she handled it well. She just laughed and said, "You've got to be kidding, Roald," and walked away. To this day, Millie doesn't admit Roald was ever rough on her and has remained firm in her admiration for him, although she adds, "He's not a man I could love."

I had been anxious for Roald to meet Harvey Orkin. I thought they would have something in common now that Harvey was a writer. I invited Harvey and Gisella and some Actors Studio friends for supper at the apartment. Roald cut Harvey dead. "There's something about you I don't like," he said pointedly. Harvey and I had been joking and shrieking our heads off as usual. Roald said he didn't want me to be "rowdy." But I always felt there was something more to his ungracious attitude. He was jealous.

Roald was jealous of Gary, too. Whenever he saw his name in the paper he would question my feelings for Gary. I admitted that I loved Gary very much, but hurried to add that our relationship could never have worked. I wasn't about to volunteer more.

The truth was, the thought of Gary was still hurting me and I didn't want to talk about him or think about him now. I had to think instead about settling down to a normal life.

There was nobody I could speak to. Both Jean Valentino and Chloe were miles away. I could confide in no one in New York, not Millie or Harvey or Lillian, who always had an opinion on everything but never said a word about Roald. Except once I heard her say that she didn't think much of his writing.

The last straw finally came. We were at Edla and Peter Cusick's one evening and Roald cut loose at the dinner table with some of his arrogant remarks. I was so embarrassed. I followed Edla into the kitchen and admitted, "There's something in him I hate."

Edla just looked at me. "Well, nobody has a gun in your back, Pat. Why don't you break it off?"

I really thought I should do just that. I confronted him with my feelings, but not to his face. We were on the phone and before I knew it I was telling him how horrible I thought his behavior was, and that I didn't think we should get married at all. If I believed Roald Dahl would apologize, I was mistaken.

"You don't talk to me that way, Pat," he warned. "Do you know what you're doing?"

"No," I wailed, "I don't! I don't know at all!"

I did agree to see him again, and I told him I thought he was rude, arrogant and nasty. But he saw his behavior merely as common sense, just putting something in its proper place. This infallibility of his left me feeling frustrated, but rather than deal with it, I just gave in.

The Children's Hour closed in the spring. I was glad to have the time for planning the wedding. I wanted a truly beautiful trousseau. I had never collected the kind of wardrobe Hollywood actresses are expected to own, and always considered myself a failure where fashion was concerned. So I went all out. I chose a color scheme of white to palest pink to shocking pink to red. Everything I bought or had made was in that color range except for a black lace nightgown. I must say it was the best outfitting I have ever had in my life, and I did it all myself.

I found, however, that I absolutely could not refuse Teresa Hayden's offer to appear in her productions of *The Scarecrow* and *School for Scandal* at the Theater de Lys. It was a wonderful opportunity to prove my mettle as a character actress, and since it was a limited engagement, I could do it without interfering with the wedding. It also put me in a working relationship with some friends from The Studio—Eli Wallach and Anne Jackson, and David Stewart, an astonishing actor. There was also a pleasant, good-looking young man who excelled in a small dancing role. I was sure James Dean had a great future ahead of him.

All my reviews were good except one. Walter Kerr still refused me a nod of approval. I was once told it was because I was a lot like his wife. I wonder.

Roald and I decided on a small chapel at Trinity Church in the city. He had been raised in the Church of England; all that mattered to me was that the ceremony be Christian. I made all the arrangements with the vicar, who was a bit solicitous about a "show business" wedding. I ordered huge baskets of flowers and sent out the invitations. Neither of us was inclined to bring our families to New York for the wedding. We simply announced the event and promised to visit them soon, the Dahls during the honeymoon and the Neals at Christmas. It would be just a small gathering of friends at the chapel and afterward a lovely party hosted by Charles and Claudia for about seventy guests. As I made a list of friends, I thought how funny it was that most of them came in pairs. Jo and Ivar, Peter and Edla, Harvey and Gisella, Ed and Marian. Now it would be Pat and Roald. That had a very comfortable sound.

The night before the wedding I sat on the edge of my bed. I was alone. *Jesus God,* I thought, *what am I doing?* Then I thought of those children, the ones in the photograph. I wanted beautiful children, too. Yes, children would be the answer for Roald and me.

July 2, 1953, dawned hotter and stickier than predicted. When Roald got up and felt the heat, he took one look at his gorgeous new wedding suit and decided it was much too heavy to wear. So he ripped out its elegant silk lining. I must say he still looked very handsome that day, but it struck me as a shocking thing to do to one's wedding garment. My wedding dress, which I had cut down from a pink chiffon evening gown, was trim fitting and hugged my thin waist and ample breasts. My hat was trimmed with tiny flowers and the bouquet Roald gave me had matching blossoms. I looked sensational and I knew it. I didn't care if it was 105 degrees in the shade.

Charles Marsh was Roald's best man and Millie Dunnock was my matron of honor. The minute the ceremony started I was aware of a vacuum. For all my conscientious planning, I had forgotten to arrange for music!

When the vicar asked, "Do you take this woman . . . ?" Roald's "Yes" was clear and sure.

The vicar turned to me. "Do you take this man . . . ?" As annoyed as I could be with him, I did have the conviction that marrying him was the right thing to do. A home and children would smooth everything out between us. He was thirty-six and I was twenty-seven. He said it was time we settled down. I had been through my great passionate love. Life was more than that.

"Yes," I promised, "until death do us part."

I would never go back on those words.

When we turned to leave the chapel, Jo Bryce began to shower us with rice. Soon everyone was throwing it. What seemed like a ton of rice went everywhere—on the seats, in the aisle, under the pews. The vicar's face grew dark with rage. "What have you done? What in God's name have you done?" I would hear his words many times in the months to come.

My husband had a rough time dragging me away from the reception. But at last he got me back to the apartment. We sat down on the sofa and Roald switched off the light. "I love you," he said softly, and touched me. I felt tears come to my eyes. They rolled down my cheeks in the dark silence. I could feel my heart breaking. I so wanted to be married, but to another man.

CHAPTER
TWENTY-EIGHT

Roald told me that he loved me on the night of our wedding. He would do so two more times in our life together. This was not a slight. This was being a Dahl, for whom demonstrations of affection were not necessary. And although I did not love him, my commitment was absolute. Whatever moral confusion I had fallen into before I married, one thing was clear to me now. My marriage would be sacred. There would be no divorce for me and there would be no sex outside my marriage bed. And there would be no regrets.

Planning our honeymoon had been great fun for Roald. He had an enormous appreciation for anything he generated. We would pick up a chic Jaguar convertible in Naples and have a six-week drive along the Italian seacoast to Rome, head along the Riviera and continue through Switzerland and France. Then we would cross the Channel to England and end the honeymoon with a grand meeting of the Dahl family in Great Missenden. I had no idea where Great Missenden was. I just thought of it as a little cork screwed down somewhere in the heart of England. It was going to be an absolute fairy-tale adventure and I was ready to take off the day after we were married.

We made our first stop in Positano. *My* first stop was the luxurious bath in our hotel room. In all the years since, I have never seen such a bath. The tub was huge and blue and the end was formed by two panes of glass that made a window onto the sea. Between the panes was a tropical paradise of tiny fish and plants. As I soaked, I could look past those exquisite fish swimming right next to me and down onto the beach and ocean and feel as if I were part of the whole Mediterranean.

I opened the door to find Roald already in bed, reading. It was such a charming room, one meant for lovemaking, with a huge comfy bed and large windows opening to the gentle sea breezes. I reached for my black lace nightie, catching sight of my undressed figure in the mirror. I loved my body. I remembered Gary had, too. I stood there admiring myself when Roald looked up from his book. "My God, will you stop that! Put some clothes on." I covered myself at once. I felt wretched, until in the dark he became, as always, a most fulfilling and considerate lover. But never again did I appear in front of him naked, not until my stroke, when he had to help bathe me.

Our marriage was put to the test immediately. On our first boat ride up the coast, the guide sailed into a deserted cove. When we reached shallow water, I pulled off my shoes and put my foot over the edge of the boat. As I touched the soft sandy bottom, I felt it move. Then a sting of pain shot through my foot. I let out a shriek. The guide pulled me back into the boat, grabbed a hunting knife and cut a cross into the flesh of my big toe, which was turning purple and swelling to twice its normal size. All the time he was shouting, but we couldn't understand a word. It sounded like "Sookeet—sookeet!" Suddenly he began to suck my toe, spitting out the blood. Then he grabbed Roald by the neck and yanked the wounded toe up to his face. "Sook eet!" he commanded. I thought Roald would gag. But he was heroic. In a crisis he was always a knight in shining armor. God only knows what poison was in that sting.

The remainder of our time in Positano was blessedly uneventful. We just quietly inserted ourselves into the warm, unchallenging rhythm of the Italian summer. We took long, gorgeous walks on the beach and long, gorgeous meals in the sweet cafés and long, very gorgeous siestas. I have often wondered how the Italians ever really accomplish anything with such a lovely, relaxing schedule.

Rome was as bustling as Positano had been restful. Roald found a hotel at the foot of the Spanish Steps and became my guide in the Eternal City. He was interested in everything and spoke with authority about the architecture, painting and sculpture. He bought gifts for his family and I shopped for everyone who had ever been good to me. I was caught up in the excitement of a new culture and becoming enchanted with the honeymoon.

But as we prepared to leave for Florence, I was abruptly presented with a bad omen—the tires of our car had been slashed. Sure enough, although we spent three days in Florence, I was hit with a tourist bug and didn't see a thing except through Roald's eyes. Then during our drive north, he began talking about all his friends we had to look up: Sir Matthew Smith in London, Babe Paley on the Riviera, and of course, we must call Lilli Palmer and Rex Harrison in Portofino. I found myself getting annoyed, because I really did not give one damn for his famous friends. I felt he was just trying to impress me. For long stretches I put my head on the back of the seat and went to sleep.

When we arrived in Portofino, we did ring up Lilli and Rex. Lilli insisted we come right over for tea. Rex wasn't there, so Roald invited her to bring him to dinner with us that night. When Lilli pulled up in front of our hotel in her jeep I was surprised that there was no Rex. She explained that she had accepted our invitation without knowing he had an urgent business commitment that evening. She brought us his profound apologies. We three walked to a little restaurant on the pier near the hotel. I remember I sat facing the water, Roald the restaurant, and Lilli the street. Suddenly her face was ashen. We all turned, and there, walking down the pier, was Rex, arm in arm with two buddies. They stopped at our table, Rex bowed from the waist, then walked on, roaring with laughter. I thought poor Lilli would die of embarrassment. Obviously he hadn't wanted to dine with us and couldn't care less that we knew it. For all my aggravation with Roald and his style of rudeness, at that moment my husband looked very good to me.

I remember Switzerland and France as a succession of petrol stations. Our great Jaguar was giving us reason to stop for repairs at regular intervals and Roald made up his mind he was definitely going to ask for our money back. In Switzerland we bought each other wedding presents, elegant gold watches, the finest we could get, Patek-Philippe. I still have mine and it still works.

Roald had been to Paris often and usually stayed at a small hotel on the Left Bank that had been introduced to him by his friend Sir Matthew. It was quaint, lovely and cheap. Quality at a good price, like all the hotels he selected on the trip.

It wasn't as if we were budgeting ourselves. We didn't keep books. Our honeymoon was a joint venture financially. He paid or I paid. That is, he handed over our money. I was old-fashioned and didn't like to see the woman paying the check.

Wherever we were, we shopped. Our prize find was a statue of St. Catherine of Alexandria. She stood about three feet high and had the noblest thin face. In her hand was part of the wheel on which she was tortured. I don't remember the price, but Roald said she would cost much more in a London gallery. We packed her up in the back of the convertible with the rest of our treasures. We were beginning to look like the Joad family.

Mimi Tellis was now living in France with her two small sons. It was my turn to drag Roald off to meet a friend of mine. She made a one-pot meal that was one of the loveliest we had in France. Roald was wonderful with her boys. I noticed that they followed him around like the pied piper. He would, indeed, be an attentive and loving father. Later, Mimi and I were reminiscing over coffee. She brought up our last visit in La Jolla, when I was with Gary. I quickly changed the subject—I just didn't want to speak of Gary in front of Roald—but I could not turn off the memories that had been awakened.

Our broken-down car finally reached the ferry at Calais. As we glided across the water, I tried to keep my mind on the present by memorizing the dismaying list of names belonging to my new English family, but my thoughts slipped back to that charming house in La Jolla and the days and nights spent with Gary. I glanced down at the lovely wedding gift on my wrist, with its inscription on the back—the date of our marriage and the huge initial R. I remember wondering just who this man was, this R, and what the hell I was doing with him.

As we drove along the endless twining roads and lanes that trace the English countryside, Roald spoke of his family. It was almost as if the English air itself was circulating memories of his boyhood. His father, Harald Dahl, had gone through a terrible ordeal at age fourteen. While replacing tiles on the family house, he fell and fractured an elbow. The doctor, a bit drunk, tried to force the arm into shape and it had to be amputated. But, Roald added with a gleam, his father was fond of bragging that the loss of an arm caused him only one serious inconvenience: He found it impossible to cut the top off a boiled egg. There was a streak of defiance toward limitation in the Dahl family that I would find indomitable.

Harald Dahl had come to Cardiff to become a ship broker. There he made his fortune and began his family. After his wife died in childbirth, Harald returned to Norway to find another to bring up the children and produce more. She was Sofie Magdalene Hesselberg, known as Mormor, and she would become one of my treasured memories of the Dahls.

The loveliest story Roald told of his mother and father was of their "glorious walks." During the last three months of Mormor's pregnancies, Harald would take her to places of beauty in the countryside, where they would walk for a while each day. It was his father's firm belief that if the eye of a pregnant woman was constantly observing the beauty of nature, this beauty would somehow be transmitted to the babe in her womb and the child would be born a lover of beautiful things.

Great Missenden is halfway between London and Oxford. The village consists of one winding high street lined with eighteenth-century brick houses. It took us all of five minutes to drive through and we were at the home of Roald's sister Else and her husband, John. Children were perched on a heavy wooden gate waiting for us, and as we passed through, they set up volleys of whoops. "That's Astri and Nicky," said Roald. I recognized Nicky. He was one of the children in the photograph. "And here comes my oldest sister, Alf, and her husband, Leslie. And there are Else and John." In a moment we were surrounded and it was like a big party, with everyone laughing and talking at once.

Then I saw a short woman carefully picking her way over the stones in the drive with the help of two canes. Her chin stuck out in proportion to her very large nose, which was a Dahl trademark. She was no physical beauty, but I would later learn that her real beauty shone from a great motherly heart.

"Hello," she said slowly with a heavy Norwegian accent.

"Hello, Mormor," I said as I reached for her hand. There was no kiss. No embrace. In fact, as welcome as they made me feel, not one of them greeted me with a kiss that day.

They immediately whisked us into the house for a feast of a supper. England still rationed food, so this was their extravagant embrace for their new sister-in-law from America. Roald's family was obviously delighted to see him home. They doted on him the way my aunts used to dote on Pappy. Through supper, I tried to get Roald's family straight in my head. All those A's! Asta and Alfhild, Alex and Ashley and Anna and Astri. And Alexandria, who, thank God, they called Baba. And not one of them lived more than twenty minutes from another!

Then came an impromptu show that was really like a children's party, with each member of the family taking turns entertaining. The highlight came when Leslie announced he would perform his "specialty," which brought great cheers from the children. He lay down on the rug, raised his legs and lit a match a few inches from his backside. Everyone got very quiet and all eyes seemed to be on me. Leslie then let out an immense fart, which caused the flame to leap and explode. It was the most amazing thing. I was both impressed and dismayed, which made everyone scream with laughter.

Else and Roald took me up to the nursery to see the twins, Anna and Louise, already tucked in their beds. Those precious faces, the ones in the photograph, that may have been the reason I had come all the way to England. They peered out at me from under their sheets. Little Anna even managed a very brave "Hello, Auntie Pat." At that moment, I remember feeling very close to Roald for the first time on our honeymoon.

I awoke early and made an entrance into the kitchen looking for all the world like a movie star in peignoir, negligee and scuffs. Mormor, already busily preparing breakfast, glanced up at me only once. She moved with a lumbering step. Roald had told me that it might not be long before she would be confined to a wheelchair. But for the moment she was still queen of her kitchen and I was a guest in her house. "I've made you some coffee," she said. I was delighted. I just lolled away the morning, sipping coffee and being waited on. The next morning, dressed in my finery, I found that Mormor had everything ready for me again. Every morning we were in Great Missenden, I let her wait on me while the brat in me just lapped it up. I had no idea I was sowing some seeds of discontent with my new mother-in-law.

Else and John gave a big party to show me to friends and neighbors. The people in that little hollow had never seen a film actress and I was determined to make a good impression. I put on my best pink dress and put my best foot forward.

Within minutes I began to see that these were real people, there to meet Roald's bride and not to collect autographs. I was meeting friends that would be dear to me for a lifetime. Roald's half-sister, Ellen, and his half-brother, Louie, immediately took my heart. I met Sir Matthew Smith, whose name had so irritated me when Roald was enumerating the famous people we had to look up, and who turned out to be the most enchanting little old man. Almost blind, he still had an impressive career as a painter. He would one day paint me. And Archie Gordon, dear Lesley O'Malley, Dr. Brigstock and his wife. And Elizabeth David, the wonderful cookbook writer. These people would stay with me long after the pink cloud faded.

Roald adored his home and wanted to share every bit of it with me. The land looked almost cherished. The Dahls were all natural gardeners. Especially Mormor. She would name each of her favorite plants with the same pride she had when she showed me every picture in the family album.

The last members of the family I met were his youngest sister, Asta, and her husband, Alex, who lived in High Wycombe with their children, Willie and Baba and the newborn, Peter. Peter, in fact, had been the reason they hadn't come to Great Missenden for our arrival. I immediately fell in love with the baby and couldn't have been more pleased when Asta asked me to be his godmother. Alex was Catholic, the only adult in the Dahl family who was. I was very surprised his church would permit it, and I felt very privileged.

We were all gathered in the tiny church for the ceremony. The priest poured the water on the babe and said the words of baptism; then, when he lifted his hand in blessing, little Peter made the hugest fart, just as loud as his Uncle Leslie's! We all burst into peals of laughter, including the good Father, who most likely had never before been rewarded with such a surge of relief at his touch.

CHAPTER
TWENTY-NINE

As soon as we got back to New York City we began apartment hunting. Roald insisted that I had been living beyond my means. I had to agree that my cavalier behavior with money was all right for a bachelor girl, but I was married now, planning for a family. We found a smaller, cheaper place on the West Side just off Central Park. It had an extra bedroom that we set up as a writing studio for Roald.

We moved most of my old things with us, which, little by little, he got rid of. Roald was never fond of the pictures I'd collected. He had quite a reputation for his taste in art. After he lost his inheritance, he began buying art and selling it to acquaintances, not necessarily for a lot of money, just enough for a small profit or perhaps a good investment tip.

Two of my paintings bit the dust first. Roald felt I should sell them because we could use the money. I was making more than my husband, but this hadn't been a major problem, except that he never seemed to think we had enough. I don't think money was his only motivation for selling off the paintings. It's possible that he simply did not want things from *my* past cluttering up *our* life.

He even asked me to sell the diamond earrings Gary had given me. I drew the line there. But I didn't flatly refuse. I just said I'd think about it.

I liked Roald's friends, especially Josephine and Ivar

Bryce. They were fantastically wealthy and owned a paradise in Nassau, where they entertained masses of guests. It was through Jo and Ivar that we met Colin Leslie Fox, the young man who had just crossed the Atlantic Ocean in a tiny boat. His bravado, charm and good looks made him the social catch of the season and opened the way for a successful modeling career. Colin became the man in the Hathaway shirt, the one with the sophisticated patch over one eye. He was not a movie buff and knew nothing of Patricia Neal, which irritated Roald no end. "You should make it your business to know who people are," Roald lectured. "Not because she's my wife. She's a celebrity."

Roald met his match in this affectionate rough diamond. "You think differently than I do," Colin chided. "You're a public figure and cater to people. I'm an iconoclast. I don't like anybody." Surprisingly, Roald took to Colin. So did I. He was like the man who came to dinner—he stayed in the family for years.

I was not the perfect wife by any means. I did appreciate my mother's teachings about a woman's place in the home—"Remember, Patsy, cooking meals and keeping a house is not a demeaning role but the privilege of a good wife, whether she works outside the home or not." I was sloughing off, though. I let the house go and saved whatever culinary skill I had for dinner parties. I did like to cook. I had never been happier than when I cooked for Gary. I loved inventing new recipes, and I began to get a reputation with friends like the Goodmans and the Cusicks for my chicken tarragon, oxtail stew and Meat Loaf Neal.

I didn't go so far as to ask Roald to make my morning coffee, but I certainly never thought about getting up to make breakfast for him.

I remember now Maureen Stapleton telling me that early on she had told her husband, Max, she wasn't making the bed. He said he wasn't, either. So nobody made it for six months. I guess I was a lot like Maureen.

But if Roald noticed my domestic failures, he wasn't

saying anything. In fact, sometimes he would go for days without talking to me at all.

That September I went on the road with *The Children's Hour*. I bought a skein of maroon cashmere yarn and began a scarf for Roald. He loved cashmere. As I knitted away in my dressing room, I was quite convinced that things between us were indeed going well. I would call him almost every night, if only to pass on a tiny tidbit of what was going on in Chicago.

I remember telling him about meeting a young man named Michael something, I couldn't recall the last name. He had come by the hotel to ask me to do a recording of one of Roald's stories for his theater group. He wanted to be an actor more than anything in the world. But he just didn't look talented and I didn't want him to end up brokenhearted. I did my best to talk him out of it.

The Children's Hour was not at all successful on the road. In a few short weeks I was back in New York. While I was gone, Roald had not been lonely. He told me he had been in Gloria Vanderbilt's company more than a few times. They had met at a party and had gotten along well. He said she had become infatuated with him, but he cooled her ardor by reminding her that he was a married man. Years later, Gloria told me a different story. In fact, she still had love letters Roald had written to her that she described as "very well done." She wanted to show them to me but her lawyers would not let her indulge my curiosity.

Up to that time, I hadn't considered that my husband might be fair game for other women when I was out of town. But I could not believe he would cheat. I trusted Roald absolutely.

One afternoon as I was passing a newspaper stand, a photograph on the front page of one of the papers caught my eye. It was of Gary and Rocky at Orly Airport in Paris. I saw in their expressions the most beautiful love. He was obviously happy without me. The next time Roald asked me to sell the earrings, it was easy to say yes. It was time to get Gary Cooper out of my guts.

I took the earrings back to Winston's, but the man said they were not interested in buying diamonds "of that quality." I insisted that they had been purchased there by Gary Cooper. He disappeared for a short while, and when he came back, scarlet-faced, he said that the earrings had indeed been bought by Mr. Cooper. They were one of three pairs purchased at the same time. He made a very low offer to buy them back, and I accepted.

I wondered if Roald would be annoyed with me for settling for such small change, but the fact that Gary had bought *three* pairs canceled any disappointment my husband might have had. He hooted with laughter and later enjoyed telling everyone who came to the apartment. I don't know why I told him.

We had promised, at the time of our wedding, to visit my family at Christmas. My people were not rich and cultured in the way Roald appreciated, but since I had taken to his family, I assumed he would respond to mine. After only a few hours in their company, he became so bored that he spent most of his time reading in our room and appeared only for meals. Mother and NiNi thought he was the rudest thing alive.

Even when he was with them he didn't try to ingratiate himself in the least. One evening during supper the question of my brother Pete's ongoing education came up. George and NiNi were pressing him to find a university he might want to attend, when Roald said, "Pete, why don't you just quit school? You could start a filling station." We didn't think it was very funny, but Roald went on listing the advantages of owning a gas station. He thought Pete would be great at it. I had been giving Mother money for Pete's education and I was sure Roald just didn't want me to continue footing the bill. By the time we left, Mother was so furious with her son-in-law that she could barely say goodbye.

Our first houseguest was Leslie Hansen, the Great Missenden farter. He had developed problems with his teeth, so Roald found a specialist in Texas. Charles Marsh would take care of it. The night before Leslie arrived, as

I got ready for bed, Roald turned to me and nonchalantly said, "Pat, I want a divorce. This marriage is the wrong thing for us."

I was absolutely dumbfounded. I couldn't believe he was serious. We had been married less than eight months. He assured me he was not joking. "But don't worry about it now," he said, "just go to sleep."

And he did just that. Only a man could tell you something like that and then roll over and start to snore.

He fixed me for sleep that night. I sat for a long, long time in the darkness. Then I got up and quietly put on my clothes.

I walked down empty streets until dawn, trying to piece together what could possibly have gone wrong. The fear of meeting violence on the dark city streets never occurred to me. Why was I so devastated? It was a loveless marriage, wasn't it? I hadn't wanted anything from it but a way out of my own grieving for Gary. Why, then, was I fearful to have it end? Roald stood against me and I respected him for that. I had to admit I hadn't given our marriage my best. I hadn't given him what he should have had from me. I knew I would go a long way before I found someone I respected as much. For all his annoying ways, he was a special person. And I did need him. Always when I found something good I fought to keep it. And, damn it, I would be too old to have a big family if I waited much longer. No, I was not going to accept a sad ending.

I decided that I simply had to find a way to make the marriage work. If I could.

I waited for the shops to open and went to the little knitting place where I had left Roald's scarf to be cleaned and blocked. Then I went home.

"What in God's name were you doing out on the streets so early?" Roald asked when I came in.

"I went to pick up something I made for you. I know you like cashmere." I held the scarf out to him. "Whatever happens to us, I made it for you."

Roald put it around his neck. It was a little short when I knitted it, but the blocking had made it long enough to reach his knees.

"Jolly good scarf," he said. I knew he was moved.

When Leslie arrived, I thought it best to tell him what was going on. Poor Leslie didn't say a word but burst out crying. I was deeply touched by this vote of confidence. Roald said crisply, "Well, it is not all that definite. I've talked with Charles Marsh and he has some ideas. I think you should give him a call, Pat."

Charles took over. Since Roald and Leslie were headed for Texas, he invited me to join him in Jamaica.

Ocho Rios was fabulous. Just its sunny warmth was enough to give me hope. For several weeks, Charles was a friend, teacher and Father Confessor. For hours and hours each day he and I met in his suite or walked along the beach and talked.

"Patricia," he began one day, "do you know what the most important thing in a marriage is?"

I ventured a guess. "Sex?"

"Do you know what that means?"

I laughed. "Our sex life is really very good. I don't think that's the problem at all."

"The problems of marriage," he interrupted, "always come down to s-e-x, but not the way you're thinking. Money is sex."

"But, Charles," I cried, "there are no problems with money. We don't have any!"

"No matter how little, my girl, you've got a problem as long as you are the breadwinner. You don't understand men, Pat. When it's a question of sex, not all of them want to be on top. When it comes to money, they all do. You can't have the balls in the family. You can make the money, but Roald must handle it. Have one bank account and let him write the checks, and I guarantee you that your marriage will be fine."

I couldn't believe it was that simple.

"There are a few other things," he added. "You must do all the cooking. You must wash the dishes and do everything in the house. You must not lie in bed. You must work hard."

"I'm willing to do that," I said, and I meant it.

I waited excitedly for Roald to join me. Charles had

said a marriage was two-sided, and he had some things to tell his young friend, too. I was very glad about that.

When they arrived, Leslie looked and felt splendid. The doctor had simply pulled out all his teeth. I don't think he ever did get dentures. He surely must have developed the hardest gums of any man alive, because he ate absolutely everything.

I happily assured Roald that Charles and I had been very successful, too.

The next morning we were surprised to see people running into Charles's room. A doctor emerged and told us Charles had been stung by a mosquito during the night and that he might *die* from it. We were devastated.

Our Charles did not die. He lived for ten years more. But the mysterious bite damaged his brain and he was never again able to speak beyond a simple yes or no. I often wondered what lecture Roald would have gotten if that terrifying insect had not taken Charles away from us.

Roald and I were left brokenhearted by the terrible accident that befell our friend, but his tragedy generated a new spirit between us. I told Roald what Charles had told me to do.

"And what do you think?" he asked.

"I agree," I answered.

Frankly, I don't think it amounted to much more than getting a joint bank account, but Roald now felt he wore the pants in the family and that was all that mattered.

Even without Charles's lecture, Roald changed. He stopped shutting me out with the silent treatment and he wasn't as rude to others. Maybe I was beginning to understand him better. Or maybe I finally got used to him.

CHAPTER THIRTY

From that moment on, I had one motivation. I wanted nothing else but to have a baby. Every month I prayed that my period would not come, and each time it did, I was in tears.

I started back to work, not on the stage or in films, but in television. It was the time of "Goodyear Playhouse" and "Studio One," and I did a show for each. I rather liked television and don't recall ever feeling frazzled by the hectic pace or pressured by performing live. I loved the challenge of learning lines quickly and working in a whirlwind of changes.

I did receive an offer to make an English film called "Stranger from Venus." I would again play an earthling who befriends a visitor from outer space. But this was no *Day the Earth Stood Still*. I didn't think much of the film. Roald encouraged me to do it because "we could use the money."

But my deep concern was not my career. My disappointment at not becoming pregnant gave way to a nagging fear that something inside me was seriously wrong. I knew I could conceive. I had already done so. But no matter how hard we tried, I could not get pregnant. Roald even had himself tested. There was nothing wrong with him. What if the abortionist in Los Angeles had taken something vital out of me? What if I could never have children?

Finally Roald and I decided I should go to a specialist in New York, a Dr. Rubin at Mount Sinai Hospital, who had developed a new treatment for blocked fallopian tubes. This, indeed, turned out to be my problem. I had to have air blown through my tubes, and it was agony. I nearly flew off the table, but if that's what it took, I was willing. When my period came again, I wept my heart out. The doctor insisted that if I would just not worry about it, things would happen in due course. So I promised to stop fretting.

Else and John wrote with news that they had found a lovely Georgian farmhouse on five acres of land in Great Missenden. It was a three-bedroom, two-story house that needed a lot of work, but it was going up for auction and the beginning bid was expected to be very low. Since Roald and I had decided to spend summers in England, we jumped for it. We offered more than the bid was expected to reach and still got it for a little over four thousand pounds. Mormor offered to pay half, and I paid the other half out of my savings. It already had a name: Little Whitefield.

We returned to England and it looked as if the visit would be a bit longer than I had thought. My agents had lined up a film for me in Italy to follow "Stranger from Venus." Yes, I took Roald's advice and signed up for that little English gem, which was eventually known, aptly, as *Immediate Disaster*.

I loved Little Whitefield. Remodeling had already started under the guidance of Roald's old friend Wally Saunders. Wally was the last of a generation that appreciated formality in service. He kept a clear line of respect and insisted upon calling me ma'am. But in his work, he was the king. Wally saw that house through more changes in the next twenty-five years than the stage at Radio City Music Hall. His first job was to make all the doors higher to accommodate Roald's towering frame. During the work we stayed with Mormor.

The English countryside around Great Missenden was alive and lush. Roald and I often walked together through the fields and I remember envying their fertility. One afternoon the bright blue sky was skirted with low-hanging clouds—like ladies removing their panties, I thought to myself. A delicious idea hit me. I was ovulating. Maybe I could get pregnant out there in the open air. So I interested Roald in sex and soon we were on the ground. I remember thinking this time it was going to work. Suddenly I felt my backside stinging. In moments I was in agony, but I was determined I would not interrupt him. What rotten luck, I thought, to have chosen a thorn patch for a bed!

When I got up, my bare bottom was covered with huge red welts. The ground was swarming with an army of angry soldier ants that had been defending their hill from our rude invasion. We laughed our heads off as I limped home.

My period came, but abruptly stopped. I waited a couple of days and then told Roald I should go in for that mouse test.

"Rabbit!" he shouted, his eyes twinkling.

The test was positive. We were going to have a nipper at last.

Of course, we always thanked Dr. Rubin, but I wonder if some credit shouldn't go to those bellicose ants. I always performed well under duress.

My mother-in-law was no longer keeping her displeasure with me to herself. She had started picking on me. Or at least I felt she was. Little things like slamming a plate down in front of me or shutting a door in my face and then hissing an insincere "Excuse me." Finally, one morning she thumped the coffee on the table and snarled, "Actress!"

I ran out to the garden crying and told Roald what had happened. "Your mother doesn't want me here," I sobbed.

Roald went into the house. "Mama," he commanded, "we are going to leave and never see you again if this continues. You may not behave this way to Pat. She is going to have a baby." Mormor's attitude changed completely after that day. She was utterly beautiful to me. This was an earthy woman who could obey with the simplicity of a faithful old dog. I loved her for that. Charles Marsh would have given her a high score.

We moved into Little Whitefield and attended to the finishing details ourselves. Roald was equally handy with a hammer or craftsman's knife, a paintbrush or pruning saw. I became a whiz with dust cloth and scouring pad. We began to choose furnishings. Some of them were authentic antiques, others simply old and comfortable. The walls began to fill up with art we both liked, ranging from ancient wood carvings to contemporary oils. Many were by Sir Matthew. It was a treasured time of sharing. Working on the house was just what we needed.

A few months later, professional commitments called us both away. Roald had to return to the States. His macabre stories were gaining him quite a reputation and Cheryl Crawford was going to produce a play called *The Honeys* fashioned from three of them, including "Lamb to the Slaughter," in which a wife kills her husband with a frozen leg of lamb, then cooks the lethal weapon and feeds it to the investigating detectives. It was destined for Broadway with the illustrious Jessica Tandy and Hume Cronyn. We were very excited.

Before our departure, we had just enough time to look up friends of Cheryl's who lived outside London. Roald felt we should make the effort to meet Brian and Maggie Dulanty before we began working with Cheryl because he really wanted her to like him.

The Dulantys were delightful. Their home looked like a charming miniature, more like a grown-up dollhouse than a dwelling. They had their own private stream and a great aviary with peacocks, parrots, cockatoos and budgies. We became fast friends.

Roald was scheduled to leave a few days before me and wasn't eager for me to stay out in the country alone. My old friend Helen Horton was now living in London. She had married her Hamish Thomson and they had a little boy named Jamie. I got myself invited to stay in their tiny flat until my departure.

The Italian film, *La Tua Donna,* was not in the least inspiring. Since I spoke no foreign language, my voice was entirely dubbed. But Rome in autumn was beautiful. I think anywhere in the world would have been. I was in love with being pregnant. The studio put me up at the Hassler, right at the top of the Spanish Steps, overlooking our honeymoon hotel. I hadn't told anyone about my pregnancy because I thought I might be replaced if they knew. I loved holding that quiet little life all to myself. As early as it was, I told Roald on one of my many transatlantic calls that I was sure I could already feel the baby's foot.

I loved to hear him gripe about the out-of-town labor pains of *The Honeys*. Although I always read his stories and gave him my two cents' worth, and he always evaluated the scripts offered to me, this was the first time he had crossed over the line into my territory, the theater, and he was having a perfectly dreadful time.

During their New Haven tryouts, the director had been fired and Hume Cronyn had taken over. Roald and Hume clashed constantly, with Roald uncharacteristically getting the worst of it.

I was very sympathetic. And I truly missed him. I was really feeling our first time apart.

As the end of the film approached, I began going to a doctor in Rome for routine checkups. On my third examination, I could see something was disturbing him. He told me there was a protrusion. I was aware of it, of course. I thought it was the baby's limb. The doctor said it might be a tumor and I should prepare myself for the possibility that I could lose the baby. He suggested I tell my husband at once.

I was panicked, but one thing was certain. I would not tell Roald any bad news about this baby. Instead I called our friend Dr. Ed Goodman in New York.

I told him everything the Italian doctor had said. Ed promised to call me back within the hour. A few minutes later the phone rang. It was Roald. Ed had called him immediately. I began weeping into the phone and Roald kept saying, over and over, "Don't worry about it. Please, just don't worry." I heard a tenderness in his voice as delicate as the life I carried. I felt my heart reach out across the ocean to him. I was beginning to fall in love with my husband.

We agreed that I would fly to New York right away. Roald was there at the airport. He had made an appointment for an immediate examination. He was positive that everything would be fine and I would carry this baby to term. When Roald said something with that certain tone of his, I could almost believe he was God.

Whatever the problem was that had so distressed the Italian doctor, it never materialized and my baby continued to grow. I can't begin to express the relief and gratitude I felt. It freed me to think of other things. I was obviously too big now to try to get any work, but I knew I had to be active. I needed to get back to the roots of my profession, which had not been stimulated by my last two film outings. I remembered my severed association with The Actors Studio, which was now under the leadership of Lee Strasberg. I called and asked if I could return. He said yes.

My first day I sat behind an earnest young actor with the most penetrating blue eyes I had ever seen. His name was Paul Newman. By the time that first session was over, I didn't feel in the least like a visitor, but was totally committed again. I loved being with talented people and I always did my best work in response to good actors. The Studio was a godsend.

During this time, a most significant relationship developed with an old supper acquaintance, Gadge Kazan. After seeing my work in a few scenes, he offhandedly said, "After that baby comes, you should try cutting a tooth on Tennessee Williams."

Roald was in Boston with *The Honeys* when I felt my first labor pains. I was sound asleep and suddenly I felt a bang! bang! bang! I waited for more signals and then called Roald, who flew home immediately. He timed my labor pains until he determined we must be off to Doctors Hospital. I've never seen a man more thrilled. But this baby of ours was not to be enticed by mere enthusiasm. I was in labor for thirty-six hours.

Finally, on the afternoon of April 20, 1955, my baby decided it was time.

I don't know what I expected in the delivery room, but whatever it was, it was not what I got. I wanted everything to be beautiful about this miraculous experience. But the two nurses who attended me couldn't have tarnished the moment more if that's what they had set out to do. I remember asking one if it was really necessary to knock me out, because I wanted to see the birth happen. "State law," she snapped. Then the other strapped my legs in stirrups and my arms to the table. Didn't she know I was having a baby, not a convulsion? But the ugliest thing was that they simply would not stop giggling about a double date they had had. I thought they were so nasty and insensitive that, just before losing consciousness, I vowed never to have another baby in New York.

CHAPTER THIRTY-ONE

Olivia *Twenty*! What do you think?'' asked Roald. We had already chosen Olivia as our daughter's first name. It had a special significance for me. Olivia was the role I had played in *Twelfth Night* at Northwestern.

''But where did you get 'Twenty'?'' I asked.

''She was born on April 20,'' he answered, ''and I'm getting twenty dollars a day expense money on the road.''

The minute Roald mentioned money, I remembered dear Charles's words: ''That is the kiss, Patricia.''

Olivia Twenty had a distinguished audience for her first public appearance. All my friends from The Studio came. Eli and Anne said this was by far my best work. Dash came, too, feigning disappointment that I hadn't kept my promise to name her Neal Dashiell. He volunteered to baby-sit anytime.

Even though Roald and I had wanted a baby so very much, we could not have anticipated the wonder we felt when we brought this new life home with us. I remember that first day I took Olivia into my bedroom. We were alone. I lay down with her on the bed and put her on her tummy next to me. I looked her over and over again. What mother doesn't count and recount every finger and toe? She was perfect. Huge lovely eyes under perfectly arched brows and the best lips I had ever seen. Only a few days old, she already looked like a little person, and a serious one at that. I turned her over between my hands. At the base of her spine was a deep dent, almost a hole. I caught myself wondering if there had once been a tiny tail that had fallen off before birth. "Oh, my Olivia," I whispered, "what kind of a creature are you?" She gazed up at me and I was overcome by such a strange feeling. It was as though Olivia was looking right through me to my very soul. Her gaze said, *I see you. I have seen you all your life and I will know you all your life*. I have never seen this look since in the eyes of any other baby. I was soon to learn it was a declaration of war.

From the very first I was an uneasy mother. For some reason I was panicky every time I had to feed Olivia or change her or bathe her or even pick her up. We had an old Scottish nurse to help me look after her, and when she left I would just sit and stare at Olivia and try to figure out what to do next. I remember thinking my uncertainty was the result of never having been allowed to touch any of the young ones when I was a child—"Don't touch, Patsy, stick to your dolls." When my real moment came, I simply did not know babies. I wanted desperately to breast-feed, but I was so nervous I didn't have any milk. I would put Olivia to my breast and pray the miracle would happen, but the most I ever produced was one tiny drop. I took this as the ultimate judgment of failure and told Roald I felt it meant I simply could not handle motherhood. He was very tender and said, "Not to worry. If you can't do it, you can't do it," and assured me that most women would be relieved not to have to bother. But at each feeding, I would still examine myself, hoping to find a sudden fountain of milk. When it didn't come, I would cry more than the baby.

Olivia seemed to sense my lack of confidence, and how she played on it. She had only one weapon and she used it. All babies cry, frequently at inconvenient times, but Olivia cried with a vengeance. She seemed to lie in wait. She could be sound asleep, but if she sensed me near, her eyes would pop open and she'd let out a piercing scream. Her timing was perfect. Day or night, she kept me constantly at the edge. Roald was a very maternal daddy and never minded sharing the shifts. But the struggle was definitely between Olivia and me.

Only days out of the hospital, I got a call from Guthrie McClintic, who had a play scheduled for the upcoming season on Broadway. It was called *A Roomful of Roses,* written by Edith Sommer, who had been at the Barter Theatre. I would play a mother who is reunited with her rebellious fifteen-year-old daughter, whom she left years before. Considering I had just birthed my first child, the role would be a little challenging. Roald and I both liked it, and the lead in a McClintic play on Broadway seemed a good choice to reactivate my career. Six weeks later, we left for England with a copy of the script tucked in my bag and a new baby in my arms.

The Dulantys found us a nurse who had the distinctive reputation of having cared for one of the Churchill babies. She turned out to be a strange bird with one fake eye and a hacking cough. I was more of a nervous wreck than ever. On the fourth day Roald fired her, saying that I had this great mother thing and really needed to do it myself. This was true. If only I knew how.

By midsummer, things between Olivia and me were no better than they'd been in New York. After five children, I can now look back and see how silly I was. But I was overcome, a bundle of raw nerves. Finally, my sister-in-law Else saw my distress and offered to take Olivia to her home to give me a rest. She promised it would make a difference to the baby, too. "Take her!" I cried. "I can hardly wait to get rid of her!" I was so exhausted that I slept for a week.

I don't know what Else did that made the difference. Maybe it was just experience—after all, she was mothering little Nicky and the twins—but somehow Olivia knew she was not the boss with Else. When Else gave her back to me after two weeks, the war was over. She cooed instead of cried. And this little three-month-old was even on her way to being potty-trained. I couldn't believe it. I could hold her on a potty that was hardly bigger than a saucepan and she would make bonks—a word I picked up from her cousin Nicky.

As fall approached, we decided that I would return to New York alone with Olivia. Mother had offered to come and stay with us during rehearsals. Roald decided to remain in Great Missenden to work and I didn't argue the point. I doubted he'd like being alone with my mother in our flat. He would come over for the opening. As the great BOAC plane soared into the horizon, I cuddled Olivia very close. I felt as if that one tiny life were the whole world in my arms.

I loved getting back to work. Rehearsals were delicious. Guthrie McClintic was a divine man and a sympathetic director who would cry when he thought a scene was performed well. He became a friend and we would often go for supper or drinks with members of the company, which included Warren Berlinger and Betty Lou Keim, who played my daughter. These two youngsters fell in love in the course of doing that show and it was great fun to live through their courtship. I was so happy for them when they got married, because I was beginning to find happiness in my own marriage.

Mother was a great help. She adored her granddaughter and loved playing nanny. To my great joy, she insisted Olivia was the picture of me.

The play was received very well but was not a great hit. The press at that time was more interested in covering my domestic bliss than the show. They filled columns on my home life with new baby and just-arrived husband, that macabre English writer *Ronald* Dahl. I was certainly not the only woman who was wife, mother and professional, but this was long before women's lib and it made news. Truly, I was performing to everyone's satisfaction, including my husband's. I wasn't merely following Charles's advice, I was following it in spades.

I rose early to bathe and feed my now six-month-old, walked her in the park and did the shopping. I made breakfast and lunch for my husband, conferred with the nurse, cleaned the apartment, prepared supper, did the dishes and made it to the theater for an 8:30 curtain. And I made sure there was always plenty of time to discuss my husband's work with great appreciation. It was an exhausting schedule, but I was having a wonderful time.

When the play closed after eighty-eight performances, Guthrie made me a gift of my wardrobe, which included a Dior suit. I was wearing it on a rare afternoon outing by myself. Walking down Fifth Avenue, I stopped to window-shop. There was a man looking in the window. I was suddenly aware that it was Gary.

Strengthened by the fact that I was looking divine in my Dior, I tapped him on the shoulder. He turned around, slightly annoyed at being accosted by a strange woman on the street, and then he recognized me.

"Oh, my baby!" he gasped.

"Hello, Gary," I answered, and we looked at each other for long seconds. We had not seen each other for three years and I could not bear standing on a public street a moment longer.

"Let's have some tea?" I pleaded.

The St. Regis was right across the street. We found a quiet nook in the corner of the bar. He looked older. Time had cut deeper furrows into his face. I caught myself adding his years to my own. Gary would be fifty-five or fifty-six. He told me I looked great and wanted to know all about me.

"I have a baby, a little girl. Her name is Olivia. I'd love you to see her. I'm married now." The words tumbled out stupidly.

"Yes, I know," he said. "Radie Harris told me about it in Europe. Not about the baby. She told me about the marriage. I'm afraid she saw how shocked I was. I told her if the bastard wasn't good to you, I'd come back and kill him. She loved that."

"I am so happy to see you," I said, matching his surprising directness. "I am happy we're here."

"Olivia," he repeated quietly, "that's a nice name. She must be a little beauty."

"There really is no need to talk around things this time, is there?" I asked.

"No," he agreed.

"You broke my heart, Gary. You really did."

"You know, baby, I couldn't have hurt Maria for the world."

"I know," I said. "I loved you so much."

"I still do," he answered.

And I always will, I thought to myself.

We looked at each other without a word. Oh God, had there been a way to have this incredible gift of love and still respect his marriage vows, I would have touched upon the miracle of my life.

We finished our tea and he saw me to a taxi and I went home to Roald.

CHAPTER
THIRTY-TWO

arly in 1956, I did a scene from *Cat on a Hot Tin Roof* at The Actors Studio with a young actor named Pat Hingle. *Cat* was then playing on Broadway with Barbara Bel Geddes, Burl Ives and Millie Dunnock, directed by Elia Kazan. Gadge saw our scene and asked me to replace Barbara, who was going on a three-week holiday. I jumped at it. Of course, Barbara's understudy had been waiting months for this chance. The night I went on, the poor woman got dead drunk in the basement. I felt bad, but not bad enough to let her take the part even once. It was a joyful reunion with Millie, that wisp of a woman who filled the stage as Big Mama.

Coincidentally, Roald and I had decided to find a larger apartment and Millie suggested the flat she was leaving across the street from Campbell's Funeral Chapel on Madison Avenue. The building had been constructed in the 1890s, which made it the third-oldest apartment house in the city. There were two apartments to a floor, each with a great high ceiling. Because of the rental rules in the building, we had to sneak in as Millie sneaked out without the landlord knowing.

As soon as my run in *Cat* was over, I took a long-awaited opportunity to go to Atlanta to show Olivia off to my whole family. Barely nine months old, she astonished everyone by starting to walk.

I was there only a few days when Gadge called. He

was preparing his new film, *A Face in the Crowd,* by Budd Schulberg, and wanted me for the female lead. "It's a great part, Pat," he promised.

I couldn't believe his words. I really never expected to be in another film. I thought I had given up on Hollywood and vice versa. Budd had casting approval, but Gadge felt sure he would agree. However, I had to go to Florida to meet him.

I left Olivia in the care of her doting grandmother, got the next flight out and that same day lunched with Budd. We talked a little and that was it. As I headed back to Atlanta, I knew I had the part.

The film would not start until August, so I was back doing scenes at The Studio. One day I was caught with no one to take care of my toddler. I remembered an old friend's promise and called Dash. He was thrilled. He walked her around his room while she held on to his thumbs, and for two and a half hours he talked to her, which was certainly more than he ever talked to me. Of course, she was too young to remember their afternoon, but, God willing, part of my heaven will be finding out about that talk from Olivia.

We returned to Little Whitefield in May and continued our restoration, this time adding a small cottage. This was meant to be used for guests, but when it was finished, Roald liked it so much he commandeered it for himself, setting it up as a workshop for restoring antique mirrors.

That was not all he was restoring. His sister Alfhild had a weather-beaten old gypsy caravan. It was just sitting in her garden falling apart but Roald rescued it and turned it into a charming playhouse for the children.

We were country folk now who occasionally got to the theater in London or the greyhound races, which Roald adored, at the White City, an enormous track outside London. We were hosted there one night by a friend from Hollywood, Bette Davis, who had been a guest at our home. She shared Roald's enthusiasm for the dog races and was terribly popular at the track. All the handicappers gave her the best tips. We always made a mint when we were with Bette.

Our life was centered on our home and Roald's family. Mormor's hips had finally collapsed into the dreaded chair, so she never went beyond her house. But I often took Olivia to see her. How Olivia loved Mormor's lap. She seemed to find all the comfort and security she needed there.

Before I knew it, I was back at Heathrow Airport saying goodbye to Roald and Olivia. It was the first time I had to leave her and I felt the tug of separation. I did not know, as I wept and waved out the plane window, that I was carrying a new baby.

It was during my costume fittings that I realized I was pregnant. I had the test and joyfully sent Roald a wire saying: HERE COMES PETER COTTON-TAIL, HOPPING DOWN THE BUNNY TRAIL. I received an immediate reply. His wire read: I LOVE YOU. It was the second time he told me so.

It was hotter than hell in New York when we began studio rehearsals and even hotter in Arkansas, where much of the film took place. I had a honey of a part. I played a woman who discovers a hillbilly singer and turns him into a popular TV personality, only to find he's become a monster. A very talented Andy Griffith played that role. Andy had catapulted to fame in *No Time for Sergeants,* which opened on Broadway the same week as *Roomful of Roses.* Working with Andy was like working with family—I absolutely loved him. The enchanting young Lee Remick was introduced in the film. And Walter Matthau had a small part. I adored working with Walter. For years after my stroke I could only remember him as the *nose,* who had the smallest part but who became the biggest of us all.

Elia Kazan does not need me to verify his genius. He is a master, a presence that breaks every barrier that could possibly keep an actor from doing his best. I remember a scene with Tony Franciosa, a Studio colleague, in which I had to hit him across the face. We got through rehearsals, carefully choreographing the blow so it would appear realistic, but just as we were ready to shoot, Gadge whispered to me, "I want you to really smack him, so hard you nearly kill him." All right, I thought, if Gadge wants me to do it, I will. Tony didn't know what hit him. He started to cry, which wasn't rehearsed. He was utterly fantastic. But when the camera stopped, he kept on crying and cried all through lunch. I felt terrible. I wanted to tell him what a great job he'd done, but he wouldn't come near me. I'm sure he thought I was a number one bitch. It was all for nothing, because Tony's wonderful tears were cut.

My big moment in the film comes at the end, when my character realizes what a bastard the singer has become. He's in the final moments of his TV show, smiling sweetly under the closing credits. Secure in the belief that the sound has been cut, he snidely berates his audience as mindless clods. I'm in the control room and seize the opportunity to expose him by turning the sound back on, allowing these fans to see what he really is. Two men in the booth try to drag me away from the controls, but I hold fast. It's a hell of a moment. "Now I want you to really grab on to those controls," Gadge told me just before the cameras rolled. "Hang on as if your life depended on it, no matter what happens."

The scene began, and when I grabbed the handles on the board, I felt the pulling at my back, my arms, my shoulders. Those two guys were strong, all right. I hung on with the determination of an animal holding fiercely to its kill. Finally, the terrifying weight from behind succeeded in pulling me off and I burst into tears, certain that I had let Kazan down. When it was over, Gadge confessed that he had used not two but eight men to overpower me.

My unborn child was certainly getting a baptism of fire. Earlier, during a scene in Piggot, Arkansas, I was making my way along a catwalk over a cattle pen when it suddenly collapsed under me. My bruises, if any, were minor, and no harm was done to the baby. You'd think such a traumatic moment would be easy to recall, but my memory of the fall is based solely on newspaper accounts.

I phoned home at least twice a week to keep up with my darling Olivia, who was now playing with dolls, and to let Roald know how things were going. There was never a question of his coming over to spend time with me during filming. He was terribly involved with a new book and simply wasn't the type to traipse around after a working wife. I was secretly relieved, for I knew he could never be just a casual observer on the set, and I was still leery of those definite opinions of his.

Also, I wasn't eager to have him see the press I was getting, especially in the South, where Roald was constantly misspelled, most frequently as "Fouald, which rhymes with you all."

With the finish of *A Face in the Crowd,* I looked forward to being with my family, content that I had had a splendid reunion with film. I couldn't wait to meet my husband and daughter at La Guardia Airport. Roald broke a Dahl tradition and kissed me hello in public.

We spent the winter in New York but returned to England so our new baby could be born there. Olivia was moving toward her second birthday and it looked as if she might be sharing the date with a new brother or sister.

But the new baby did not wait for Olivia's birthday. On April 11, I was admitted to Radcliffe Hospital in Oxford and met a young nurse. She probed and listened and then matter-of-factly announced, "It will be a girl, Mrs. Dahl."

"How can you tell?" I asked.

She replied, "A girl has a different heartbeat." So began a long friendship with Nesta Powell.

When the contractions started, Nesta said, "Don't be afraid to express your pain. You have a right to say how you feel about this thing."

Maybe one should groan, I thought to myself. So I was lying there going "Ooough! Ooough!" when Dr. Hawksworth walked in.

"What is going on with you?" he demanded. "Will you please stop making all that noise!" I quit immediately. I never made a noise again in labor.

He was a lovely doctor, but I do think he stole a bit of my birthing rights.

Chantal Sophia Dahl was christened soon after her birth, with Betsy Drake as her godmother. Betsy had to hold the new infant over the baptismal font for the rites. It was immediately obvious that she had little experience with babies. Betsy stood there smiling down on the newborn, whom she was holding at a forty-five-degree angle, the tiny feet high in the air and the small head buried in the crook of her elbow. I kept motioning to Betsy to lift the baby's head. She kept nodding and smiling back and lifting the feet higher and higher until I thought Chantal Sophia would be standing on her head. Through the years, Betsy could not have been a more faithful and loving godmother.

Her godchild, however, lost her Christian name three months later when Roald realized that Chantal rhymed with Dahl. He was determined that his daughter would be spared the teasing and changed her name to Tessa.

As one might have expected, Tessa quickly established herself as a little tiger. No "glorious walks" through nature had formed this one. She had been molded on the catwalks and hot studio sets of *A Face in the Crowd*. Tessa was going to be very different from Olivia.

Shortly after Tessa was born, I was invited to attend the European premiere of *A Face in the Crowd* in Scotland. It was to be a grand affair, but Roald decided he'd rather see the dog races instead, so I went alone. Roald made a killing at the races, which inspired him to make up for his slight by buying me some expensive antique turquoise jewelry.

The next week, we went to a fabulous party and I wore my new beads. Everyone was quite impressed and Roald just beamed. One man, a duke, I think, took a very close look, and Roald picked up on his expression. As soon as we were alone, Roald grabbed a pin and stuck it smack through a bead. It was paste. He sent the bogus gems right back to the dealer with an outraged letter. He got his money back.

But the thing that really got to Roald was that man knowing the Dahl jewels were fake.

My next job was for British television, the BBC production of *The Royal Family*. I was very pleased because I had not yet established myself professionally in England. Working there would keep me close to my sprouting family and my income on the rise. Roald's writing was not yet pulling in very much. I was delighted to be in the company of that fine English actress Fay Compton, who had been married to Ralph Michael, with whom I'd worked in *Hasty Heart*. Fay loved my fake jewelry story and insisted on giving me her own necklace of real turquoise, which I have to this very day.

The Royal Family was the first of several good BBC outings. Over the next few years I would do S. N. Berman's comedy *Biography* and two plays by Clifford Odets, *Clash by Night* and *The Country Girl*, the latter with my friend Eddie Albert. Regardless of what lay in store for me in America, it looked as if I was going to have some kind of a career in my adopted country.

CHAPTER
THIRTY-THREE

We were settling in. Roald did the planting and I did the weeding. I cooked and kept house and he refinished his antique frames, which were in every room. He tended our roses. We had over a hundred varieties now. We were turning Little Whitefield into a beautiful home. There was an open atmosphere. Everything centered around the downstairs sitting room, where Roald's discerning eye for beautiful furniture and paintings had created a peaceful and lovely environment.

We had built a kind of summer house for outdoor teas, but when Brian Dulanty gave us some budgerigars, the little teahouse was closed in with wire and became our aviary. This was Olivia's special place. She loved to come with me to feed the birds and help me clean. Her favorites were the rare, pure white and yellow parakeets that somehow were always disappearing. I'm sure it was the work of some animal, but for Olivia, these vanishing beauties were like tiny angels who could evaporate at will.

Roald also had Wally Saunders build him a hut in the apple and pear orchard. There Roald set up his office with a large leather armchair and the wood and green felt writing board. He would sit for hours and create. He kept a regular schedule in his hut, from ten to noon and from four to six every day, even in the coldest weather, when you could find him bundled up in a blanket with a thermos of hot tea or coffee and an ashtray brimming with butts at his side.

I loved the way he looked when he was writing. When we were first married, he was already starting a Shakespeare forehead, with great wisps of hair growing over each ear. By now he was settling into his forties with a decided resemblance to Virginia Woolf, whom I always thought of as Roald Dahl in drag. He never looked as if he cared much about his clothes and usually was attired in gray trousers, striped shirt and cardigan. It was a studied casualness, however, because the shirts were custom-made in Scotland, when he felt he could afford them, and the sweaters would be of the finest English wool or cashmere. Underneath these outers he was always naked as a babe.

He was then compiling a book of his magazine stories and searching for a title. "Remember that phone conversation between your friend Jean and her husband? 'Kiss-kiss'?" he mused. "I always thought that would make a smashing title. And, by the way, Pat, this one will be dedicated to you." There was no argument from me this time. I was very touched.

Roald graciously invited my mother to visit us, and although I was delighted at the prospect, I couldn't help but feel it would be the Hatfields and McCoys again. I was not wrong. It wasn't long before the old antagonisms began to show. They never actually squared off, but they needled each other constantly.

Mother was openly critical of what she perceived to be Roald's fondness for the rich and famous. "Pat," she would ask pointedly, "why do you always talk about who has money and who does not? We never valued things like that in our family. Whom did you get that from?"

When she insisted upon cooking some of her southern specialties, Roald went out of his way to let her know it was not his favorite food. Unfortunately his displays rubbed off on the girls, who began complaining about her pork chops and black-eyed peas before they tasted them.

Poor Mother never had much of a chance to prove herself with her granddaughters.

Roald did, however, bring Mother and Mormor together. Mormor could not get out to Little Whitefield at all anymore so Roald arranged for Mother to spend an afternoon at her home. He saw that Olivia and her nurse went along, and Mother was certain that the nurse was meant to bring back reports about the meeting. The two women got along quite well and Mother's visits were repeated, always with the nurse in attendance. Finally, Mormor called Mother herself and invited her to tea, and she made a point of telling Roald to keep the nurse home. Well, the two had a great talk, woman to woman. Mother told me later that Mormor was aware that Roald was a difficult man to live with. As was his father. She said Mormor never went to bed without a comb under her pillow because her husband didn't appreciate her waking up with her hair mussed. I assured Mother that there was no comb under my pillow. But I wasn't prepared to discuss the fact that I still never appeared naked in front of my husband.

The Thames flowed somewhat near our house and we loved to spend some of our precious summer days boating and picnicking by the water. The children were always part of our enjoyment on these outings, and there was a bunch of them now. Besides our two there were Nicky, Louise and Anna, Astri and Willie, baby Peter and Baba. On one occasion our crowd rented a great cabin cruiser together and the whole tribe was aboard. As we grown-ups sat talking, little Louise came up and said, "Baba has gone down under the water." No one paid any attention, so she repeated it. "Baba has gone down under the water!"

We froze in the realization of what she meant, then raced to the rail. "Where, baby, where?" we cried, and she pointed to where a bright ribbon was floating. Roald plunged his hand into the water and grabbed the ribbon. He pulled the poor child onto the boat by her hair. Baba spat out some water and within minutes was begging to

Back in Kentucky with Aunt Maude, Aunt Josephine and Mother.

With John Garfield, filming *The Breaking Point*. Not the most celebrated film from a Hemingway novel, but the most faithful.

In Argentina with June Haver. She gave me my first taste of the Catholic Church.

The Day the Earth Stood Still and second of three *very* tall men in my life.

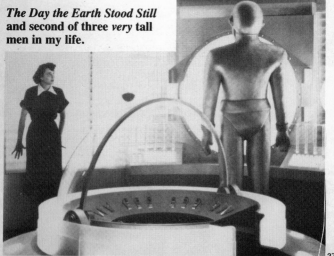

Diplomatic Courier. Espionage, intrigue and
Ty Power.

Onstage in Korea. Stringy hair and dripping with
sweat, but the boys didn't seem to mind.

Back in New York and *The Children's Hour,* with Kim Hunter. Lillian Hellman gave me this fabulous job when I needed it most.

40

As Lady Teazle in *School for Scandal* in 1953.

41

The honeymoon. Roald and I at the Colosseum in Rome.

At the Roman Forum. These statues of the vestal virgins were famous for the beatings they took.

With my beautiful Olivia when we left for New York and *A Roomful of Roses*.

A *Roomful of Roses*. Betty Lou Keim, Warren Berlinger and I through the eyes of Hirschfeld.

During the filming of *A Face in the Crowd*, with Andy Griffith and the genius—Elia Kazan.

47

A work break on location for *A Face in the Crowd*.
Lee Remick, Andy, Gadge, Budd Schulberg and
tearful Tony Franciosa.

48

My big moment in *A Face
in the Crowd*—being dragged
away from the TV controls.
There are only two men
shown but I swear it took
eight.

49

Pregnant with Tessa
at Little Whitefield.

Tennessee Williams's *Suddenly Last Summer*, in London. My favorite performance.

With Anne Bancroft, Patty Duke and Torin Thatcher in *The Miracle Worker*. Helen Keller's story became an inspiration to me during difficult times ahead.

Happy days at Little Whitefield. I adore this picture.

53

With my Theo, before the accident.

Breakfast at Tiffany's. I love Audrey Hepburn
looking at George Peppard looking at me.

54

In 1961 with Roald and my darlings back in England— safe. We thought.

Tessa, Theo and me.

Roald in his hut, with writing board, blanket and an old suitcase for a footstool.

57

58

The BBC production of *The Country Girl,* with wonderful Eddie Albert. It was called *Winter Journey* in England.

Olivia's grave.

59

As Alma in *Hud—
the* role at last.
That's Paul Newman,
need I say.

62

With Melvyn Douglas on the set of *Hud*. What a beauty of a man he was.

63

A lucky lady and the four little ones in her life— Theo, Ophelia, Tessa and rattling Oscar.

At Ophelia's christening. With the beautiful twin nieces, Louise an Anna, and my beloved Harvey Orkin.

64

In Harm's Way. The second and happier time I worked with Duke Wayne.

65

In Harm's Way. A marvelous reunion with Kirk Douglas.

66

continue the games with the other children. I remember wondering with amazement how Louise had the sense to keep repeating her message. And I looked at Olivia and the baby Tessa and thought of how shatteringly uncertain life is. How could we possibly protect our children?

For all of our early turmoil, Olivia and I were developing a grand relationship. She helped me with the housework and tagged along wherever I went. She wrote poems as soon as she learned that words could rhyme, and we would take all the dolls down to the lake, where she would attempt to teach them those rhymes. Roald and I started a zoo of miniature glass and ceramic animals in her nursery, and Olivia constructed toy villages and parks for them to roam. She was beautifully imaginative, painting pictures that told stories of her private world. One day I watched her do a rainbow with a child walking over it, and I remembered a rainbow from my childhood that was always visible at Cumberland Falls.

"Why, that's me," I told her.

"No," she corrected, "that's Olivia!" That painting hangs in my New York apartment.

A later "Olivia" hung over our mantelpiece at Little Whitefield for many years. The significance of its marks and symbols was known only to her, but it had a compelling aura that rivaled the work of the professionals hanging alongside it. It was worth more to Roald and me than any Constable. It would be the one our souls would struggle over.

We took our summer vacations in Norway. For two or three years in a row we went to Fevik and Hankø Island, where the cliffs meet the shore in a dramatic clash. Norway was a haven for Roald, and I found myself loving it, too. Our days were spent fishing or yachting or diving, complete with oxygen tanks. I admit they never got me into one of those getups. It took enough courage just to swim. There were rare places where one could walk for a long way and the water would never come up over your head. That was my style.

I added exotic names to my address book—great friends like Tull and Sverre and Gunvar and Lillerie—but when I think back on our summers in Norway, I think mainly of Roald's sister Alfhild, because she and I still share the wonderful memories of that time today.

A Face in the Crowd had not reestablished me as a sought-after movie actress. I wasn't even offered the film version of *A Roomful of Roses.* But I was working continually in television and usually in quality shows. It gave me a chance to get back to "my people." As lovely as my new friends were, I got lonesome for theater folk, for the freedom of our kind of talk and laughter, and for the gossip.

California always seemed Gary Cooper country to me, but nevertheless I liked returning to Hollywood to do shows like "Playhouse 90." I usually stayed at the Chateau Marmont, a small but pleasant hotel above the Sunset Strip that was considered "in" by visiting New York actors. It was also cheaper than the Bel-Air, and expenses for TV were pretty modest. These occasional visits gave me a chance to see good friends for happy times.

And good friends for not so happy times.

I had not seen Jean Hagen for ages. She and Tom had a lovely home in Westwood, complete with swimming pool and the other symbols of success. Jean had started out with a bang at MGM with an Oscar nomination for *Singin' in the Rain* the same year Gary won for *High Noon.* But Hollywood had left her nursing hopes of fulfillment, and when the teat dried up, she started on the bottle.

On one of my work jaunts to the Coast, Jean invited Millie Dunnock and me to Sunday brunch. When we arrived, we found a wreck of a human being. She was completely smashed. Nothing had been prepared and the house was a mess, dirty dishes stacked in the sink. Millie and I washed them and straightened up a bit and left. I didn't know what else to do to help. Jean never liked people meddling in her affairs. Eventually Tom left her. My dear friend did finally quit drinking, but there were many heartbreaks to come before she made it.

CHAPTER THIRTY-FOUR

n midsummer 1958, I got a call out of the blue from Herbert Machiz. He was planning a production of Tennessee Williams's *Garden District* and wanted me to make my London stage debut in the role of Catherine Holly in the second half of the bill, *Suddenly Last Summer,* one of Tennessee's most intense good-versus-evil dramas. Herbert warned me that I would have to do it for love, that there was no money in it. There had been a successful off-Broadway production, but I hadn't seen it. Herbert sent me a script, and at first reading, I knew I'd do it for love.

We rehearsed in a rented hall in London and Herbert was right. My salary just about covered train fare to and from Great Missenden and no extras. Once I was so tired after a performance, I slept right through my stop and had to give a cabbie three days' pay to drive me home from the next town.

But how I wanted to do that role. If for no other reason than the last scene, which is, in fact, a fifteen-minute monologue. I was back to my roots. Herbert staged this scene very simply, with only a single spotlight on my face. I remember I acted my heart out to that single beam of light shining down on me.

On opening night, the curtain went down slowly and there was what seemed an eternity of silence. Then the applause came, rolling over us like thunder. It was the crowning moment of what was, for me, the most thrilling acting experience of my life.

I got the best reviews of my career. At least I *think* I did. Kenneth Tynan wrote in *The London Observer*:

I must pause here to salute Patricia Neal, the American Method actress. The power and variety of her dark brown voice, on which she plays like a master of the cello, enable her to separate the cadenza from its context and make of it a plangent cry from the depths of memory. Rhetoric and realism, in this harrowing performance, not only fuse but fertilize each other, and I was more than once reminded of Maria Casares' incomparable Phèdre.

This time I was absolutely sure I'd get the film. The man who would produce it, Sam Spiegel, saw a newspaper ad for our show on his way to London and came to see the play. He was so impressed he called Tennessee Williams that same night and bought the rights. He also raved about me. He sent several associates to see the play, and night after night I would be called for in Rolls-Royces and taken to supper after each performance. I was so confident that I did not go after it. I didn't ask my agents to pitch me and I didn't hire a press agent to publicize my success. I had been counseled to hire a publicity man after *A Face in the Crowd* to get my movie career going again, but I have always felt that if you do good work, people know.

So one day I picked up a paper and read that Elizabeth Taylor had been signed for *Suddenly Last Summer*—the greatest stage hit I had ever had. Losing that film was the hardest professional blow of my life. I still cannot talk about it without tasting bitterness.

I had an offer to do another play on Broadway. The whole family packed up and we returned for our winter in New York. But when I arrived I found that the producers had decided to go with Shelley Winters. I was so hurt. Those are the moments in this business you really hate.

So it was back to The Studio for me, and another stretch of housewife duty.

Roald, however, was busier than he'd ever been, working on his first children's book, *James and the Giant Peach*. He had a foolproof system for developing his tales. He would tell them to the children and if they asked to hear one again, he knew he had a winner. This one was to be for Olivia and Tessa.

The apartment above us was owned by Clifford Odets and sublet by a young actress named Valerie French, who let Roald use one of the rooms as his studio. It wasn't his hut, but he was grateful to have a place of his own. We were getting to know most of the other tenants in the building and found our neighbors just eccentric enough to make them interesting. Mrs. Whitehead was a dear old lady who treated all the tenants as if we were guests in her home. The Hafers were the shortest people we had ever seen and rumor had it that they took their even shorter children to some gym on the West Side to be stretched. On the eighth floor were the Kadinsky sisters. They kept monkeys and cats, and Olivia liked them because they gave pet treats instead of candy at Halloween. One family had two of the ugliest little boys, whom Roald referred to, fortunately in private, as guppies.

One morning Roald was waiting for the elevator with Tessa when a neighbor and her daughter joined them. Roald looked down at the little girls and, pointing to her toddler, asked the mother, "How old is *that?*"

"*That* is two," she batted back.

Roald pointed to Tessa. "So is *that*."

And that is how the Austrians, Geoffrey and Sonia and their Susie, came into our lives.

Phone calls between the second and fourth floors were constant. If Sonia and I weren't gossiping about the neighbors—Sonia knew absolutely everything that was going on—it was the girls. I used to get such a kick out of hearing that tiny voice say, "Hel-leu, Sew-sie. Tes-sah he-ah." It made me realize I was the only one in our household who sounded American.

Sonia and I were real New York mothers. We walked our kids in the park or took them to movies or the zoo. I recall one Saturday afternoon when we all went to the circus in Madison Square Garden, and, as all children everywhere, ours had to have souvenirs of the big event. Olivia had become transfixed by the chameleons. Nothing else would do; she had to have one, and the vendor happily pinned the ghastly thing to her coat. When our taxi pulled up at the apartment, the chameleon was gone. A frantic search ensued, with the driver removing the backseat and combing the springs for the elusive animal, all while double-parked, of course. Eighty-first Street soon started to vibrate with honking horns, but the driver insisted he would find the thing no matter how long it took. I thought it was very kind of him until Sonia pointed out that the meter was ticking away like mad. Olivia's little cammy was finally uncovered, turning out to be the most expensive animal I had ever bought for her.

We returned to England early in the spring of 1959, and I was at Elstree Studio when I heard someone mention that Gary Cooper was on the lot shooting a film with Charlton Heston. Chuck was a fellow Northwestern alumnus, graduating in the class of '45, which would have been my class had I stayed.

In England, socializing on sets was not encouraged, but I went to the soundstage anyway. I was not only allowed in but graciously shown to a chair at the foot of a great boat set looming over me. The two actors were rehearsing, but when Chuck saw me he whispered to Gary. Gary shut his eyes for a moment, then continued rehearsing without looking down. When the director called a break, Gary finally looked over and smiled. He climbed off the set and dropped into a chair beside me. I remember nothing of our conversation that day except that we mentioned one of his films I'd missed. I had just had Tessa when *Love in the Afternoon* was playing. I heard it was about a May–December affair and I was curious as hell.

Soon he was called back to work, and walked me to the car.

"I'm glad you stopped by," he said, and he took my hand between his palms.

"I just wanted to see you again," I answered.

He kissed me on the cheek and helped me into the car.

As the car pulled away I did not look back. Gary had been a part of me. But he was no longer my life. I knew I had taken the right course. There were no more regrets. But the touch of his great warm hand lingered.

That was the last time I saw Gary Cooper.

A few months later, Roald and I were with friends at a club in Manhattan. The room was absolutely jammed with people. As I looked around I suddenly saw Maria Cooper, now a young lady, sitting at a table near the wall. She was glowering at me. I don't know how one look could cut through that sea of humanity. I turned away, pretending not to see her, and closed my eyes, remembering a little girl on a road in Aspen. After all these years, the wound had not healed. Would I ever be reminded of Gary and not feel bittersweet pain?

CHAPTER THIRTY-FIVE

t was April in 1959 when I heard from Arthur Penn, the director. He was casting William Gibson's *The Miracle Worker*, about the young Helen Keller. Everyone knew it was bound to be one of the biggest hits of the season and the vehicle of a lifetime for the actress who played Annie Sullivan, Helen's teacher.

The only problem was, Arthur was not offering me that part. He thought I would be wonderful as Helen's mother. It was not a starring role, but I hadn't done a play in the United States in four years or a film in three. I was in no position to command the star spot and I knew it. I could fantasize all I wanted, but if I was to keep working I would have to go with what was offered.

The star of *Miracle Worker* was Anne Bancroft. Like me, Anne had left Hollywood and returned to New York to make a new start. I first saw her at The Studio and admired her as an actress. Later I got to know her socially at the Strasberg parties. She was great fun and I liked her very much. Our paths were destined to cross many times.

We were in rehearsal only a few days when Anne and Arthur invited me for a drink. Arthur asked me quite candidly if I resented not playing the star role. I was equally candid. I admitted that I did, indeed, find it tough to step down, but I was trying my damnedest to do it graciously. They breathed sighs of relief. Both of them thanked me for being honest and assured me they knew how difficult it was. I can truthfully say that the fact that I adored Anne and Arthur helped. I felt better than I had in days for having gotten it out. It was one of the happiest companies I ever worked with. It also afforded me a reunion with Phyllis Adams, of my pavement-pounding days. Phyllis was now married to George Jenkins, our set designer.

Near the end of rehearsals I saw Fred Coe, our producer, in the auditorium with a man and a woman. I couldn't see their faces from the stage, but the man kept waving at me. Finally I walked down the aisle to see who he was.

"Do you recognize me?" he asked with a tinge of wickedness. "We met in Chicago."

I searched the familiar face for a name.

"I'm the fellow you told not to go into show business."

"Oh yes," I said, nodding. "Michael . . ."

Fred helped me out. "Nichols."

The woman with him, of course, was Elaine May.

I had gone six weeks without my family and we were just beginning out-of-town previews in Boston when Roald arrived with the girls. I could not wait to see my babies, and as they got off the elevator, I bellowed my welcome. Olivia looked at me with fright and Tessa let out a terrified wail. They obviously had no idea they were coming to see me and, in fact, did not seem to know why I had been absent from their lives for so long. I was annoyed with Roald for this oversight, but later, when all was well and we laughed it off, I scolded myself for making too much of it.

Eventually Roald came to the show. Following the performance, Arthur appeared at my dressing room. He was shaking with anger. "He's quite a fellow, that husband of yours. He doesn't think we have much of a play. Of course, he gave us his recommendations. We'd appreciate it if you'd see that he doesn't come again."

I was humiliated. And so angry that when Roald came

backstage, I seethed. "This has nothing to do with you. Will you keep your fucking nose out of my business and let me make my own enemies!" We did not speak again about the progress of the play.

The Miracle Worker opened on October 19, 1959. Our reviews were as great as everyone hoped. Especially for Anne and little Patty Duke, who played Helen.

I got pregnant on opening night. Obviously Roald did not hold grudges.

Patty was older than the six-and-a-half-year-old Helen she portrayed on stage. I used to take her home with me and she was the perfect guest, completely charming and gracious. She loved to read stories to the girls, who adored her. Her visits spurred Olivia's pestering to come and see Mummy act for the first time. I arranged for Sonia to take her to a matinee but asked that she be kept in the lobby during my first scene, fearing my frantic screams for my stage child might set up a howl from my own. After the performance, she looked at me very seriously and said, "I loved you, Mummy. You were jolly good." At that moment I didn't mind that Anne had gotten all the reviews. I had just gotten the most important notice of my life.

CHAPTER THIRTY-SIX

By March I was too pregnant to continue in the play. God knows when I'd have had to quit had I played Anne's role. Her nightly battles onstage with Patty, although carefully choreographed, were so rough that they both wore padding under their costumes.

My acting was limited now to morning sessions at The Studio. I remember I did a scene from *Romeo and Juliet*. I had always wanted to do Juliet and had been disappointed that it was not the Shakespearean play chosen to follow *Twelfth Night* at Northwestern. I would finally do the balcony scene many years later on a cruise for the Theatre Guild and be told it was the most romantic Juliet in memory. I would be fifty-eight years old at the time.

I did a scene with a new young actor who had just made his Broadway debut. George Peppard was handsome and sexy—my happily pregnant state made me particularly sensitive to his boyish charm and energy—and I was convinced he had a real future.

We were all enjoying our yearly winters in America and summers in England, but no one looked forward more to our return to Little Whitefield than I. For the first time one of my babies would finally experience Grandfather Harald's "glorious walks." Roald now had over two hundred rosebushes on our land and we would stroll among them, letting our unborn absorb the almost poetic loveliness.

Theo Matthew Roald was born on July 30, 1960, seven pounds, three ounces, with artistic hands and dark chocolates for eyes and the longest eyelashes I had ever seen on a baby. "I was quite conscious through the whole thing," I wrote Sonia, "and knew when the head emerged, the shoulders and then, my dear, the balls!"

Ivar Bryce was Theo's godfather and, by the day of the christening, had already enrolled his godson at Eton. One of the godmothers was our new nanny, Susan Denson. She had been a teacher and wasn't particularly experienced in nannying, but she was young and enthusiastic, if a little cocky, and Roald and I liked her.

On the heels of Theo's birth, I received my first Hollywood movie offer in years. I had really come to believe I would never work in films again. Dick Shepherd's wife, Judy, suggested me for the role of the other woman in Dick's new movie, *Breakfast at Tiffany's*. My character was a society matron known only as 2-E, the number of the apartment she maintains for the struggling young writer she's keeping. The writer would be none other than George Peppard, who had started his conquest of Hollywood. The role was mine on one small condition. I would have to dye my hair red so I would not distract from the dark-tressed Audrey Hepburn, who was playing the lead. The whole family thought it would be jolly good fun to have a flaming red, carrot-topped mummy. Of course, I agreed.

2-E just about squeezed through as a decent part. The director, Blake Edwards, was beautiful to work with, as was Audrey, who was the queen of Hollywood in 1960. Only gorgeous George seemed to be champing slightly at the bit. His character was written with a battered vulnerability that was totally appealing, but it did not correspond to George's image of a leading man. He seemed to want to be an old-time movie hunk. Gone were the humble days of truth at The Actors Studio. He and Blake locked horns through most of the filming, almost coming to blows at one point. In the end George played the role as he wanted, and I always felt that had Blake stood his ground, the film would have been stronger. And so would George Peppard.

I had only one scene with Audrey, but she was quite friendly and even invited me to her house for supper. She was then married to Mel Ferrer. I remember our supper was on a work night. Mel was very strict with her during production, so the evening was one drink, a light meal and good night. I don't think the sun had even set by the time I got home. But I sure knew how she kept her looks and figure.

During the production in Hollywood, I got to be good friends with my benefactress, Judy Shepherd, and spent a lot of days off sitting around her pool. The Shepherds often invited me for meals and it was at their home that I was introduced to a lovely man named Charles Carton. "*Doctor* Charles Carton," Judy said. "He's a genius."

"I am very glad to know you then," I smiled. "What is it you fix?"

"Heads," he answered. "I'm a neurosurgeon."

"Well," I laughed, "I hope you never have to operate on me."

CHAPTER
THIRTY-SEVEN

finished my three-week stint in *Breakfast at Tiffany's* just as Theo passed his fourth month. Olivia and Tessa were enrolled in a nursery school up on Ninetieth Street at Fifth Avenue, about a ten-block walk from us. In her first year Olivia had an awful time adjusting and I would hear her howling each time I left her for the day. Tessa was picked up at lunchtime, but she would have happily stayed through the whole day.

It was a crisp December morning. The fifth. The daily cleaning woman was busy with her chores when I left with Susan to pick up Tessa. I had quite a lot of shopping to do, so Susan, walking Theo in his pram, went on ahead to collect Tessa. I was in the A&P on Madison when I heard the shrill blast of a siren. At that moment a police car whizzed by and I remember sighing, "Thank God," without knowing why. I must have sensed they were rescuing someone. I left the grocery store and started to walk toward the corner.

"Mrs. Dahl!" Someone was shouting my name. *"Mrs. Dahl!"* Our cleaning woman was waving at me frantically. "Mrs. Dahl," she cried as she ran to me, "I'm so sorry to tell you your baby was hit by a taxicab. The police took him to Lenox Hill Hospital."

The brown bag slipped from my hands and groceries spilled out all over the street. I heard the sickening sound of glass shattering on the sidewalk.

I ran all the way to our building and rushed up to the Odets's apartment, where Roald was working. I rang the bell so relentlessly that it pulled Valerie out of her bath and she answered the door dripping wet. "I need Roald!" I said, and without stopping ran down the hall to his workroom. "Our son!" I cried as I pushed the door open. "Our son! The police have taken him to the hospital. He was hit by a taxi!"

Roald looked at me incredulously. He put down his pencils and moved with calculated deliberation. "What about Tessa?" he asked.

"Tessa and Susan are at the hospital, too, but they're all right. Oh my God! Olivia! I'd better ask Sonia to go for her!"

It took only minutes to reach Lenox Hill Hospital. Our baby was still in the emergency room. Someone told us where Tessa and Susan were. When we walked in, Tessa was standing in the center of the room, crying. Susan was weeping too, almost uncontrollably. "Oh, Mrs. Dahl—I saw the light turn green! I saw it! I saw it!" she wailed over and over.

I took her by the shoulders and tried to calm her. "I'm not angry with you, Susan. We need to know what happened. Can you tell us?"

Susan was on her way back from the school with Tessa. She had seen the signal turn green on the corner of Eighty-second and Madison. As she pushed the pram out over the curb, an anxious taxi jumped the green light. It smashed into the pram, wrenching it out of Susan's hands. The carriage was hurled forty feet across the street with Theo still inside. It slammed into the side of a bus, pinning our baby's head between pincers of metal as the carriage folded in on him.

The doctor came in and called us aside. His expression was grave. "We are doing everything we can," he said. Then he added, "He is going to die."

We sent Tessa and Susan home and followed the doctor to the intensive care unit. I can remember the sound of my heels on the hard floor, an odd clicking noise that echoed down the hollow passageway. We trailed the white-robed entourage behind the doctor, passing through heavy doors into a room filled with massive equipment, which seemed to me a horror chamber of tubes and dials and monitors. My God, what was my baby doing here? The doctor motioned us to his side. I looked down into the hospital crib at Theo. He was unconscious and his tiny head was swathed in bandages. I did not have to see through the layers of white. I knew the head was shattered. My precious doll was shattered.

The hours that followed were simply hell.

Roald notified everyone, including Mother, who would come as soon as we needed her. Mormor and Roald's sisters could not possibly come from England, but begged to be notified at every turn. Sonia and Geoff took the children and Valerie spent the night in our apartment taking phone calls.

Our own pediatrician, Milton Singer, was called in and, after further X rays, gave us the only hope we had that whole day. He said that Theo's condition was critical. But he did not say Theo would die.

After that there was nothing to do but wait.

I don't know how the hours passed. At some point I was sitting outside Theo's room, working on a needle-point cushion. It was a rose. A great rose. I kept thinking of those precious hours I had spent walking in the quiet rose garden back in England with our son in my womb. Why must this flower be crushed before it blooms? Why such a big thorn for such a tiny baby? What God does this?

In and out I mechanically passed the needle through the tapestry. If Susan had been walking our Theo through the rose garden and not on a New York street . . . if she had waited just one moment. I had not let my anger show while I was talking to Susan, but I felt a sickening clutch of hate block my throat. How could she have been so stupid? What a stupid, stupid girl. I wanted to kill her. "Ouch!" I cried. The needle's point had jabbed my finger. My work was stained with blood.

I looked up as Roald came from Theo's room. He was so angry. "I think the nurse in there is batty. The first thing she did was show me a newspaper clipping about the accident and say how thrilled she was to be on the case. I saw her give Theo a dose of an anticonvulsant. She was giving him a tremendous amount and when I questioned her about it she said it was quite all right . . ."

But before he could finish, I saw the doctor rush into Theo's room. That nurse had, in fact, hideously overdosed the baby. She had given him enough to kill him within minutes. The doctor called for a stomach pump. The thought of that tiny thing in such critical condition having his stomach pumped was too much for me to bear.

We kept a vigil at Lenox Hill for the next three days. By chance I overheard a nurse mention that my dear Dashiell Hammett was in that same hospital. I knew he had been ill, but I had not realized how seriously. Cancer on his lung was now taking its final toll. Each time I felt I could steal a few moments from my son I would slip off to Dashiell's room. I would sit and we'd smile gently at each other. His silence this time was not by choice. Both Dash and his grieving Lillian had room in their hearts for my sorrow and felt deeply for little Theo.

The hospital's neurosurgeon notified us that he simply could not have *all* those other doctors in, meaning, of course, our pediatrician. By this time, Roald and I were frantic. Ed Goodman's friend Dr. William Watson arranged for us to move Theo immediately to Ed's hospital, where he might at least have a chance. We didn't even wait for approval from Lenox Hill. We wrapped our baby in blankets and carried him out through an army of protesting nurses.

Outside, it was snowing like mad. Suddenly out of nowhere, my beloved Harvey Orkin materialized. We piled into his borrowed car. Harvey maneuvered through the blizzard to Columbia Presbyterian Hospital with divine guidance. For all Roald's past dislike of Harvey, he was sincerely grateful and applauded him over the years for his performance that night. "I wasn't keen on him and he wasn't fond of me either," Roald would say, "but he was the sort of friend who would drive through a storm to help. There was no long line of cars at the curbstone, just Harvey's.''

Theo remained at the hospital for ten days, and then we were able to take him home. I was confined to bed, terribly ill with the flu, and could not go near him for fear of giving it to him. Roald kept saying all through that first day that he did not like the way Theo looked. His eyes were groggy and unfocused. Roald called Dr. Singer and they rushed him back to the hospital, where they discovered he was blind.

For a week they stuck needles into his head to drain off fluid that was collecting there. And then they had to operate anyway for a subdural hematoma, which they explained was a swelling caused by bleeding into the brain. They had to open the whole left side of his little skull to remove blood clots that had collected in spite of the needles. After three weeks in the hospital, Theo looked worse than he had after the accident. It was clear that he was in for a long siege.

Theo's head had indeed been shattered. Because of the multiple injuries to the brain, he had developed hydrocephalus. Theo's surgeon, Joseph Ransahoff, explained what this meant. It seems that cerebrospinal fluid accumulates around the brain, causing an enlargement of the head and compression of the brain. If the fluid can't escape, blindness, retardation and death will result. The treatment for this illness consists of inserting a tube, or shunt, that runs from one ventricle of the brain down into some region of the body where the excess fluid can be absorbed, like the heart. It is a brutal kind of therapy, but there was no choice. They put in the tube and we waited.

The Austrians insisted on taking care of Olivia and Tessa because both Roald and I were keeping a steady vigil at the hospital. From the moment we realized that the first doctor's shattering conclusion was not true, we worked in a real complement. We ate, drank and slept in sync to be sure one of us was always near Theo. We went nowhere we couldn't be reached in an instant. It was, paradoxically, one of the most married times in our life together.

We decided to keep Susan in our employ. Roald felt it would be cruel to fire her in the midst of everything, and, though I had mixed feelings, I agreed. I was still not entirely convinced that she was not to blame for the accident, but for the moment it was easier to blame the obscure cabby. I couldn't help feeling, unreasonably perhaps, that whenever people talked to her about the accident, she seemed to like being the center of attention.

We waited and we watched. The shunt, for its gift of saving Theo's life, had a terribly demanding life of its own. At least three times a day, for as long as Theo would have it in his body, the valve had to be manipulated by hand, pressed in and out twenty times to be sure it was open and the fluid flowing. He needed continual supervision. I began a new relationship with my son when he came home.

On the tenth day the same agonizing symptoms appeared and he was once again blind. But now he was also running a fever. It was snowing—why was it always snowing?—when we rushed him back to the emergency room. The shunt had clogged again and he had to undergo more surgery to reposition it. Dr. Ransahoff said this time they were going through the fontanel right across the cortex of the brain. He assured us that they would stay out of the motor areas and work only in an inactive part. I could not understand the technical jargon about what was happening to my baby, but I knew very well there could be just so many places to put that damn thing down into him.

They went down through the right jugular vein and then the left one. They went through the pleura, which is the membrane covering the lungs. Each time, the baby's reaction was more frightening. He would run a fever, convulse, his head would swell. And each time we had to be prepared for it to happen again because little bits of brain tissue constantly got into the tube. Roald got angrier and angrier. "With everything science has come up with," he would rail, "why can't they produce one little clog-proof tube?" Every time we had to take him back for surgery, Theo would look up at us with those huge, desolate, bewildered eyes that asked, Why are you doing this to me again?

I don't know what I would have done had I known we would go through eight such operations in the next thirty months.

CHAPTER THIRTY-EIGHT

The people in our building were wonderful to us. From the very moment Valerie answered that door, she was on call for anything. She stayed at our apartment and manned the phones. The Hafers and the Wilsons cooked dinners for us. The Kadinsky sisters started Olivia on piano lessons. Sonia, bless her, took care of both girls a good part of every day. Tessa had a particularly special place in her heart.

On top of everything, I was worried about the blow this whole incident might deal to the psyches of my girls. But children have a way of integrating shocks and a resilience that adults have left behind them.

January 20 was my thirty-fifth birthday. All the small fry in the building got together to put on a play as a surprise for me. There was no script and I doubt there had been much rehearsal. They were all dressed up in costumes they had thrown together out of old potty paper tubes and beer cans from the alley. The play was a great, happy frolic inspired by their naive impressions of the funeral parlor across the street. The children saw the profusion of flowers constantly being delivered and the elegantly dressed people who attended the services and thought the greatest of parties must go on inside Campbell's.

I held up pretty well under the strain of those first weeks. I did not cry a lot. I functioned. But I always had to talk things out in order to keep going, and I certainly couldn't talk with Roald. He was doing everything he could just to keep moving and he did not need an extra burden from me. Roald and I rarely discussed our individual needs anyway. Dr. Watson, the man who had helped us when Theo was hit, offered to help again. He was a psychiatrist who specialized in crisis intervention. I met with him several times and he helped me a great deal. I never received a bill.

I was anxious for work because our insurance did not cover all of Theo's medical care. But the money was only one consideration. Work always helped me to keep my focus. I got one TV job on "The Play of the Week" in New York, and another out on the Coast, where I was able to tell cherished friends face to face how much I valued their concern.

Roald also got a regular job. He was hired as the host of a new TV show called "Way Out," a very well received dramatic series that specialized in the eerie, of course. He was kind of the New York answer to Alfred Hitchcock. He wrote the opening play, and our Millie Dunnock was gorgeous as a dominated wife whose deceased scientist husband has left his brain preserved, still active, still watching her every move through an attached eye. I can still see Millie taking her cool revenge by blowing forbidden cigarette smoke right into his single surprised eyeball. Roald adored being an "actor" and it helped pay the bills.

Out in California, I confided to Judy Shepherd that I just couldn't seem to get both oars in the water. I was aware that I was still struggling deeply with my resentment toward Susan. I could not stop feeling that she was responsible. Judy steered me to Dr. Arthur Clinco, a psychiatrist in Beverly Hills. He was a godsend. After my talks with him, I honestly thought I had stopped blaming Susan for Theo's accident.

Jean Valentino and Chloe Carter felt Gary should hear from me.

"I see him every week at St. Charles," Chloe told me. "Did you know he's Catholic now? If you'd like, I'll take him a message." I did want to tell him about Theo myself, so I wrote him a note that Chloe discreetly passed to him. She said that as Gary was leaving mass, he fell. He got up quickly, but she sensed that something was very wrong.

I did not hear from him.

While I was away, Roald had been busy researching the shunt problem. I should have known that his exasperation with its performance would not be the end of it. He searched out institutions and groups that helped hydrocephalic children, but found no leads to a clog-proof tube. He did learn that thousands of other children suffered as our little boy did and, even more devastating, that doctors gave no hope that any of them would ever be able to live without this tube.

By Easter Sunday, Theo had survived five incredible weeks without complications. After all the grueling time he had endured, it was a miracle. I bent down and stroked him under the chin and sang him a little ditty from my childhood, "Me and my buddy gonna pick a bale of cotton." He actually smiled back at me and his beautiful brown eyes twinkled. Though one eye was not as straight and direct as it once had been, my baby was alive and we were moving on.

The shocking headline of the evening paper read: GARY COOPER DEAD FROM CANCER. May 13, 1961. I remember thinking it was just a week after his birthday. There was a Catholic church very near and I stopped in and said a short prayer.

I felt a strange, remote sense of relief. A tempting voice whispered to me, "You will never again have to look twice when you see a tall, lanky man with a certain stance. You will never again step a little closer to see his face. You will know he can never again be there. Now you can rest."

How wrong the voice. How incredibly wrong.

CHAPTER THIRTY-NINE

Since Theo's accident, Roald had become more and more convinced that England would be a much safer place to raise a family than the streets of New York. He was sure that had we been living in England, our son would have been spared.

He didn't mean we should just extend our time beyond our usual summers, but that we should move there permanently. We discussed the possible advantages in terms of the life and education we wanted for our children, agreeing that English schools probably would be better, and life in England, with its subsidized medical care, would be cheaper.

Personally, I wasn't entranced by the thought of moving away from New York and all our friends. But professionally, it would be only a minor handicap. I was used to traveling for my work, and England, after all, was not the end of the world. There was the apartment, but it could always be sublet and Sonia and Geoff would surely keep an eye on it for us.

And, since I was certain that Roald had already made up his mind, I agreed we should make the move.

Before we left, I got a wonderful role on "The Play of the Week," in an adaptation of Strindberg's *The Stronger*. It was a two-character play and I didn't say a single word through the whole thing. My character only reacts to the constant stream of dialogue of the other woman, played by Nancy Wickwire, who comes to realize that I am having an affair with her husband. Delicious! I've always wanted a copy of that one. But it was on kinescope and I understand it was destroyed.

Mother came to see us before we left and she was terribly moved by the plight of her grandson. It was a good visit. She and Roald even made an effort to get on.

Some simple goodbyes to friends, and we were back in Great Missenden before summer. Mormor was devastated to see what had happened to her grandson, and as she cradled him in her arms, she said over and over that he was home safe, and for good.

Almost at every turn we encountered simple and heartfelt concern for our baby. I was very touched one afternoon to receive a visit from the vicar of one of the Great Missenden churches, who came to offer his consolation. But the dear man took one look at Theo and almost gagged. I thought he took the prize for gauche behavior. Every time I saw him after that, I looked the other way.

Life in Great Missenden was very much the same routine, but there was a difference now that the family was going to take root. We talked about returning to America —the girls especially were missing their friends—but deep down I wondered if it would ever happen.

I had little time for speculation or regret. My days were filled with constant caring for Theo. He had further operations and treatment at Great Ormond Street Children's Hospital in London, and when he was home, the tube still had to be monitored three times a day.

I watched him for any sign that would tell us what permanent damage had actually been done. There had been no predictions from any of the doctors. Only life, it seemed, would disclose how much our son would be able to accomplish. There were still times when he would wake screaming and vomiting in the middle of the night, times when he couldn't keep a bite of food down for days, but generally he was doing pretty well.

At one year old he weighed almost two stone, about twenty-four pounds. He was gay and loving and very lively. He couldn't support his own weight, but he could use his stomach muscles to get into a sitting position, where he would pivot on his bottom. But he covered no ground. We got him a little walking chair, which he maneuvered very well, and a jumping seat that hung on a spring from the ceiling. The only trouble was, he got so used to it that whenever we would hold him he immediately began jumping. He had learned to take off his shoes and socks and kick off his pants. He understood a great many words but said only a few, like "mama" and "papa" and "bye-bye," and nothing else that didn't sound Chinese. I continually measured his small skull, which didn't seem to be growing large enough. I would write Sonia, giving her his latest measurements, and ask her to measure Sarah, her youngest, for comparison.

Not too long after our return, Olivia came down with the flu. That poor child was so sick. I remember thinking that when that one got ill, it was always on a grand scale and always to the bitter end. She had adjusted to the move better than Tessa and seemed very content with her English school, especially with her teacher. Her love for animals absolutely engulfed her now. She seemed to spend more and more time in her birdhouse.

How she adored her father. She would trail after him everywhere, in the garden when he was pruning the roses, in the workshop while he refinished his frames. She had begun writing little stories. I remember one she brought home that began, "Once upon an African day." Isn't that good? Of course Roald was pleased no end. It was evident that Olivia was becoming so like him, not only in his artistic sensitivity but in the temperament department as well. Like her father, she could be very stubborn. When their wills clashed, Roald would give his adored child the spanking of her life. Spankings in our home would diminish as our family grew. Tessa got fewer than Olivia, and by the time we had five, the last one got none.

Tessa started out missing Susie Austrian so much that she took it out on us by refusing to go to school and wetting her bed. Luckily her defiance did not last long. She was quite thin and becoming a rather chic five-year-old, wearing knitted skirts and tops, so very British. She would tell everyone, "I'm half American, half Norwegian, and *all* English."

Roald kept busy, working toward an October publishing date for his new nipper's book. He installed a wire to his light in the hut and hooked it up to a button just outside our back door, which I would use to call him to the house. We set up a signal. One flash meant he had a phone call or a visitor, or that I wanted to speak to him. Two flashes meant he was needed right away. I was to use that signal only in an emergency.

We still never knew when or if that damn tube of Theo's was going to clog and this continued to prey on Roald's mind. "The problem is only a matter of precision hydraulics on the smallest workable scale," he would say, convinced that a clog-proof tube could be designed. He remembered a friend named Stanley Wade, who used to fly model airplanes with him near Amersham. Roald would fly graceful gliders, while Stanley developed tiny hand-built, engine-operated planes. Stanley had gone into the business of manufacturing hydraulic pumps and Roald would pass his factory while driving the girls to school each morning. He was certain he and Stanley could figure out a tube that would not clog.

And indeed they did, after months and months of work and the eventual help of Kenneth Till, a neurosurgeon at Great Ormond Street Children's Hospital. The gadget was a flexible tube about the size of a drinking straw with all kinds of screens and valves in it. It was thirteen pieces and only an inch and a half long. It was called the DWT Valve—for Dahl-Wade-Till—and by the end of 1962 it would be in the heads of eight children and working perfectly.

My love for my husband grew as I observed this practical expression of his love for our son. We were, no doubt about it, growing closer. It wasn't a spoken thing. It was a matter of knowing we could count on each other.

As for me, I seemed to be in early retirement. I had decided that I simply would not be away from Theo for any extended period of time. Susan was still with us, but

I did not want to leave her in complete charge. That unresolved worry had come back and I couldn't shake it this time. Actually, she was being courted by two young men, and I hoped she would marry one of them and move on. There were offers for television shows that would take me away for only a few weeks, but since I had gotten a reputation for doing good television, I was picky and turned them down.

But I wasn't missing show business a lot. I didn't have time. I was too busy being mother, mistress and manager at Little Whitefield.

One morning my daughters were watching as I changed Theo's diapers. Suddenly, the baby's naked penis became a fountain. "Oh, Mummy," cried Tessa, "why can he do that and I can't?"

I could see that it was time for a few of the facts. So I sat them down and explained that Theo was different because when he grew up he would have to make a seed to plant in a mother's body so that another new baby could come. "This is how a Mummy and a Daddy express *gr-r-eat* love," I concluded.

Tessa screamed with laughter. She thought it was a hysterically funny notion. Olivia, however, was very serious and became quietly thoughtful. The next day she asked, "Is that true, about what you said happens?" I told her it was. "Thank you," she said. And that was that.

The house itself took a lot of attention. We were adding central heating to the place after years of using those darling little coke stoves. Shopping would take hours. With no malls or supermarkets to ease the chore, I had to prowl dozens of shops clustered on High Street—the greengrocer, the dairy, the butcher, the chemist. Dear Charles would have smiled approvingly at my domestic expertise—and laughed at my early rising. Indeed, I was getting up early, many mornings in time to watch the great sun rise over the hills. I loved those moments.

I was sinking into the village life of Great Missenden, not really socializing yet except with a few like the Dulantys and the Kirwans, but meeting the people—Claud

Taylor and his wife, Grace, and Frankie Conquy, who came into my life much the way Sonia Austrian had— through our children. Her daughters, Sarah and Amanda, were my girls' closest friends.

Claud Taylor was the town butcher and a devil after my own heart. Claud owned cows that grazed in our orchard. One of them came in heat, and he was damned if he would pay a stud fee to our neighbor, who owned the only bull in town. One night Claud talked Roald and me into helping him get this cow up the lane and through the fence without the neighbor's knowledge. I remember how silly we felt as we watched the coupling and how frightened I was that the bull's passionate bellowing would awaken our neighbor. It was over in a flash, however. I finally knew the meaning of "Wham bam, thank you ma'am."

I finally got an offer to do a good role in a good television play in New York. I was ready for a work break. I would be away from home only for three weeks, and back in time for Christmas. The show was *That's Where the Town's Going!* by Tad Mosel, which had a wonderful cast that included Jason Robards, Jr. and Kim Stanley. I hadn't talked to Kim since that day, sixteen years before, when she snubbed me because she thought I was hot for Bruce, whom she had eventually divorced. This time she couldn't have been nicer. We played sisters and began a mutual admiration society that has lasted to this day.

Another thing I did in New York was get a new agent. Harvey Orkin had joined the ranks of the ten-percenters and I was thrilled to have him represent me.

I arrived home, my suitcases loaded with gifts for Christmas, including glass animals for Olivia's menagerie. It was a happier holiday than the previous agonizing year, in spite of the fact that Olivia came down with the flu, which, of course, Theo got. But we shoved phenobarbital into them and got on with it.

My Christmas present came from the BBC—the lead in *The Days and Nights of Bee-Bee Fenstermaker,* a fantastic part. Bee-Bee was a gal from a rural town whose romantic dreams of love and success in the big city fail.

She was southern, sloppy and drank too much—what more could an actress want? This time I could commute from home, so I wouldn't be away from Theo, who was now walking! Granted, it was very much like Charlie Chaplin, but he was walking. I was pleased with Bee-Bee Fenstermaker—she got me a nomination for best performance.

As I look back on those months following Theo's accident, I realize that for all the agonies we felt, it was one of the most beautiful periods of my life. I will never understand people rejecting a wounded or disabled child. For us Theo was a centering force, not only for Roald and me but for our daughters as well. Having to give up their preferences because of his needs was a hard but valuable lesson that I would not fully recognize until I saw Tessa with her own children.

I looked at my husband, hair a little thinner now and his lean face showing the first wrinkles, and I was glad I had fought for this marriage. I had not become the greatest actress in the world, but I had not been deprived of a career of some stature. I had been blessed in two worlds; what woman could ask for more?

CHAPTER FORTY

Theo had been well for almost an entire glorious year. His balance was still a bit questionable—he staggered and fell down a lot—but he was exceptionally lively. His speech had improved—you could really call it talking. All in all, he was a cheerful and adorable child. But he had such a temper. He got so angry with Roald one day that he called him a "wasps' nest." Brilliant!

Else often drove with me to pick up the girls from school. On one afternoon, Olivia handed me a note that bore the elegant script of the headmistress at Godstowe. "This is to notify all parents that measles are in the school." A strange feeling crept over me as I crumpled the paper into my pocket. Well, I thought, we'll just play it safe and have all the children vaccinated.

Inoculation against German measles was commonplace in America, but we soon found that gamma globulin was rare in England, almost unobtainable. It was kept on hand mainly for pregnant women who had been exposed and not as a preventative for schoolchildren. I felt uneasy and called Roald's half-sister, Ellen, for help. She was married to Sir Ashley Miles, who was the head of the Lister Institute. Through Ashley I hoped we could get some vaccine for the children. I pleaded Theo's vulnerable medical history and our concern for Olivia, who always got wiped out when she was sick. Ashley was sympathetic, but felt he could not justify breaking the rules, even for us. "Let the girls get the measles. It will be good for them," he laughed, trying to reassure me that we were not in dangerous waters. "But of course we can get some vaccine for Theo." Theo got the precious serum, but Olivia and Tessa did not.

Sure enough, three days later Olivia had the measles. We brought her into our room to separate her from Tessa and tried to cheer her by saying she was our fantastically polka-dotted daughter. But right from the beginning, she had no energy. Roald tried to read to her and make up stories, which she usually loved, but she didn't respond at all. The only thing we could do was hope it would pass through the family in a normal manner.

It was the fifteenth of November, 1962, and Olivia had been sleeping for twenty-four hours straight. I called Dr. Brigstock, who came right away and said that everything was all right. "Sleeping sickness" was apparently a normal aftermath of measles. We were not to worry.

But the following day saw no improvement. She was still drowsy and very weak. On the seventeenth, Roald tried to get her to play a bit. I remember he'd gotten some brightly colored pipe cleaners and made little stick animals for her. But she just sat and stared. I pulled the sheet up to her chin and looked down into almost lifeless eyes. I was frightened. I called Dr. Brigstock, and again he said she was all right, that she just needed a little more time than most children to recover.

Else was coming by as often as possible to break the dreadful anxiety she knew I was feeling. As Olivia's godmother, she was as concerned as I.

It was twilight, that time just before you turn on the lamps, when Else made her daily visit.

"I want to show you some clothes I got the twins for Christmas," I told her, also wanting a quick moment to check on my patient. I quietly opened the door to our room and knew at once that something dreadful had happened. Olivia's body was still, her eyes open in a fixed, walleyed stare, her mouth gaping limply, oozing spit. "Oh my God!" I cried. "Oh my God!"

I fled downstairs and pushed frantically on the button to the hut.

Roald came at once. We dashed back upstairs with Else close on our heels. He took one look and called Brigstock. Else sat next to Olivia and turned her head to one side. "She must not be allowed to swallow her tongue." I ran to the bathroom for a washcloth. I couldn't find one. It was too dark. When I switched on the light I saw myself in the mirror.

From some unknown place, I knew. It was not a premonition. I knew my daughter was dying.

I remember that the doctor's face was ashen as he called for an ambulance. I tried to calm Tessa and Theo and told Susan to keep them in the nursery until we had gone.

The wailing siren seemed unnecessary. This was not New York. There was no stream of cars on Eighty-second Street, no traffic lights to run. The blare would not smother that silent message. My Olivia is dying.

They put Olivia into a private room. Nurses and orderlies slipped in and out and when I caught their looks, I could see the fear in their eyes. "She will be all right, Mrs. Dahl," they said. No, I thought, she will die.

I watched the quiet little face on the pillow. Olivia's eyes were closed and she looked as if she were asleep, but I knew that sterling little mind had been corroded by seizure. Even if she recovered, what would be left of it? *Let her go.* A mystical voice within me cried, *Let her go.*

We stayed for over five hours, but she did not regain consciousness. Roald called Dr. Philip Evans, a fine pediatrician who had treated Theo. He promised to come at once. I knew I had to go home to the other children. They would be terrified by now. Roald drove me home and headed right back to the hospital. We would again take shifts with a sick child.

Everyone in the house had finally bedded down. I looked in on Theo and then on Tessa, curled up in a ball under her covers, and at the empty bed next to hers. Then I went downstairs.

Frankie Conquy came and sat with me for a while. "She is dying," I kept saying to Frankie, "I know she is dying." My dear friend took me in her arms and tried to console me.

After Frankie left to care for her own Sarah, I just sat in the empty room. The phone's bell startled me.

"I must speak to Mr. Dahl," the voice said. "This is the doctor."

"He's not here. He's on his way to the hospital."

"This is Mrs. Dahl, isn't it?"

"Yes."

"Mrs. Dahl, Olivia is dead."

I couldn't speak.

"Did you hear me?" he demanded. "I said Olivia is dead."

"Thank you," I said, and hung up.

I walked about the house for God knows how long, then into Susan's room and shook her from her sleep. For all the times I had wished her out of the house, I was glad not to be in Little Whitefield alone that night.

"What is it?" she whispered.

"My Olivia has died."

"Oh, Mrs. Dahl, I'm so sorry."

I left her and went down to the sitting room. I sat there in the dark until I heard our car pull up. I heard the door slam and the scuffle of shoes on the drive. Roald came in and walked toward me. His face told me it was true. He put his arms around me and I could feel heavy sobs spill onto my shoulder. I wept back into his embrace.

Roald was just destroyed. I knew he needed to be alone and I persuaded him to go to bed. Then I walked from room to room and turned out lights and checked doors.

The night was so still as I looked out the window toward Olivia's birdhouse. There was no movement. All was quiet. The tiny birds would all be sound asleep with their heads tucked under their wings. I prayed, "What do you see in this night, my little Olivia? How can I let you go?"

The sun appeared. Slowly the curve grew and pale morning light invaded the room until it became a magnificent ball of fire. "Jesus!" I cried out loud. "How dare you rise when my beautiful, beautiful daughter is dead. *How dare you*!" I wept and wept. "Oh, my Olivia, what will I ever do without you?"

When Dr. Evans arrived, he was so sad. He had driven for hours but had gotten to the hospital too late. I knew there was nothing he could have done. I cooked breakfast for him, and he told Roald and me that Olivia had died from a rare complication of the disease called measles encephalitis. Large doses of gamma globulin, had it been available, could well have saved her life. The landslide of anger and frustration that would all but bury Roald and me in the months to come began in those first hours.

I kept cooking, first for them, then for the family. All morning I just kept cooking and cooking.

Roald collapsed in bed that day. I knew he wanted to die. I kept going like a madwoman. I planned the rest of the day's meals, then called my mother. She said she'd come right away, but I assured her we would be all right. She was working now, as a housemother for a fraternity. Later she told me that all the boys had knelt down to pray when she told them about Olivia. I thought that was an amazing thing for them to do. I made the necessary calls to friends in New York and California and London. I found a chest that Roald had brought from Africa and started to put Olivia's things away, but then Roald's sisters were there and adamant that they should take care of all. They would plan the funeral—everything. It was a family crisis and I was learning what this meant to the Dahls.

When Tessa woke up, I sat with her on the bed. How do you tell a five-year-old that her sister has died, when just hours before you assured her that she was only asleep and would be able to play in a few days? I pulled her up onto my lap. "My darling Tessa, our Olivia is dead." She looked up at me with disbelief. "God decided to take her to heaven to live with Him," I told her, holding her close. She didn't say a word for several moments. Then she gazed around the room.

"Does that mean everything in here is mine?" she asked. She squirmed off my lap and ran over to the toy chest and opened it. I was utterly horrified. I watched her pull out things that belonged to her sister. My mind told me that she really didn't understand. What else could a five-year-old do? But as I left the room, I was in such pain that I could not speak.

There was no way anyone could really console me over my loss and any effort just left me more devastated. Except for Mormor. Mormor was a religious woman, but with overtones of spiritualism and folklore. She had a kind of crystal vision and very often amazed us by predicting some unexpected event in advance. Indeed, she had accurately predicted the family Roald and I would have, two girls, a boy, then two more girls, exactly like her own. She would later predict my own recovery the day after my stroke, citing a dream in which she had attended a service for me wearing *brown* shoes, so it could not have been a funeral.

Mormor had lost a baby daughter too, her firstborn, also seven years old. Mormor had no grand words for me but I knew the ache in her breast was like mine. "Don't try to understand now," she said simply. "You will get through this. I know." Perhaps this was the moment in life when I really met my mother-in-law.

Roald's three sisters took charge of the funeral arrangements. He was simply not able to cope with it and I was not to be burdened. They chose the casket, they chose the music, the flowers, and they, not I, saw that little body prepared and dressed. It would do me no good to be there, I was told. I must not see her dead, but remember her as a living child. A body in death changes. I thought of Daddy. I thought of my dear Dashiell. In life, even in the throes of his illness, Dash looked like a familiar friend. At his funeral, I thought I would see that old friend lying in his coffin, but he was a fearful stranger. Maybe they were right. Maybe I should not see Olivia.

The graveyard was in Little Missenden, an even quainter version of its big sister town. The church was Norman and a thousand years old. The funeral was very simple, just family and a few friends. Else composed a poem in remembrance of the day.

> The church bell tolls for Olivia
> As the slow snow falls from above,
> Enfolding the grave of Olivia
> With love.
> A blanket of snow for Olivia
> And garlands of flowers for her shroud,
> And those who have known Olivia
> Are proud.
> We will ever mourn for Olivia
> But anguish and tears will cease.
> For eternal youth is Olivia's
> And peace.

The small casket was unopened. I never saw my beloved child. The sisters assured me she looked lovely. As we walked away from the grave, I kept myself from turning back. What if I had followed what my heart told me to do? To run back and rip off the lid and hold that cold little body between my breasts and weep on that divine face until my pain was absorbed into the hardness of those cheeks. To tell her that I would bury her within me. That she would be born again. That was my right as a mother. They had taken it from me. But no, I could not blame anyone but myself. I had let it go.

I swallowed my rage and finally looked back over my shoulder. Men had begun working by the graveside. Olivia's coffin was being lowered into the great embrace of a new mother. Graceful flakes of snow were just beginning to fall. It would snow all night long.

CHAPTER
FORTY-ONE

Dear Dr. Clinco,
How good of you to telephone me and then to write as well. Know that we are, and will be, all right. We have to be.

Tessa's reaction was shock and total disbelief. Then it was as if the vultures had arrived as she realized her new position and gain. (This hurt me but I "understood.") But soon she realized her loss. For three nights, even with the aid of sleeping pills, she was awake and wildly restless. She is sleeping now, and her nervous system seems quieter. But she is a very sad little girl.

My husband, who truly wanted to die as well, is better every day and he will "work it out."

I should like to tell you a bit about how I have felt.

She was my firstborn. No child was ever more wanted, more adored. I had a very special delight in her, cuddly closeness with her, and understanding of her. My husband had developed a wonderful, beautiful relationship with her.

The horror was not to be able to do a thing. At five o'clock she was fine—measles, but fine, and asleep. At midnight she was dead. During those hours I saw my bright, beautiful child's mind unmistakably overcome and destroyed. I did not want life at all costs. My husband did.

When Theo was hurt, we discovered for the first time that we were vulnerable—that terrible things *could* happen to us. But then, we could put up a fight. And indeed we did.

Now we have seen that life/death is not in our control *at all*. We cannot protect our children. All three have been, in some way, damaged.

I have now returned to my natural, original mystical self. I absolutely believe in a soul. And I long to let her go, to free her—and *hope* she will be born again to me. But I am very earthbound—and it is hard.

My fear is—or fears are—many.

What does one do? How many body blows can one endure? Don't think I expect you or anyone to answer that. In fact, please don't think you must reply to this. I simply wanted to write it.

> Bless you.
> Patricia Neal Dahl

I was more brave than honest when I presented Roald's situation to my good Dr. Clinco in California. Roald all but lost his mind after Olivia died. I don't think anything in his life ever hit him so hard. He had always been the one to steer the family since 1920, when his eldest sister, Astri, died from appendicitis at age seven. Yes, just Olivia's age. He was haunted by the coincidence. His father had died only six weeks later. Everyone said Harald had perished from pneumonia, but they all knew it was from grief. He simply did not want to live after his little girl died. Roald wondered if there was a pattern and if he would soon follow Olivia. I would bring him tea and try to get him to talk about his pain. But that Nordic strain of deep restraint kept him from reaching out to a wife, even in the aftermath of death.

My mystical self was finding a sense of God in the deep purification I experienced through pain in the days after Olivia's death, and in having to remain strong. It was a time of grace, but that did not mean I was without suffering. I still felt bitter and cheated at not having seen Olivia

253

after she died, and there were agonizing moments when my conscience tortured me with thoughts that God was punishing me because I had taken the life of my first baby. Alone at night, when the family was in bed, I would cry my heart out. It was a luxury to cry then, because during the day I had to be strong. I cried because I wanted to be with Olivia again. I knew there must be someplace where I would see her. My head did not have to believe in heaven. My heart would accept no other choice.

I tried to share my new feelings with Roald but to no avail. He said he wanted to believe, but he had to be convinced. Our search took us to the Archbishop of Canterbury, who was once Roald's headmaster. The "boss" of the Church of England, as Roald used to call him, probably knew more about God than anyone else in the country. But when the great man said heaven was a place for human souls only, he lost Roald completely. Roald simply told him that if there were no animals in heaven, Olivia surely must have refused to go.

That was the end of religion as any possible consolation for Roald. He would accompany me to church, but took no active part except when he joined me in giving our statue of St. Catherine, in memory of Olivia.

The day after Christmas, Sonia brought Susie for a visit. I knew it would mean the world to Tessa to have her friend near, but I didn't realize how much it would also mean to me to be able to sit and talk—and cry—with Sonia.

I selected a headstone for Olivia's grave and the cutter began carving the inscription I had chosen: SHE STANDS BEFORE US AS A LIVING CHILD. Roald proposed building a rock garden with miniature plants at the grave site as a memorial and I agreed. Valerie Finnis was an expert gardener and recommended just the right plants, dwarf Japanese evergreens, minuscule hybrids and wild mountain flowers, many that Olivia herself knew by name. Roald drove to dozens of nurseries and quarries throughout the district in search of proper plants and rocks. Together we set the plants, nearly two hundred specimens, arranging them in natural groups. I helped him add a dozen or so small porcelain animals from Olivia's menagerie.

The job consumed Roald for more than a month, and when he finished, he had created a small mountain garden that one could look at for hours. Roald himself seemed better for the work. It was as if the pure physical effort brought with it a release. I hoped so.

We had been thinking about what to do with Olivia's money. We had started a fund for her at birth, as we did for each child, and didn't want to just absorb it back into the family account. We wanted to do something meaningful.

At this time, a very welcome Marjorie Clipstone came into my life. I had seen Marjorie in the village. She ran the Christmas charity shop. She wrote me a most beautiful letter and I knew I had to meet this lady. She was a widow, having lost her husband only two years before, and so was particularly sensitive to the unrelenting sting death inflicts. I told Marjorie about our dilemma over Olivia's money. She suggested starting an organization to help orphans. I thought it was a fine idea and invited her to supper to discuss it further.

When dinner was over and Roald had excused himself, Marjorie and I sat and talked. She said that she believed she and her husband would be together again someday. I confided that I also believed that I would see Olivia again, but *someday* was too far away. "What do I do *now*, Marjorie? I didn't know until she was gone the treasure I had."

"Stop it! Stop it!" Roald was standing in the doorway, his face wild with anger. The anguish within me now flooded my eyes. I ran up the stairs to our bedroom. I slammed the door and the dam burst. Roald followed me, his anger gone. "I'm so sorry, Pat," he said, "but I just cannot stand such trashy sentiment. My daughter is dead. There is nothing more to be said." I looked up at him but I was not moved. "Can you hear me?" he cried. "*My daughter is dead!*"

He turned and left the room and did not hear my reply: "She is *my* daughter, too."

I was afraid that as a family we were doomed if I did not keep us moving emotionally and financially. I had no idea how much money we actually had but there always seemed a need for more. And we had to have the stability that comes with knowing life goes on. I no longer had any great aspirations for my career, and I felt a terrible twist at the thought of leaving to go anywhere for work, but I knew it was necessary. I made up my mind to take any job that came along, provided it was only a few weeks' work at most.

CHAPTER
FORTY-TWO

The first offer I got was for a segment of a TV series, the bottom of the barrel, but the money was good.

Martin Ritt called a few days before I finished my work on the show. I had known Marty from the early days at The Studio. "I'd like to send you a script," he said. "I hope you won't think the part is too small." The thought of working in a film again fired my engines, and if Marty was involved, I was sure there was something good up his sleeve. The script was titled "Hud Bannon."

I flipped through looking for my scenes. Irving and Harriet Ravetch, the writers, described the character: "Alma Brown is a tall woman, shapely, comfortable and pretty. She has an indulgent knowledge of the world and it makes for a flat, humorous, candid manner." So far, so good.

Marty was right, it wasn't a large part, but it was the only woman in the picture, which was a plus. And although Alma was a brief role, it was strong. She was an earthy, shopworn gal who had been handled badly by life, which had made her wise and tough but not invulnerable.

Alma had no real highs, no dramatic monologues, and she played mostly in the background to the other characters. But I knew her in my bones. I had thought the days when I would be offered a part like Alma were over.

The story itself was arousing, a drama of moral combat

centering on a young boy who must choose between the way of life of his grandfather, an aging cattleman, and that of his uncle, a 1960s specimen of the I'm-going-to-get-mine breed.

The heartbreaking thing was that it would be at least a two-month commitment and there was no way I could leave Roald and the children for that length of time. Marty asked me if it would make any difference if I could go home in the middle of the shooting, between the Texas and Hollywood locations. It was too good to be true. I took the script back to England, and when Roald read it, he agreed that I had to do it. Roald had started work on a new children's story. I was so happy. It meant he was moving away from the tragedy. He was getting on with it.

The *Hud* company met at Paramount Studios for rehearsals before going to Texas. I had met our Hud before when we were studying at The Studio. And Paul Newman had brought his wife, Joanne Woodward, to the Paramount makeup department one morning to meet me during the filming of *Breakfast at Tiffany's*. The superb Melvyn Douglas was the grandfather and a very talented young actor, Brandon de Wilde, was the nephew. I could tell from the first reading that this was going to be special. Even the ad campaign would be revolutionary. "Paul Newman IS Hud" introduced a generation of "is" movies.

I just plain loved working with Marty. For the first time since working with Elia Kazan, I felt I could do anything a director asked. At the first rushes, I remember him grinning and saying, "The minute I saw you handling those pots and pans, I could tell you were a woman who knew your way around a kitchen." So I did.

The entire company got along extremely well. Not that there was much time for intimate bonding. It was a rare moment that found Paul and me sitting alone one Sunday by the pool at the Texas motel that housed the company. It was early in the location shooting. We had not yet played a major scene together. In fact, we may have been discussing the work to come. Suddenly, I found myself not talking about the picture at all. I was telling him about Olivia. I went on about her loveliness and talent and her fragility and how much I loved her. I pulled out Else's poem, which I always had with me. But it only served to reopen the wound I carried.

"My sisters-in-law took charge of everything. They did not let me do a thing. I didn't even see Olivia," I found myself admitting. "Do you think that's right?"

Paul didn't answer.

"I just saw that damned closed coffin. I should have taken a stand at the time, don't you think? I was her mother. I had a right to see her."

Paul finally looked at me. For a long moment, he just stared through me with those blue eyes. Then he got up and said quietly, "Tough," and walked away.

I couldn't believe it. I had shared the most intimate secret I carried, something that had cut deep, and had been met by almost brutal indifference. I vowed I would never talk to him like that again.

Whatever chemistry mixed between us that day, Paul and I worked together beautifully. On the set he was an ace, thoroughly professional and completely in character at all times. In fact, he and young Brandon would tear around the small Texas town at night, much the way their characters did. I began to realize that although I had poured out my heart to Paul Newman, it was Hud Bannon who had responded.

In the years that followed, I have known only kindness and consideration from Paul, and my heart went out to him at the time his own son died.

Halfway through *Hud* is an important scene between Paul and me. Alma is straining curds through cheesecloth at the sideboard when Hud comes up behind her and begins to fondle her shoulder and kiss her neck. Just as Paul moved in, a huge, furry green horsefly began to crawl up the porch screen. I couldn't take my eyes off it. "I've done time with one cold-blooded bastard," Alma says. Instinctively I grabbed a dishtowel. "I'm not looking for another." And zap! That bug went flying.

"Cut! Print!" called Marty. "Perfect. The fly was great!"

My favorite scene, the one moment I loved most about Alma, was when the boy Lon asks her what life is all about anyway. "Honey," she tells him, "you'll just have to ask someone else." That scene hit the cutting-room floor. Naturally.

Back at home in England, there were old problems to face. Theo was going through a terrible period when all his ghastly symptoms—not eating well, running a temperature, looking groggy—seemed to return. One afternoon he fell and became unconscious. Again we rushed him to the hospital, where he was tested over and over again. Kenneth Till finally suggested that perhaps the hydrocephalus had arrested and the shunt itself was causing the trouble. We agreed to try an experiment. Remove the shunt. We knew the risk. We had tried it twice before and both times the symptoms returned and they'd raced to put it in again. Kenneth thought that if Theo could get through thirty days without the shunt, he would be in the clear.

So our little boy had his eighth craniotomy. The shunt was removed and we watched and waited, every second of every day. One by one, the thirty days passed. And we knew his case had arrested and that he would live through this thing for sure.

SHE STANDS BEFORE US AS A LIVING CHILD. The stone marker for Olivia's grave was finished, but Roald could not bear to look at it and refused to have it installed. I was secretly sorry. There was truth in its message, which was consoling to me, but he was so adamant I didn't argue. It was banished to the back of the garage, face to the wall. I don't know what became of it. Instead we used the tiny metal marker that Olivia had used to identify plants in her own little garden.

In the spring, Godstowe would have its annual high jump contest. Olivia had been their 1962 champion. I found the cup I had been given the year before as Tennessee's "Woman of the Year" and had a jeweler erase my name and inscribe "The Olivia Cup" in its place. I gave it to the school as the prize for that year's winner. It is still handed down.

I never had to face the question of firing Susan. She had chosen one of her beaux, and it wasn't long before she left to get married. Another ad went into the paper and we chose a lovely twenty-one-year-old Scottish lass, Sheena Burt.

I wanted desperately to have another baby. I was thirty-seven, and that was late to have a child. But I was going to try, even if it meant another one of those horrible tube-blowing sessions.

In May 1963, *Hud* opened to sensational reviews. I was genuinely surprised by the attention I received. I knew I had turned in a good performance and secretly hoped that Alma would get me more work, but I was unprepared for accolades. Not that I thought they were wrong.

We had a special showing of *Hud* in Aylesbury, with the proceeds going to International Help for Children, the organization Marjorie helped us found with Olivia's money. I was thrilled to see a fat check go to an orphanage in Bari, Italy.

With *Hud,* offers did come—a firm one for a thriller called *Psyche 59,* and a not-so-firm one for *The Pumpkin Eater.* There was no doubt in my mind which I preferred. The latter was no pumpkin; it was a plum. But the producer wouldn't make the offer definite and the money for *Psyche 59* was right there, so I went with it, hoping that the *Pumpkin* people would wait for me. They didn't. They went with my old friend Anne Bancroft, and she was wonderful. My movie was not a particularly happy experience and it was a forgettable film. I should have taken my chances and waited.

But if I wasn't making film history, at least I was making medical history. I had my tubes blown again. Afterward it was discovered that I was already pregnant! The babe had survived this violent procedure, which was intended to offer an access to life, but which, in fact, had almost destroyed it. I wrote Sonia that, considering the circumstances, we thought the name Curetta or Curate most fitting. I was being cheeky, but I was not really laughing. It had been a close call.

I felt a change in all of us once we knew there was a new baby on the way. We never expected a new child would replace Olivia, but there was a healing promise anyway in this new life. We discovered among some old papers that in its original deed, Little Whitefield had been called Gipsy House. We decided to give the old name back to our home. A new name signaled a new beginning, and an end, we hoped, to the anguishing days that had torn us to shreds.

CHAPTER
FORTY-THREE

Toward the end of the year the rumbles started. I was named best actress by the New York Film Critics for *Hud*. Nothing could keep me from attending the awards. It was a whirlwind trip and I was home in little more than a day. There was a message from Otto Preminger waiting. He wanted me for *In Harm's Way*. It would certainly be a major film, with an all-star cast headed by John Wayne. And talk about perks. It would shoot on location in Hawaii! Unfortunately, with the baby coming, there was no way I could do it. I called Otto immediately and told him so. He said the nicest thing. He said, "I'll wait for you."

I also had an offer of a Broadway play that I had to turn down. It was such a good play, too—*The Subject Was Roses*—and I liked the character of the mother. I would go through a lot more living, and dying, before I would play Nettie Cleary.

Hard on the heels of the New York Film Critics, the National Board of Review named me best actress, and then the British Academy of Motion Pictures said I was the best foreign actress of 1963.

I was in the Caribbean with Roald when I got a call from my agent. It had taken him hours to track me down. "Patricia," he shouted, "you've just been nominated for the Academy Award! Best actress!" I couldn't believe it.

No part as small as mine had ever been nominated for best lead performance. Just coming out on top for a change felt damned good.

All in all, *Hud* raked in seven nominations, though not for best picture. I was so happy that Paul Newman, Melvyn Douglas, the Ravetches and our cinematographer, James Wong Howe, had also been nominated. The one nomination that pleased me the most, though, was Marty Ritt's.

The ceremonies in Hollywood, or, to be specific, Santa Monica, were scheduled for April 13, 1964, and there was no question of my attending. I would be way too big by then. This didn't concern me, because if the advance predictions held any water, the battle would be between two Hollywood favorites anyway, Natalie Wood and Shirley MacLaine. I thought Leslie Caron would win. Rachel Roberts and I had to be the dark horses. Roald, however, had no intention of giving up hope and insisted I select someone to collect the Oscar if I won. He thought that Annabella Power would be an excellent choice. Since we had met in my early days in Hollywood, she had become a good friend. She had also known Roald—quite well—before our marriage, which did not in the least put any strain on our friendship.

The thirteenth came, about eight hours earlier for us than for Los Angeles, which meant we'd be comfortably in bed when the Oscar ceremonies began. We would read all about it in the morning papers. But wouldn't it be great fun, I thought to myself as I tucked Theo into his bed. He had been to the eye doctor that afternoon and the doctor had told me Theo was the most intelligent child of his age he had ever met. I kissed my son goodnight. "You did so well today. We are all proud of you." The Dahls turned in early.

About five in the morning the telephone rang. It was Charlcey Adcock, my old school chum! "Patsy," she screamed, "you won! *You won!*"

"I won the Oscar!" I shouted in Roald's ear. "Isn't it *great*?"

When I finished talking with Charlcey, my agent rang. "Sorry," I kidded, "but you're not the first." Then the phone started to ring off the wall. I think I must have talked to everybody in the world that morning. I know I talked to everyone in Atlanta. The family all said that because Melvyn Douglas, Sidney Poitier and I had won, the South was laying claim to the Oscars.

We just forgot about any more sleep. Everyone was up now and cheering and hugging, none more energetically than Theo. In the midst of the celebrating, he asked, "What is an Oscar, Mummy?"

"It's a great golden boy," I answered, "who whispers in your ear what you've known all your life."

Somehow I managed to find the time that hectic day to cable Marty. The message was simple: IT WAS NOT TOO SMALL.

Arrangements were made by the studio for me to meet the press in London that same afternoon. As I rummaged through the closet for something to wear, my hand stopped at a familiar jacket. I took it out and slipped it on. The jacket was still beautiful and gracefully cowled my very pregnant form. It was the mink Gary had left on my doorstep twelve years before.

On the train to London I could hardly contain myself. Not only did my whole industry think I was good enough, but now, finally, a fabulous new career was just around the corner. And we'd make a fortune.

After the initial "How do you feel about winning the Oscar?" question, the tragic note that had set a new theme to my life during the past twenty-eight months dominated the interview. "How did you handle it?" "How did you keep going?" I answered as honestly as I could, feeling the frightening edge of a new public personality forming around the actress who had been honored for a professional performance, but was being asked to give witness to another kind of performance.

My last outing before the baby came was a quick trip to Marylebone Station to pick up a special-delivery pack age from Annabella. The stationmaster knew what was inside. "I'm from Buckinghamshire, too, ma'am," he grinned, as if the whole of the county had won. "We're all so proud of you. You're a lucky woman."

Yes, I thought, looking down at the great round curve of my stomach, I was a very lucky woman.

CHAPTER
FORTY-FOUR

Ophelia Magdalena Dahl was born on May 12, 1964, and we were thrilled with our beautiful, all-pink daughter. Especially Roald. I think he finally came out of his despair when she was born. Ophelia was a blessing on the Dahl household and we all felt it. Theo immediately nicknamed her Don-Mini.

Ophelia's godparents were the now very grown-up twins Anna and Louise, and Harvey Orkin and Colin Fox. I remember Colin telling our children the most fanciful bedtime stories, running all the familiar fairy tales together so you might have Goldilocks and the Beanstalk. The children loved them. And although Colin was invading his domain, Roald could not dismiss his flair.

Now I had two new offspring to show off, Ophelia and Oscar. There was something special—or at least unusual—about my Oscar. He rattled. I thought there must be a loose screw or something inside, but never bothered to check. I would tell visitors not to just hold him, but to shake him. It was always a great gag when Oscar would rattle like a baby's toy.

Our visitors were not all familiar friends. Some, attracted by our family's recent publicity, were people who sought advice about their own brain-damaged children. Most people wrote—and we did our best to answer every letter—but some called or simply dropped by the house. One afternoon a strange American couple appeared on our doorstep. They wanted to talk about Theo because they also had an ailing son at home. During our conversation, I played my rattling Oscar game. They were shaking away when I left them alone to get tea.

A day or so later, when we shook Oscar there was no sound. I turned him upside down and was appalled to find the green felt pad on the bottom had been poked out. Those bastards, I thought, they must have stuck their fingers through to get at whatever was making the rattle. I couldn't imagine anyone being so crude. What did they think it was, I angrily wondered, a diamond? Then I realized, for all I knew, it might have been. After that I put Oscar high up on the mantel, out of reach.

This will come as a surprise to some in Hollywood, but Otto Preminger may have been the most generous man I ever knew. Not only did he keep his promise to wait for me for *In Harm's Way,* but he also invited me to bring the entire family to Hawaii and picked up the tab. I arrived in Honolulu with Roald, Tessa, Theo, six-week-old Ophelia, and Sheena Burt and Nesta Powell, who had become family to us. Otto arranged for huge accommodations, complete with a great veranda overlooking the sea. He even provided playmates for our children. His wife, Hope, who did the costumes on his films, brought their twins to the location.

In Harm's Way was a personal drama of military men and their women set against the bombing of Pearl Harbor. It brought me back into a working relationship with John Wayne, whom I had not seen since *Operation Pacific.* Those days were not pleasant for either of us and we had both been through a lot since then. He was certainly a better man for it, much more relaxed and generous. This time we got along splendidly.

I had another reunion, a very warm one, with the film's other star, Kirk Douglas. Much had changed for him in the intervening years, too. Like me, he was now happily married and raising a family.

I loved my role of Maggie. It wasn't what you'd call a

great challenge. She was very much me, I thought, and I slipped into her character like an old bathrobe.

Roald and the kids thoroughly enjoyed Honolulu. Tessa and Theo took swimming lessons. I remember that on the first day, Theo's teacher started to toss him into the deep water, and he cried, "Don't throw me in. I am only a little boy!" But in he went and he learned to swim. Roald prowled greenhouses for orchids to introduce to the Gipsy House garden. He was also making new friends. Robert Altman and Jackie Cooper had come to Hawaii to seduce Roald into writing a screenplay. At the end of a week of carousing with them, he had agreed to write an original script entitled "O Death, Where Is Thy Sting-a-ling?"

I was finished in seventeen days. Never had I made so much money so easily. Roald expected to turn out his script quickly, so rather than return home right away, we stayed on for a bit. This gave me a chance to see Honolulu, too. I thought it was a bit honky-tonk, but you can't take away the water, and those rainbows, and that air.

I spent time strolling the beach with Ophelia in my arms, and I remember thinking her "glorious walks" had been at the time of my professional triumph. It had taken me a long time, much longer than I had expected when I made that first trip from Knoxville to Hollywood. But finally I was sure I would be able to write my own ticket as an actress. The plums would be mine now. How ironic the title of this movie seemed. *In Harm's Way.* I had been living—surely we all had—in harm's way. I looked at my daughter. She was the only one who had not been hurt. "Please, God," I prayed, "don't let anything happen to this one."

We were home for Christmas, and in the Dahl clan Christmas was truly a joyful family occasion. It was always at Else's house because Mormor lived next door and because they had the biggest tree. Presents were opened at Christmas tea. The final surprises were saved for the next morning, after Father Christmas came in the night and filled the stockings.

During *In Harm's Way,* I signed to do John Ford's new

film, tentatively titled "Chinese Finale." It was slated to start shooting right at the beginning of the new year—1965. Since it would be a ten- to twelve-week schedule, we again decided to bring the entire family—this time to Los Angeles. Being in California in winter would not be hard to take. We rented Marty Ritt's home in Brentwood while he and his wife, Adele, were in Europe. During our absence, Gipsy House would be redecorated. A British home magazine offered to do this for a layout on our country cottage. It would cost us nothing, so I leapt at it.

Altogether, seven of us moved into the Ritt house. It was not an ostentatious home at all, which pleased us very much. Roald immediately attended to some practicals. The house had a lot of flagstone, and in the center of the living room stood a rock pillar on a wood base—all sharp surfaces and corners that meant potential danger for Theo. Roald carefully padded everything that might cause a problem.

I went into the studio for my padding, too. I would be wearing pants throughout *Seven Women,* the John Ford film's new title. My part was that of a medical missionary in China who scandalizes her Christian sisters with her worldliness—a morality that later allows her to save them by sacrificing herself to the ravages of a Mongol barbarian. I think the story must have been better than it sounds now.

I was very happy to be in a film directed by the great John Ford and, in our very first meeting, felt I understood him perfectly. He was the boss and no one would cramp his act. I thought he was a darling. And again I was in first-rate company—Eddie Albert, Margaret Leighton and, the most wonderful gift of all, Millie Dunnock.

But there was no shooting schedule, no start date. Something to do with a strike, or impending strike, I forget which. Normally a production delay would not have distressed me, but I had reason to worry. I was almost three months pregnant.

I told Roald people would think I was crazy to have two babies in fifteen months. But time was running out and I wanted all the children I could have.

Two weeks later, on Valentine's Day, filming finally started and my high spirits returned. Our location was the MGM back lot, on sets that had been built years earlier for *The Good Earth*. If the ladies in the cast had any qualms about John Ford's reputation as a grouchy tyrant, he dispelled them the first day, when he arrived on the set accompanied by the music of an Italian accordion player. Apparently this musician was on every Ford film, heralding the great man's first entrance of the day with strains of "Bringing in the Sheaves." He also provided mood music for the players before every scene.

No one knew I was carrying a baby, so the first three days were strenuous. I spent the entire fourth day, February 17, riding a donkey!

I don't remember being tired in the least when Millie dropped me off at home after work. Ophelia was already asleep, but Tessa and Theo wouldn't rest until I had told them all about my donkey ride. Even before Roald brought me the martini I had been looking forward to, I was besieged by questions. What donkey? What *is* a donkey? How high? How fast? Theo was especially interested to know if I had fallen off. I told him I had not. A trifle disappointed, he asked, "Not even once?" This continued until I was reminded we had a dinner date that night. Sheena took Theo up for his bath, but Tessa wanted me to bathe her that evening.

I soaped the cloth and began rubbing her shoulders. It was a special moment with my daughter. She was almost eight, and it wouldn't be long before her body would be changing. She'd be a young woman so quickly. She would need to know her mother's approval of all those things that happen to our bodies. A nanny cannot do that. This was my real work.

A pain shot through my head. *Maybe I overdid it today,* I thought, *I shouldn't be bending.* I stood up.

"Mummy, what's wrong?" Tessa asked, a bit frantically, I thought, but she had special antennae.

The pain grew more intense and I staggered into our bedroom. Roald was on his way in with my martini. "I've got the most awful pain," I told him, "I think there's something wrong."

He helped me to the bed. "I've been seeing things, too," I said.

"What sort of things?" he asked. I couldn't tell him; I had forgotten.

"Is the pain only in one place?"

"Yes." I pressed my hand to my left temple. "Right here."

I was aware that he reached for the bedside phone. All I could hear was the sound of my heart beating. The last thing I remember thinking was, I have children to care for. I have another inside me. I can *not* die.

CHAPTER
FORTY-FIVE

All the stories I have heard, all the things I have read, including my husband's writing and Barry Farrell's book and the movie about my stroke, say the same thing. I was as one dead. Gone. The UPI even put my obituary on the wires and it was picked up and published by several newspapers.

I lay in a coma like an immense vegetable. No one detects any movement in a vegetable except, perhaps, the shrewd gardener who knows its roots are reaching deep into the earth. So, perhaps, was my unconscious body reaching into the wellhead of raw existence. Everyone has said the first thing I saw was Roald's face looking down at me. It may have been so. He said I opened one eye and looked at him for five seconds and shut it again. He said my hand was squeezing his. I hope so. He told me that one of the first things I tried to do on the brink of consciousness was reach for his cigarette. I don't remember.

My recollections are secondhand. Roald kept a diary of those four weeks in the hospital and the few friends who saw me have shared their feelings.

Only two memories are my own.

At some point I knew that I was not alone in the room. A haggy voice kept calling, "Patsy. Hello, Patsy." There were other beds, but I remember only a woman who kept waving and calling my name. She was old and crazy and

I felt such loathing in me. Then she was gone. They said she died. I didn't care. I was glad she stopped tormenting me.

I had a terrible pressure in my abdomen. I knew what that meant. There was a woman in my room named Jean. I saw two of her, but I knew she was only one. She was there to take care of me. I tried to say, "Toilet. Pee. Potty," anything to get her to help me go to the bathroom. Nothing came from my mouth. I felt my clothing get hot and wet and stick to my bottom and I began crying. Jean and someone else got me out of my wheelchair, but by the time we got to the toilet I was starting to bonk all over the floor. I heard raucous sounds. They were laughing. They were covered with shit and so was I as they tried to pull me down onto the potty. A wash of anger swelled in me. I felt my spirit sucked into a whirlpool of humiliating laughter, roaring *inside* my head.

But it was not in my head. It was just the toilet flushing.

Then I was alone on my bed in the darkened room. There was nothing but that sound—*wubble-wubble-wubble*. That strange sound would flush through my head several times a day for the next two years.

I learned later that I was in the intensive care unit of the UCLA Medical Center. The call Roald had made was to Dr. Charles Carton, the man I'd met at the Shepherds'. He and Roald had been in conference about Theo's shunt a few days before and his number was still pinned to the mirror by the bed. Apparently he was horrified when he learned Roald was calling about me. Roald described my symptoms and Dr. Carton sent an ambulance immediately.

The household stood frozen in shock, Tessa still wrapped in a towel, as I was taken on a stretcher. "What are the names of the children in this house?" I demanded to know. "My God, I've got an early call tomorrow. I have to be at the studio at seven-thirty." That was the last coherent statement I would make for weeks.

I suffered three strokes altogether. One at home and two in the hospital. The third was the one that did me in.

No one believed I would make it. Even so, precautions were taken during X rays. Lead aprons were placed over me to protect the baby. A team of six doctors, led by our friend Charles Carton, conducted an operation that lasted seven hours. They opened my skull and found I had suffered an aneurysm.

Blood runs through an artery for years, and you don't know there is a weak spot getting thinner and thinner. Then a blister in the wall of the artery, like a spot on a weary bicycle inner tube, explodes and blood seeps into the brain. The blood destroys the nerve cells. It destroys the oxygen that feeds the brain. The blood clots and presses against brain tissues. This is one reason they had to cut a four-by-six-inch trapdoor in my head, to remove the clots.

The aneurysm was congenital, meaning it ran in my family. My life had been slowly building to that moment while bathing Tessa. For thirty-nine years I had lived with no knowledge that some evil force lurked in my head, just waiting.

The operation was an apparent success. Then came the days Roald waited for my coma to end. He spent that time talking to me. "Pat, this is Roald. Tessa says hello. Theo says hello. Don-Mini says hello." He squeezed my hand constantly, and finally, he says, I squeezed back. He told me later that this tiny signal was his first encouragement that I was not going to die. He had exclaimed to Charles, "She's going to live! I'm sure of it."

"Yes, she is," Charles had answered. "But I'm not sure if I've done you a favor."

My right side was completely paralyzed and I had been left with maddening double vision. I had no power of speech and my mind just didn't work.

As soon as I was fully conscious, Roald gave me the whole story, even to the point of assuring me the liquid food I was being fed through a tube was delicious. He never said how he knew.

He described the entire operation in detail. Millie Dunnock, who had also been at my bedside, didn't think that was such a good idea and said so. Roald was unruffled.

He told Millie, "Pat's learned enough about neurosurgery since Theo's accident to get the complete picture of her condition. I've held nothing back because I want her to know that her chances of recovery are very high." Millie was not convinced. She had seen him slap my unconscious face in search of some response, and had been shocked and angered. Of course, she had seen the doctor do that, too, but Millie's an actress and knew there were slaps and then there were slaps.

Once I was off the critical list, Roald began to take care of our domestic affairs and was even able to accept some dinner invitations from concerned friends. Still, he monitored my every move, keeping in constant touch with the doctors. He also kept tight control over my visitors, many of whom had been keeping a vigil outside my room, carefully screening them, admitting few. Lillian Hellman. Cary Grant. Hope Preminger. John Ford. When I saw them, I knew them. I was even able to smile at them. But I could not remember their names.

Some who had been there night after night later told me they had never been admitted. Jean Hagen. Chloe Carter. The Shdanoffs. Betsy Drake. Arthur Kennedy and his wife. I don't know why.

The Jean I had been aware of earlier was Jean Alexander, my nurse. Very soon after I regained consciousness, I remember Jean was washing my feet and singing, "I could have danced all night, I could have danced all night." Suddenly I chimed in, just for one word. After twenty-two days of silence, one word. So Jean sang her head off and I found more and more words to join in, to everyone's relief, since it showed neither my voice nor speech was destroyed. The whole hospital would come to hear me. It was the only singing engagement I ever had in my whole life.

Every day troops of doctors would come in to tickle the soles of my feet with pins and feathers. "Do you feel this?" they would ask again and again and I'd tell them with my eyes that I could; what now? I was given an eye patch, which brought merciful relief from coping with two of everything. I was fitted with a brace on my right leg, which would guard against my falling and endangering the baby. I wore very British-looking oxfords, the right one attached to the brace. Sensible shoes, Roald had called them, and insisted that everyone would know how smart I was because I wore them. Marvelous, I thought, but they looked like the boots I wore in Korea.

Millie had told Theo and Tessa about the stroke, but how can children be prepared to meet the shell of their mother? When Roald smuggled them into the hospital and I first saw them, I tried to tell them how much I missed them, loved them. "Love!" I tried to say. But only ugly sounds came out. Tessa looked at me from some terrible distance. She was frightened and hurt. She wanted a mother, not a vegetable. But Theo smiled shyly and seemed intuitively to know the wound we now shared.

Notably absent those first days was my mother. Roald told me that she did not want to come right away, that she had an ear infection that prevented her from flying. NiNi and George came immediately. NiNi was horrified, not only by my condition, but by the fact that no one was keeping the cards and telegrams and letters that were pouring in. Roald had a lot of things on his mind and saving my get-well messages was not one of them. My family saw this as a bitter slight. NiNi began making sure that everything would be kept so that eventually I could see for myself the outpouring of love and concern from all over the world. Even so, the bulk of the mail was destroyed.

"Hundreds of those letters and cards were from your friends in Knoxville," NiNi complained.

She was just as distressed that Roald would not even show me a card with a religious message on it. He'd throw it in a wastebasket and say, "You don't want that, Pat."

On that note, he anticipated me correctly. I can remember what was left of my shambled brain bitterly reminding me that God had done this to me. And I hated God for that. I was angry and I would be angry for a very long time.

CHAPTER FORTY-SIX

t was one month to the day when I left the hospital. Leaving turned out to be a bigger event than Roald had foreseen. For over an hour we said goodbye to flocks of nurses and nurses' aides. Everyone smiled and wept and said they thought I was very brave. I thought I was just terribly tired and heavy. The thought of leaving Jean had left us more than a little anxious. I had come to depend on her and she had completely won Roald's favor by giving him detailed reports of every inch of my progress. He invited her to come by the house as often as she could.

Millie had borrowed a wig from MGM to cover the scar on my head and the fuzz that had grown back since the operation. Poor thing, she tried so hard to get it to look like something, but when she held up a mirror all I could think was that I looked like Harpo Marx. I left the hospital wearing a scarf. My four-month baby was visible under the maternity dress I wore. I looked down on that little round form. But I could not remember what the roundness meant.

Back at the house, Roald carried me upstairs. He really did. It was so good of him. He had a very bad back, and besides, it was not his style. Only once in our entire marriage did he even hold the car door open for me. He carried me up and downstairs many more times in the next days, but indeed, it was the only way he did carry me. His approach from the very beginning was to get me to do it myself.

Once I was settled on the bed, they brought Ophelia to me. My sweet Ophelia, who would soon be a year old. At last I would hold and rock my baby girl and finally know everything was going to be all right again. I reached for her and tried to stroke her, but my hand wouldn't obey. It moved in clumsy, prodding gestures. Ophelia looked at me and began howling in terror. Sheena picked her up and quieted her. I could feel hot angry tears flood down my face. "That is *my* baby," I wanted to scream, but no words would form.

It would be days before I said my first sentence. "My mind is wrong." I did not say it sadly. I said it victoriously. It was, after all, a sentence.

There were literally hundreds of messages at the house from names familiar to many and some familiar only to me. But each name touched me. Roald had saved the ones from friends in the industry. There were flowers and wires and gifts from Katharine Cornell, Judy Garland, Annabella, Robert Stack, Ann Sheridan and Scott McKay, who was my stage brother in *Another Part of the Forest*. Harry Kurnitz and Frank Sinatra sent a phonograph and records. NiNi made sure I saw the messages from friends who went all the way back to the Barter Theatre, like Bob Porterfield and Phyllis Adams Jenkins.

Even further back than that. One wire, saying: ALL OF US ARE PRAYING FOR YOU, was signed YOUR CLASSMATES AT PARK LOWERY GRAMMAR SCHOOL, KNOXVILLE.

Otto Preminger phoned from London to offer us the use of his fully staffed house in Beverly Hills. But Roald preferred not to disrupt the already shaken household with a move. Marty had let us know that he would not accept any further rent from us. The Dahl family called from England. The only thing they could do for us was to oversee the remodeling of Gipsy House if we still wanted the magazine people to continue. Roald wrote back, "Continue." Anne Bancroft wired, "Call me if there is anything I can do." There had been. Just two days after the stroke, John Ford pressed her to step into my role in *Seven Women,* which she did.

I shall never know how to thank so many in Hollywood who helped us in those days, not by splashy show but by wonderful, thoughtful things. People like Robert Altman and Carolyn and Alex March came to Marty's house just to cook a meal for us. Keith Urmy, Millie's husband, took the children out to Disneyland. Eddie and Margo Albert frequently invited me to be with them when all I could do was sit and stare. Dear Jean Hagen came to offer a hand. Even my Peter Douglas came, bringing his beautiful wife, Virginia.

After a stroke, anger grows with awareness of what you have lost. The fog of unconsciousness that held you prisoner from the outside world was, in fact, a blessing in disguise. First you're like a soul with no body, but the soul is drugged. Then the soul awakens into a body you cannot command. You are a prisoner in a private hell. Everybody is just pushing you around. They push your arms and your legs, your body. They say things, shout things, look at you with expectation, and you don't know what they want.

Each minute brings new reminders of the terrible gaps between you and every single thing you have taken for granted all your life. Brushing your teeth, swatting a fly from your face, getting a drink of water, going to the bathroom in the middle of the night.

I would want a cigarette and Roald would put it just out of my reach. "What do you want?" he would ask, and I would think, Cigarette.

"I want a . . . I want an . . . oblogon."

"Somebody get Pat an oblogon," Roald would order.

"Stop it! I don't mean an oblogon. I mean a . . . crooked steeple. God! You know!"

"You mean a cigarette?"

"Ah, I love you! A cigarette! I'll go crazy if I don't have one. I'll jake my dioddles." Then I would forget as promptly as I had learned. "What did you call it? What word did you say? Inject me again."

Everyone would laugh and I'd have to smile, too. It

was funny. A martini came out a red hair dryer or a sooty swatch. A spoonful of sugar was a soap driver. Sometimes it was not funny. Once when Theo ran into the room, I noticed the straps on his Merry-Mites needed buttoning. I pointed and made signs. I knew the word. Button. I knew the meaning of it. I knew exactly what to say. But my mouth would not say it. All that came out was "Ah . . . ah." And my right hand would not reach out. I could not obey myself.

I would fall back on my pillow, exhausted just from trying to make the sounds of words I knew. Roald would say, "You're 60 percent better today." I would look at him and smile. And try my damnedest to remember his name.

Then I knew. It was Papa.

It was time for the Academy Awards. But for the stroke, I would have been on the show presenting, as the previous year's best actress, the best actor with his Oscar. I had been told that Audrey Hepburn would bestow the honor in my place and I couldn't wait to hear all the nice things she would say about me. "There! There!" I pointed to the TV when Audrey was introduced. But suddenly she was handing Rex Harrison his award, and she hadn't said a thing about me. It had to be a mistake. I pounded on the table with my good hand. "God! God! Me! Not me!" Someone asked if I was annoyed because Audrey hadn't mentioned me. I bloody well was. Roald told me later he was encouraged by my outburst. He thought it clearly was the "appropriate emotional response," which he had been warned was usually lacking in stroke victims, and it pointed to a healing process going on inside my head. He also pointed out that it was a healthy reminder that my illness was not the most important thing in the world.

After Theo was damaged, we worked with him with flash cards that had pictures and names of the objects printed on them. Roald was determined that he would not fall behind because of his accident, and at four and a half he was reading beautifully. Theo was my great inspiration. I had seen him blind and failing, and here he was, an active and outgoing child, undeniable proof of the brain's magic gift for healing. Theo didn't seem perplexed by my tangled speech. He was ecstatic when he learned I was a fellow student of the alphabet. He overheard an ABC session with my speech therapist, and as soon as she left, he appeared with his collection of giant flash cards and began checking me out on the words he knew. SISTER, CAKE, ORANGE, TROUSERS. Roald would let him go on with these games even when I grew tired. The therapist had warned that an hour of intense intellectual effort was about all I was up to in a day. After that it would be self-defeating, even harmful. But Roald felt that idleness was far more dangerous than fatigue. And anything was better than vegetating.

The speech therapy sessions were little different from Theo's games, and everything I learned in these lessons was something I already knew, something hidden and rediscovered. Physiotherapy was less of a game; it was more like trying to run through water. The exercises were repetitive and boring and there were no sudden triumphs. The muscles in my right leg would take years to rebuild and my right hand would never again be really limber.

One afternoon an old friend from my early New York days came to call. I had kept in touch with Gloria Stroock, now Mrs. Leonard Stern, through the years, and although I was touched to see her, I was fearful, too. Fearful of what I would read on her face. I wasn't so far gone that I couldn't recognize pity or sadness or even repulsion. Sometimes, as with Gloria, there would be a moment of shock and then a genuine embrace that was like a great drawbridge thrown over a hideous gap.

We chatted, that is, Gloria chatted while I struggled to make sense out of what she was saying. Then she mentioned her sister, Geraldine Brooks. "Gerry married Budd Schulberg. He wrote your movie?" "I know! I know! I know!" I cried. I was so proud. I had understood. I had remembered. Just then, Roald came in and asked if we'd like tea. Gloria wrote me her impressions of that tea:

Roald stood back and observed. He was not partici-
pating. He was being the stage manager. I had the
feeling he was going to direct traffic. I poured the
tea, which you handled very well . . . the teacup, I
mean. You took a sip and made a face as though it
was very bitter. You put the cup down and started
for the sugar. Roald interrupted. "What do you
want, Pat?" You shrugged your shoulders and he
asked again, with a hard, emotionless tone, "*What*
do you want?" I remember I was very angry with
Roald and wanted to say, "She wants sugar, what
do you think she wants?" But you did not show
anger. I watched your reaction, which was most
clever. You took a sip of the tea and smiled like a
pussycat, and put the cup down as if you did not
want anything. Roald said again, "Do you want
sugar?" and I cried out, "Yes!" I must say I admired
his fierce unrelenting approach, but as I left, I could
not help but think it reminded me of the way one
trains a dog. Sugar? Sugar? You say sugar and you
get a pat on the head. I wondered if the Patricia Neal
I had known could submit to that.

Roald had taken a *Ladies Home Journal* assignment to
write about my illness. He had not been keen on doing
this, but we needed the money. This time we really did.
The Screen Actors Guild had paid most of the hospital
bills and because of Marty's generosity we were living
rent-free, but we were still out something over a hundred
thousand dollars. The loss of my income for *Seven
Women,* five times more than I had gotten for *Hud,* made
every expense threatening. In California we were running
through thousands of dollars a month and Roald feared
we would exhaust all our savings. We would have to
return to England soon. The *Journal* piece would at least
see us home.

Partly to show appreciation for the care she had given
me in the ICU and partly because we had both become
so fond of her, Roald invited Jean Alexander to come to
England with us for a year and to bring her roommate,

Gloria Carugatti, along. It would be simple enough to get a spot for them in a good hospital through Kenneth Till or Sir Ashley. They were both fine nurses. The only question was the airfare. Roald called Anne Bancroft, and reminded her of her offers to help. She sent a check.

Jean came from the hospital almost every day and I think I was more relaxed with her than with anyone. Jean had seen me at my worst and I felt no obligation to be bright for her.

Many of my visitors left me tired and frustrated. I know that it must have been very difficult for them to figure out if my lagging conversation was caused by speechlessness or simplemindedness. Some guessed speechlessness and talked nonstop the whole time they were there. Others, fearing that the stroke had thrown me back to childhood, spoke in baby talk or pidgin English, which made me furious. It was all right if I called myself an idiot. But I didn't want anyone else to.

The frustration seemed to increase in proportion to the number of people in the room. I rarely attempted to speak if there was more than one person with me. Trying to listen to two people was like watching a tennis game, and a roomful of guests was like being on a firing range, words shooting past me like bullets. Once in a while there would be a word I understood, and for a second I knew exactly what was being said. But before I could focus thoughts and trap words of my own, I would forget what I had heard.

Not that it was always a torture. I found myself frequently amazed at how brilliant everyone had become. I remember thinking that Roald was a bloody genius. And at times I felt sheltered by my silence. I became quite good at pretending to listen. I would sit leaning forward and smile a little and, without knowing either the names of my visitors or what they were saying, appear to be a part of the conversation.

At the end of April, two months after my stroke, I made my first journey out of the house. It was for dinner at Anne and Mel Brooks's. Anne Bancroft had become one of my best friends. We were also close in age and even appearance—Roald called us "weathered beauties." We often came up for the same parts. Indeed, she had just been nominated for an Oscar for *The Pumpkin Eater*. Annie had come by the house often. She was another with whom I felt totally at ease. Annie knew when to talk and when to shut up. She and Mel had expected me to arrive in a wheelchair, but I walked in. It was a fine evening. I couldn't follow a word of the conversation, but in my heart I knew I was with good friends, and that was a joy.

Mother finally came and wanted to stay with me until I returned to England. She insisted that it had been Roald who did not want her to come earlier. But in all fairness to Roald, it was true that her ear had been infected. The Ritts had a gorgeous little guest house in back with its own sauna and Jacuzzi, and she moved in. She wanted so much to care for me and to cook for the family, but Roald insisted the house was going to be run the way he wanted it. Things came to a head over the simplest matter, as they often do. Mother wanted to cook a steak as a special treat for me. She went to the store herself and bought a delicious cut, which she carefully prepared and placed before me at supper. Roald took it away from me, cut it into tiny pieces and passed it around the table. "She should share with everybody," he said. "She should not be treated special."

Mother was horrified. "Your daddy would never have treated me like that," she said. "George would never treat Margaret Ann like that." At the time, I bowed to Roald's insistence that everyone should be treated alike, sick or not. It would have been terrible to sit with a great steak in front of me while everyone else had pork chops.

Just at this time, Roald learned that Marjorie Clipstone was in the States and invited her to come for the weekend. She agreed, so Roald asked Mother to vacate the guest house for Marjorie and move into the little upstairs room Marty used as an office. Mother was ready to make the move when she learned that Roald had let the nurse go and expected her to take the woman's place. She was truly frightened that she wouldn't be up to the responsibility—after all, in addition to everything else, I was heavily pregnant—and she told him so. That severed once and for all whatever thread of attachment may still have existed between them. Mother left before her intended departure.

Fortunately, Marjorie could handle being nursemaid. On her very first morning she was petrified at having to help me in and out of the bath. I also picked that morning to shave my legs, and she stood helplessly by as I slashed away with clumsy, uncoordinated swipes. But the sight of blood didn't faze Marjorie. She came for a weekend and stayed to help for a month.

Marjorie clearly looked to Roald for every cue. Only when I had done as much as I could myself did she dare offer her active help.

Roald did not encourage leniency with me. I got up every morning at seven-thirty by myself and found my clothes. I put on my shoes and brace and made my own way downstairs. From the very beginning I could not bring myself to ask any sympathy from him. I suspect I knew I would not get it.

I remember I would often wake in the dead of night. Pregnant women have to go the bathroom often. I would hear Roald snoring next to me, but I would never rouse him to help. He felt a night nurse was not needed, so there was no hired help in the house after dark. I would slip out of the bed onto the floor and scoot, scoot on my bottom to the bathroom. I'd crawl my way up onto the seat in the dark and then try to find a way to flush the toilet with my left hand without falling off. Then I'd slip down onto the floor and scoot, scoot back to bed. I never woke Roald. He had had enough. All day he had everything to do and he deserved his rest.

But I was also afraid to waken him and ask for help. I did not want to hear him say "No, you can do it yourself." It had nothing to do with whether or not he was right, that maybe doing it myself was healing me. It was my dread of feeling rejected.

Roald must have been experiencing his own hell, too. We were sleeping together, but sex hadn't entered my mind. So when his hand touched me I was stunned. He had been reading next to me as usual and reached over and turned out the light. Then I felt that touch. I did not tell him he couldn't do that, but I hoped he would hear my silent signal. Half my body was paralyzed and the other half rigid with tension. But he was tense, too. I could not say no to him. Where would he go if I refused him? He must have feeling for me, I thought, something in him that said we have to get back to normal. I closed my eyes and did not move. I did not scream. I wanted to. It was agony. Agony.

CHAPTER
FORTY-SEVEN

On May 12 we celebrated Ophelia's first birthday and a week later we were set to leave for Washington, D.C., en route for England. A press conference had been called at the airport. It would be my first public appearance since the stroke. I was actually excited at the prospect of talking to reporters again and it was very important to Roald that everybody get the impression that I would have a 100 percent recovery. One hundred percent had been his prognosis and it would be nothing less. For my part, I didn't want to appear like "an enormous pink cabbage"—that was Roald's phrase and I didn't much like it—so we rehearsed for the conference. We went over and over questions he was sure the reporters would ask and I practiced my answers.

Three months to the day after the stroke, Cary Grant drove us to the airport. I did not want to be wheeled into the press conference. I walked in—on my own. I shall never forget the sight of all those newsmen and photographers. Far more than when I received the Oscar. They all stood up and applauded. Roald answered a few preliminary questions and asked the reporters to speak slowly.

"How are you feeling, Pat?" came the first question.

"I feel fine." My words were drawn out but clear.

"When do you think you'll be back to make a picture?"

"I'll be back to work in one year. The baby first."

"What have the doctors told you about the baby?"

"The prediction is . . . the baby will be . . . fine."

Prediction! We hadn't rehearsed that word and yet it slipped into the sentence so smoothly. I could see Roald was amazed.

And, in fact, that *was* the prediction, although I was not sure I believed it.

We had a happy time in Washington. We house-guested with dear Claudia Marsh, who was now living in D.C. Charles's spirit was still very much in our lives and would continue to be for some time. Our Ophelia would one day study medicine and work with his Public Welfare Foundation, which helped the blind and poverty-stricken in Haiti.

Ethel Kennedy invited us to lunch at Hickory Hill, which surprised me because we did not know her. It came about because our former nanny, Susan, had a friend who looked after the Kennedy children. I felt sorry to think Ethel had gotten roped into playing hostess to us. But it was a magnificent party with masses of people from Washington paying their respects. I sat by the pool, decked out in my eye patch and brace, trying my best to keep the stature of the Queen Mother and being constantly amazed that so many people thought I had come back from the dead.

Had I been Charles Lindbergh and flown the plane myself to England I could not have had a greater welcome. There seemed to be hundreds of people crowded into the reception area at Heathrow. In every direction, flash-bulbs were popping and cameras were whirring. Most of the family was there. This time we all hugged. And I found myself crying, sobbing. It was the only time since the stroke that I had.

The rest of the family and all the neighbors were at Gipsy House to greet me. Baskets of flowers from every garden in the village lined the entry and the table was heaped with homemade cakes and all kinds of food. Everyone was splendid and said over and over how wonderful I looked. Years later, Nesta Powell told me that after she and the Hawksworths saw me, they went away and wept.

When I got a chance to look at our home, I couldn't believe my one eye. The place looked as if it had been hit by a stroke, too. The magazine people had, to say the least, taken liberties. I thought I was in a pit. The walls had been painted dark brown. The carpet was brown and so was the furniture, which was now bamboo! Huge flowered curtains of varying shades of brown hung everywhere. Walls had been knocked out. The nursery was now a sitting room and the kitchen wasn't where it used to be. The beautiful old doors and floor tiles had been replaced by shiny modern ones. As a final insult to Roald, bookcases with fake books—just covers with no insides—had been installed. His sisters had indeed tried to warn him about what was happening, but Roald simply wasn't up to handling it from California.

Papa was furious with me. It had been my idea. I felt so guilty.

Our gloom was dispelled momentarily. Mr. Thurgar, the village chemist, and his wife had sent a bottle of champagne. Roald filled our glasses. "To the pleasure of being home again at last!" was his brave toast. I took one gulp and looked around the room. It seemed to me that something had changed. I pulled down my eye patch, and for the first time since my stroke, I could see normally.

"It's gone!" I yelled.

"What's gone?" he asked.

"The double eyes!"

"Jolly good," he said, filling my glass again. "I wonder if the medical profession would be interested in our cure?"

Each morning I would awaken to a new awareness of what the stroke had taken from me. I would look in a mirror and see my hair growing in wispy, crazy shapes. I could hardly be persuaded to brush it. My face looked haggard and old to me. There was no way to put lipstick on. I couldn't find my mouth. Each day I would discover a new way to experience jealousy, to feel a hate go through me. Other people could slip on a sweater if they were cold or crank open a window if they needed air.

I had to learn to read all over again like a toddler. Roald tried to get me to read to the children, but even the easiest book, like *The Tale of Pigling Bland,* made no sense to me. The children were bored to death and I sensed that my attempts were only aggravating an already fragile bond between them and me. Theo simply took the book out of my hand when he could bear it no longer.

With Tessa, the breach was even more complex. She felt more consciously deprived of her mother. She did not need me to read stories, she needed me to talk to, to talk with. She turned completely to Roald and he let her. Even when I was with them, she would lean over and talk into his ear—Daddy this, Daddy that—as if I was not even there. Finally I would say sharply, "Talk to *me!* I have something to say!"

And Roald would ask, "What do you have to say, Pat?"

And I would sink back and answer, "I forget."

What could I possibly say or do for my daughter? Help her with her studies? Fix her dress? No, it was Daddy who did that. It was Daddy now who took them for walks to the witches' tree, to Beacon Hill, to the toy shops. It was Daddy who helped them feed and water the budgies and the dogs. It was Daddy who did the shopping and weeded the garden and chose the wine for supper. Daddy. Daddy. Daddy. Was I jealous? God, I was electrified with jealousy.

I wanted to be a wife and mother as always. I wanted to put my mind to it and do it. I would try to feed Ophelia and I could not get the spoon to her mouth properly. She would look up at Sheena and cry for her. I remember one day I was determined I would get that spoon into her mouth. I kept missing and food spilled all over the child. But I would not quit, even when Sheena demanded it. Ophelia was *my* baby. Finally Sheena brought her hand down full force, smacking my face. I looked at her in rage. I was so humiliated to be treated that way by my own paid servant. But I did not have the authority to fire her. If I had been myself, Sheena would have dealt with me on that slap. But then, if I had been myself, she would not have dared slap me.

The final humiliation came when I heard Roald tell the children that Mummy could do things for them if only she *wanted* to. The one thing I grew to hate most was being told that I could change the horrible mess I was in if only I worked at it harder.

I did want so desperately to please Papa. But I was becoming so fed up with him. He would tell me I was 42 percent better than yesterday and 51 percent better than last week. God, I was so sick of his percentages, his plans, his programs, his world. It was Papa's world now. He was a hero and I was hating him. And yes, I was hating the good Dr. Carton for saving my life. And I was hating God. How could He have done these beastly things when I hadn't been beastly myself? And I hated myself for hating.

Papa never said, "I love you, Pat." But why would he? I was the most unlovable mess in the world.

"My mind is gone," I would say over and over, "it's so evil." But I had not lost my mind. If I had, things would have been easier. Then maybe I wouldn't have cried my heart out when I was alone at night—for fear that I had lost it.

As I think back on it now, just to have been able to sustain jealousy or anger for any length of time would have been a gift. As it was, I gave up caring. Even about my home. Other women now attended to my domain. And when it came down to it, I didn't care. That was the heart of it. I simply did not care anymore about anything.

And that is exactly what Roald perceived in me. He knew if my motivation was gone, it was the end of everything for me. He decided to call in neighbors to set up a program that would literally keep me occupied every minute of the day.

Every morning I would have a reading and writing lesson with a volunteer helper. Afterward, a hired girl would take me off to the RAF Military Hospital in nearby Halton, where I was put through a series of exercises for my right arm and leg. Start, stop, up, down, push, relax, two, three, four. I felt as if I were in boot camp.

Then I would go to the Stoke Mandeville Hospital, where I would do laps in the therapy pool.

From the moment I got back from the hospital, neighbors would begin to come for an hour at a time and virtually reteach me to live. I was not allowed to sit and stare. Else tried to teach me to cook again, and friends like Marjorie and the Kirwans—Brigadeer, Patricia and their daughter Angela—and Frankie Conquy would come and talk or play dominoes or tic-tac-toe, anything to get me to recall numbers or how to spell simple words like "cat" or "dog." It was difficult for them because they had known me as a friend who played bridge, and now they were my tutors. And it was hard for me to face them as little more than an idiot.

From the time I got up in the morning until I went to bed at night, everything I had to do fought my natural inclination, which was to just lay myself down and let it all work itself out. Fortunately, I believed Papa implicitly when he told me that hard work alone could save me.

Joan Maynell, an English actress, and that wonderful actor Kenneth Haigh came to read plays with me, but I didn't relate to much except their good will. Helen Horton visited and helped me answer letters. Roald must have already answered at least a thousand of them, many from stroke patients that poignantly conveyed encouragement. It was certainly proof of friendship on Helen's part, because it would take me forever just to get one tiny note written. "Dear Mrs. Smith, Thank you for your letter. Sincerely, Patricia Neal Dahl." I would write one or two and then turn to Helen and ask, "How do you spell 'dear'?"

Life magazine wanted to do what is known in the trade as an "in-depth" piece on my recovery. They sent Barry Farrell, a very good writer on their staff who had lost his own son three years before. The editors thought that profiling the Greek tragedians of Great Missenden would help him, and Roald hoped that whatever was left of the actress in me would respond to a writer and photographer following me around.

He was right. I liked Barry. Intuitively I knew he did not understand me, but he knew how to get to me: through movies. I could remember being under contract and that I had a fur and that I'd been naive and that I left Hollywood because I'd been in love and it had—what was the right word?—not worked. And then I would teasingly ask, "Do you know *who* it was I was in love with?"

Oddly enough, Barry turned out to be more of a help to Papa than to me, for which I am grateful. He adored Roald and Roald needed that. Barry eventually developed his magazine piece into a book, *Pat and Roald,* which was Papa's story of the stroke. Had I been more with it I could have suggested he title it *The Cabbage and the Giant.* We had the right to approve the manuscript, but Roald assured Barry we would not even look at it until it was published.

My memory was selective. I had no trouble recalling moments of great trauma. Theo's accident and Olivia's death remained vivid in my mind. I could also recall things from the distant past, but couldn't remember whom I was with. One day Theo joined us with his flash cards and I kept calling him "the boy." My own son, and all that came to me was "the boy."

One day out of the blue I asked Barry, "How long are you buried . . . before you . . . come apart?"

"What do you mean, Pat?" he asked. "In the grave?"

"Yes. How long are you in the grave before you're just a . . . you know, just bones?"

"Just a few months, Pat," he said. "Inside a year it's all over, no matter what kind of coffin or embalming."

I let out a moan. Roald came into the room to see what had happened. Barry was shorn. "She was wondering about Olivia. How could I have not remembered Olivia?"

Papa changed the subject. "How about the tapes? Did you make a tape for Betsy this afternoon?"

"We did!" I answered, my grief forgotten in a moment. "You must hear it."

Betsy Drake had sent a tape from California a few days

before. Her farewell gift to me had been a tape recorder that matched her own so we could keep in touch without the need of writing. There was noise in the background that sounded like a party. Betsy spoke first and then a parade of familiar voices.

Papa had prepared a pile of cue cards for my reply. I must have made a dozen attempts before I managed to get through the whole thing in a single try.

Hello, Betsy, my dear, dear friend. Everyone here is well and fine. I am working every day and getting much better. Everyone says I am amazing. I am dying to birth my baby, but I still have to wait. Papa says it will be soon now, but it seems a long time to me. Life is going to be like it was, so don't you worry, my friend. Everything's going to be all right, all right.

CHAPTER
FORTY-EIGHT

At first I just joked about suicide, usually to Barry—that I would do it except I didn't know *how*. But I had started to think about it. Everything was being stripped away. Papa had taken over the running of the house. I had lost my place in my children's lives. Ophelia didn't even seem to know I was her mother. I was sure that they could only feel sorry for me or, worse yet, ashamed. I saw how few things were within my range, saw my responsibilities pass me by. I'd ask Barry how many sleeping pills it took or how many aspirin. He would tell me it took hundreds and hundreds, trying to discourage me. One thing I knew for sure. I would wait until after the baby came.

One night at supper I mentioned suicide in front of Papa. I made my usual joke about wanting to but not knowing how. Papa turned on me, not in a fury but with a laugh, and said, "Well, if that's all that's stopping you, your problems are solved. We've got knives that will do you up fine. And there are my razor blades. Or else you can lock yourself in the car and turn on the engine, and before you know it, Bob's your uncle!"

But it must have concerned him more than he let on, because he decided that I should see a doctor. He made an appointment with a psychologist in Aylesbury. I have practically no recollection of that day except that I was with the doctor a long time and that at the end he told me I didn't need him.

Roald was firmly convinced that the depression I was feeling was due to the worry and strain of carrying the baby. At the time of the stroke the child inside me gave me something to live for, but now, he reasoned, the pregnancy was retarding me. Indeed, walking was now extremely difficult and tiring, and I had lost all hope about my appearance. He was certain that the birth would be the great lift I needed. It would reawaken my strong maternal instinct.

Even in normal circumstances, the odds against a thirty-nine-year-old woman delivering her fifth child successfully had to be high, but there were those additional handicaps. The eleven hours of anesthesia, all the drugs and medicines and the coma itself. Then there were the *sixty* X rays. I had heard stories of radiation effects on pregnant women and knew very well that the lead aprons thrown over me gave no guarantee that the babe in my womb would not emerge a monster. Timidly I asked Roald, "Will it have a reformed face?"

"*De*formed," he corrected me, but he wasn't smiling.

Too, there was the possibility that it had been deprived of oxygen, which would result in brain damage. This baby could be worse off than I was.

Still, I was anxious to get it over with, even though I knew that someone else would nurse this one. Someone else would change it, put it to bed, be its mother. For days on end I would sit and stare blankly at the children's playhouse, the old gypsy caravan, and past that to the scarecrow in the garden. It was an old doll of Tessa's, given to her years before by Andy Griffith, that had been repainted for its new job. It would grin back at me with its smeared stupid smile.

One of the few things I looked forward to each day was the postman. On one particular day, an envelope inscribed with a noble hand caught my attention. I cannot describe the feeling its short but generous greeting imparted and would share the letter now if it had not been burned. But I will never forget its three most important words: *I forgive you*. It was from Maria Cooper.

Although desperate to be free of carrying the baby, I was stricken one evening when, in my bath, I suddenly saw the water turning red. Screaming for help, I tried and tried to crawl out of the tub. I was pouring blood. I wrapped myself in towels. I was so frightened that I was miscarrying. Papa finally came and rushed me to the hospital, where the crisis was quickly diagnosed as only a broken blood vessel.

At Papa's request, Dr. Hawksworth agreed to induce the birth two weeks early. I had stopped my sessions with the physiotherapist when I became too ungainly for exercise. Papa decided we could afford to suspend the rest of the lessons as well until the baby came. I had become such a bad student, so apathetic and unresponsive, yet good friends like Jane Figg and Judy Knivett-Hoff and Audrey Rae-Smith were too kind to stop coming.

As soon as the date for birthing was set, my mood changed. All anxiety seemed gone and I astonished everyone, myself included, with my energy and good disposition. My speech was animated and full of words that had been beyond me only a few weeks before. It seemed to Papa that my depression had hidden a continuing progress. Even our sparring, a kind of wicked ticking each other off that used to give us great pleasure, showed signs of returning.

"You're getting a bit long in the tooth, you know," Papa chided. "When you go into the hospital to have this baby, I think I'll nip into London and find myself a girl—someone not quite so fossilized."

I was able to hit the ball back. "No girls, Papa, that would not be good."

"Oh? Why not?"

"Because you might have a . . . heart attack."

I spruced myself up a bit the day of my departure to the hospital. Papa had alerted the press and I honestly cared about the way I would look. I remember it was raining, but quite a few photographers showed up, so I went out anyway. "I love anyone who will take my picture," I said and posed under an umbrella. When Papa came out, the photographers asked for a shot of him helping me into the car.

"A splendid idea," I said. So Papa held the car door open for me as I lumbered in.

"What you have there is a collector's item," Papa told them. "It's the only picture in existence of me holding a door for Pat."

"He's not kidding, either," I laughed. "It's the first time since I've known him that he did."

Lucy Neal Dahl was born at 8:23 the morning of August 4, 1965, one hundred and sixty-nine days after my stroke. Inducement had not been necessary after all. My labor had lasted less than four hours and the birth itself was easy. Right afterward, Papa, Barry and the *Life* photographer, Leonard McCombe, all in surgical masks and gowns, were in the delivery room.

"I can't remember when I've felt so good," I announced to one and all.

Nesta Powell laid the small bundle in my arms, and as Leonard snapped away, I got my first glimpse of the little face deep inside the blanket. She was perfect. "Oh, Lucy," I sighed. "You're whole and you're fine and you're my last baby."

I did not know then that that decision was no longer mine. Roald had asked the doctor to tie my tubes after the baby's birth. He did so because of my condition, assuming I would not have argued the point. He was right, I wouldn't have. Not then. Only years later did I feel the outrage.

Roald called his mother and sisters and sent telegrams to my mother and friends in Los Angeles and New York. Barry contacted the wire services. Soon the whole world knew I had given birth to what the media called "the miracle baby." To commemorate the occasion, Roald gave me a lovely gold ring. It was Greek, from the fourth century B.C. It just fit my little finger.

I was delighted over Lucy's name and I knew Mother would especially like the Neal part. Using the family name might even smooth the rough patch that existed between her and Roald. I told Else and Alf, "In the South she would always be called by both names, as in, 'Lucy Neal, you git on in heah and eat yo' grits!' " They seemed to love the fact that I was once more trying to make a joke.

Papa came to the hospital every day to see the baby and help me do my thank-you notes. Nearly everyone had been heard from, many explaining their silence the past months by saying that up to now they hadn't known what to say. It was an absolute feast of affection for me and I shamelessly insisted that the mushiest of tributes be read aloud again and again, stopping Papa only long enough to interject, "Now that one really knows what he's talking about!"

The next thing to do was remove the brace from my leg and take my first unaided, if clumsy, steps. I lifted one foot like a puppet and planted it, then the other one, in a jerking and halting manner. Down the corridor I clumped, Papa on my tail, urging me on like a drill sergeant.

Gipsy House was ankle deep in sawdust when I returned. Papa was having the nursery and kitchen restored as well as building a two-story wing to join the main house with the guest house.

Again, everyone was there to greet us. The children were all impatient to see and touch their new sister. I was so pleased that amid all the excitement, Tessa noticed my brace was gone. She thought it was "supah."

Lucy, however, was not the miracle for me that Papa had hoped for. I was still no homemaker and still no mother. I would just sit by her bassinet and look aimlessly into space, not knowing what to do, while our new nurse, Klara, tended her.

It was clear that there was no way we could keep the apartment in New York, and our tenants wanted it. They promised to put our things in storage, but years later we found that only part of our belongings had been stored. Some items, like my silver, were incorporated into their own household and much was just thrown out.

Papa lost no time in rounding up my team of amateur

therapists. He couldn't have asked for a more loving demonstration of neighbors helping neighbors. It took only a half-dozen calls to book a full week's time.

My lessons started again the morning after I returned from the hospital. These dear friends had their work cut out for them: how to keep my interest without making things so difficult that I would be discouraged or so simple that I would be insulted. Which books, for example, do you read to a mature woman whose reading level is somewhere below her eight-year-old daughter's? They decided on newspapers. The short lines kept my eye from straying and I could also benefit from an awareness of the world. Papa found another advantage. I would also be reminded that the world indeed continued to spin without me.

My speech improved, or at least that's what everyone told me. Any sense of progress, of moving forward, was all but lost on me. I found the pace hatefully slow. I still spoke in formulas. Everything was either *very good* or *evil* and I tended to stretch out everything. I didn't just say I was going to take a bath. I announced it. "I am . . . *very* . . . sorry . . . to tell you . . . that . . . I am going up . . . to take a bath." Or "It would be . . . a *very* . . . good thing . . . if . . . we . . . had a cup of tea."

One of my teachers thought it would help me if I memorized poetry. I had always been good at memorizing lines. But my attempts were disastrous. I would reverse words or omit whole stanzas and lack any awareness of having made a shambles of it. More often I would draw a complete blank. "It's gone, it's gone," I realized. "I'm through with acting. I can't remember lines."

Lucy Neal Dahl was christened in the same church as the other children. Annabella was her godmother and, in absentia, Charles Carton her godfather. It was the first time I had been inside a church since returning to England, but this did not mark a truce with God. God was not bothering me now and I was not bothering Him.

High on the wall near the altar was the carving of St. Catherine that we had given in Olivia's memory. It jutted

out like the figurehead of a ship and my eyes kept returning to it.

One day Papa felt the time had come for me to face the
challenge of going to the grocer's for our supplies. It was
not a complex chore. Even Theo could be trusted to run
down to the store, and he would accompany me. Although the double vision was gone, I was never able to
see out of the side of my right eye. Part of the road was
obscured to me and an odd stone was my waterloo. I fell
headlong into mud. I was a sight as I tried to pull myself
up out of the mess, but I could not get to my feet. Darling
Theo was too uncomplicated not to laugh. Thank God a
kind neighbor drove by and came to our rescue.

When we got to the store I looked a proper mess. I felt
wretched and was more confused than ever. I stood there
staring at all those labels. They were only splinters of
color, the writing had no meaning to me at all. I had no
idea what to buy. I began to pull things off the shelf. Theo
must have helped me because I did bring back a few items
we needed. But there were also some twenty or more
boxes of Jell-O.

The people in Great Missenden who knew me were
always more than kind, but not everyone who saw the
bumbling figure staggering after a child that day stifled
laughter. I heard it and thought I must look a simpleton.
It was hell. I remember thinking, I will never laugh at
anyone again. Only God knows what is going on inside
someone's head.

Other excursions out of the house had varying degrees
of success.

My first real outing was to Tessa's school for Games
Day. All the children, including Tessa, competed for The
Olivia, the cup I had donated. She tried magnificently to
win it back, as did Ophelia and Theo, but that honor
would be reserved for their new little sister, who would
bring the cup back home seven years later. For all the
fun, it was a hard afternoon. It brought back the pain of
Olivia's death and left me very sad.

Papa began to take me with him for supper at his club
in London. Before ordering, I thought nothing of asking

diners at nearby tables, "Is that good, what you are eating?" I had always been curious about what other people ate in restaurants, but before my stroke, I would never have asked a stranger if his dinner was any good. It's not a bad idea. I still do it and I get better food.

I also wanted to see a movie, so Papa took me to the Beatles' new film, called *Help!* The title expressed my feelings exactly. I could not make sense out of one thing that was going on and it was no comfort whatsoever when Papa told me you were not supposed to.

And I went to the airport to meet my wonderful nurses, Jean and Gloria, when they came for their visit. Papa had secured jobs and lodging at a hospital near us and they would spend weekends at Gipsy House. It was fun having the girls with me again. They knew how to cheer me. Whenever I was moping around, giving in to my limp, they would sing, "A pretty girl . . . is like a melody. . . ." Up would go my chin, up would go my shoulders and I was back on that ramp, parading for George Petty in the Syllabus Queen contest again.

The girls witnessed a minor catastrophe—a picture fell off the wall while I was reading to Theo and its corner cut my scalp. We headed immediately to the hospital, but the car ran out of gas. Papa and Gloria went for help and Jean and I walked to find refuge in a farmhouse. Jean later wrote about the unexpected gift of that night.

> Remember that very shy couple at the farm? They became so relaxed with you. You didn't tell them who you were or that your head was hurt. You talked to them about their child who suffered seizures. You even talked to them about their puppies! I marveled at the "new Patricia" who was so genuinely interested in the problems of others.

Jean's image of me was certainly not my own worm's-eye view, but she made me aware that the old Patricia, who she thought was "new," was trying to rise from the ashes.

I am happy to say, especially to stroke victims who

may be reading this, that the old Patricia's appreciation of sex had also revived. It was not a sudden return, more a gradual reawakening over many months, but sex was, once more, a part of my life.

Life magazine was thrilled with Barry's story. They hosted a grand party for me at my favorite restaurant, The Bell in Aston-Clinton. Vidal Sassoon sent his best hairdresser to cut my short hair even shorter. Everyone near and dear was there and said I looked lovely and transformed. Stanley Holloway sang "Get Me to the Church on Time." My faithful Harvey Orkin brought Marty Ritt, who bragged about me. "She's a first-class actress, free, unafraid. She'll try anything. She's stylish in the best way a woman can be stylish," he said as he lifted his glass in a toast. "That is, very womanly." Those words came at a very good time. And that dinner seemed to mark an end to the deepest worries everyone had about my recovery.

CHAPTER
FORTY-NINE

> . . . felt approaching foot-
> steps. I stretched out
> my hand . . . Someone
> took it and I was caught up and held close in the
> arms of her who came to reveal all things to me.
> —HELEN KELLER
> *The Story of My Life*

I did not know that complete recovery was within my
grasp until the day Valerie Eaton-Griffith walked into my
home and took my hand. It was a fortnight since Lucy's
birth when we were introduced. And I knew, as surely as
Helen Keller had, that my teacher had come. This is the
one, I said to myself. That is not something I can explain,
even now. I only know that is what I felt.

When I began sorting out memories for this book, I
asked Valerie to write me about our first meeting.

When I walked into the room, your face is what
caught my attention. You were not going to get anywhere with that tragic face. I had never known anyone with a stroke before. Our mutual friend, Patricia
Kirwan, thought we might possibly help each other.
You see, I developed an imbalance from a parathy-
roid operation and, like you, had to quit my job. I
could not walk for three years. I had to live through

305

the agony of wondering if I would ever be able to use my legs again. I did not meet you as a superior being, Patricia, not by any means. I met you as a peer. I didn't think you would want to come and work with me. But you did. You started coming to my house every day for many hours.

You were sort of hollow. You did not talk, really, except in pet phrases and clichés. If the coffee was cold, the coffee was "evil." It just meant that it was not quite right, but you had no other way of saying it. You could not handle money at all. You did not know an English bill from an American one. You handled shapes pretty well and you could tell the time.

One of the first things you said to me was, "My mind is gone." That was not true. I realized that there were masses of things, the intellectual functions that you learned from babyhood, that were still there. My first lesson was to learn, bit by bit, what you could do and what you had to rediscover. I tried to reverse roles and think, Suppose I were you, how would I feel? Inside I am a conscious, thinking individual. Inside I am myself. I just have no ability to get that self out. Inside I *know*. But I can't talk or express a gesture.

It was purgatory.

Roald encouraged Valerie to work with me. It is surely to his credit that he recognized he was not a teacher. He knew the wonderful, generous people who had given me so much of their time were crucial, but he also knew that was not going to be enough. Roald and Valerie liked each other immediately, but their mutual respect would be challenged by a difference in approach that was poles apart.

There were many people around you who did not see the little bit that I saw. You were not getting the respect of a normal human being.

I had no idea how she knew this, but I can remember thinking *Bravo. Thank you.*

You were knocked down all the time, not intentionally, but even by your own children. After all, they could read and you couldn't.

So we would read and do mental arithmetic—add 7 and 9 and 4 and take away 3—and you would get so bored. You would try to say something you wanted and you could not fill in a word. I would try to think of it for you and you would shout, "No, that is not what I wanted to say." I was learning a great deal, too. We were on this journey together.

If you had had a good bit of wine the night before, you would not have a good morning. If you were not in good spirits, we would just have a cup of coffee and look out the window and talk about the trees or the weather. There was no point in pushing. We would just do less.

For my part it was back to the drawing board. But there was a difference. I found that I really began to look forward to my time with Valerie. Even the walk to her house every morning felt good.

We would look at magazines together and she would ask me what colors were in the pictures and what the pictures reminded me of. She would put coins on the table and we'd name them. We'd work jigsaw puzzles. Afterward we might play cards with her father, Eaton, and her sister, Daphne. I felt good with the three of them because they never overlapped their conversation, so I could follow. I felt that I fit into their company.

You fought me more when you got tired. Once I infuriated you by asking so many questions about the past, and you were getting fidgety. I had to ask several times, "What did your husband do for a living?" and finally you pleaded you were simply too tired to go on. "Excellent," I said, "then let's go shopping. The walk will do us good." Together we looked over the shelves and you relearned the labels. Soup. Milk. Coffee. Butter. Cottage cheese.

"Now, before we go home," I reminded you, "did you tell me what your husband did for a living?"

You snapped, "He didn't work, I did!"

I never knew what to expect from you. There would be this little smile on your face and a moment of peace and then it would melt and we would have war. Oh, they were never big wars, but small ones.

"How did your day go at home, Pat?" I would get no response.

"Is there something you want to say to me?" Still no response.

This would go on like twenty questions and then suddenly you would fire, "Tell me, Valerie, are you a virgin?"

I had to govern my responses, and early on I learned that I must not blame you for being obnoxious. You felt so ineffective and angry. Just stripping me by a rude question could be a way of asserting yourself, even for a moment. The one thing I found was that whenever you had been hurtful, you never would leave before mending it.

Valerie has forgotten how *furious* she was with me at that moment. I have never seen anyone as angry. Much later she brought it up. "You asked me a question, do you remember?" I did indeed. "Well," she said, "I thought about it and I have decided not to answer you."

And then there would be days when we would hit the jackpot. I had seen something in the paper and I asked, "Is there someone named Louella Parsons?" You roared with laughter. I pulled out her newspaper column and it made all the difference. You had to have material that really interested you, that would give us a way to talk together. Louella was a great find.

It is true. I have always adored Hollywood gossip.

You could tell me that you worried because you were not good-looking anymore—you did look like the dog's dinner, I have to admit—and could not hold the people who had loved you. You were insecure about any kind of love at all.

Valerie began emphasizing that I was an actress. But she disagreed with Roald on my potential to return to acting. "All this talk about getting back to work is too early," she counseled. "You can't look too far into the future because the future is too frightening." But she did feel that acting was my "mother tongue." We began reading a little play by Charles Cooper called *Everything in the Garden*. Every line was just one sentence. She would read one line and I would read one.

I remember one day we were working with some maps. I was taking you through basic geography and we started with the USA, since that was your country. I looked for the capital, hopeful this would give you a possible success. Small successes were very necessary. "Where is Washington?" I asked. You pointed to the far western edge of the map. "No, no," I said, and I pointed out D.C. But you insisted and kept agitating until I looked for myself and there was the state of Washington. That was not just a small success, Pat, it was a major triumph, and not just because you were right. The triumph was that you outwitted me. It was a very important triumph because you were the person who knew nothing and could do nothing, who was always the fool. After that day I used to engineer a few triumphs for you, but none ever worked as well. This one was genuine and you knew it.

It was a big day for Valerie when I stopped using the old pet phrases, like saying everything was "evil." When I could begin to make up new phrases to say what I meant.

Roald did not want to believe that you were as bad off as you really were. He would ask you to make dentist's appointments for the children or buy shoes or something he felt would stretch you back to your old reality. In your house there seemed to be this frantic thing to make you better and to pretend that you were better than you really were. Sometimes I thought your children were convinced you were acting and that if you just put your mind to it, everything would be different. It created a feeling of blame that you were not a good mother.

How did she know? Of all the bitterness of those days, that was the essence.

I felt confident with Valerie. Long before I was able to perceive any lasting bond of friendship, I felt a bond of security that allowed me to tell her some of the things that bothered me and then, finally, gave me the freedom to transfer my hurt to her.

My old antique table has many blows from your fist. So many individuals way back in your life who hurt you—a doctor in New York, an actress who took a part away from you—they all came out on my table. Only slowly did you get to the point where you could remember the good things.

I was learning that encouraging you, challenging you, was in itself an art. To tell you that you should dress better or comb your hair or to speak more clearly, to dominate you by "shoulds" only aggravated you. To tell you that you were brave was all right, but you did not need to have that said to you. You had to be left with every tiny bit, every teeny-weeny bit that was yours.

That was it. Valerie summed it up. A master can tell you what he expects of you. A teacher, though, awakens your own expectations. There was no doubt that I needed a master like Roald to demand I aim for the sky. But it would take a teacher like Valerie who could kneel down and help me lift myself up out of the cabbage patch.

67

The Dahl family en route to California in January 1965. I would not come home the same way—ever.

Film Actress Patricia Neal Dies at 39

HOLLYWOOD (UPI) — Actress Patricia Neal, who won an Academy Award for "Hud," died Saturday at UCLA Medical Center where she underwent brain surgery for a massive stroke.

Miss Neal was stricken with the first of two strokes Feb. 17. She was taken to the medical center, suffered another stroke and surgery was performed on the 39-year-old star.

The blonde, blue eyed actress was unconscious for days following the attack.

Miss Neal was taken ill after returning home from work at Metro Goldwyn Mayer studios where she was co-starring in "Seven Women." She played a North China missionary in the movie being directed by John Ford.

The beautiful star, who was named best actress of 1963 for her portrayal of the slatternly housekeeper in "Hud" with Paul Newman, came here from England Jan. 23 with her husband, English writer Roald Dahl.

The couple, who live in Buckinghamshire, England, have three children, Tessa, 8, Theo, 5, and Ophelia, 8 months.

Mark Twain said it best: "The reports of my death are greatly exaggerated."

Three months to the day after my stroke we returned home. Cary Grant took us to the airport.

Theo helps me read the simple words of a child's book.

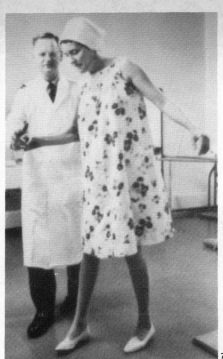

Taking my first steps without the brace.

Angela Kirwan was one of the Great Missenden friends who gave true meaning to the word *neighbor*.

Roald samples my homemade mayonnaise.

Leaving for the hospital to birth Lucy. The rain didn't stop me from posing. I love anyone who will take my picture!

72

73

Martin Ritt toasting me at The Bell—my favorite restaurant in England. His words meant much at a time when I was feeling discouraged.

74

Mormor holds court in her greenhouse.

75

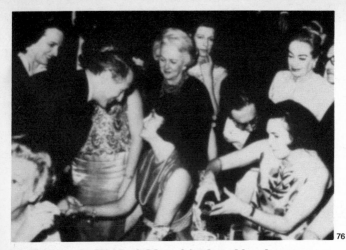

My night at the Waldorf. Many friends and loved ones attended, but it was a special joy to see Peter Cookson and his wife Beatrice Straight there.

The Subject Was Roses. A *working actress* again, in the
company of two great—and generous—actors, Jack
Albertson and Martin Sheen, and a compassionate
director, Ulu Grosbard.

**Oscar night 1967.
My comeback in
Hollywood. I'm
wearing the mink
Gary gave me.**

80

**At Sardi's following
the New York
premiere of *The
Subject Was Roses*.
A second meeting
with Tallulah
Bankhead.**

81

At the Hollywood premiere of *Roses* with the man who saved my life, Dr. Charles Carton.

With my teacher, on the set of *The Night Digger*.

84

Olivia Walton in *The Homecoming* was one of my favorite roles. And the nippers were wonderful.

85

86

Roald, Val and I in Hollywood for "Stroke Counter Stroke."

87

In *Eric* with John Savage, who played my son, just before his devastating accident.

Around the old gypsy caravan in 1975. To the world we were still an idyllic family.

A joyous reunion
in Knoxville
with my first
drama teacher,
Emily Mahan
Faust.

Widow's Nest. Loved the makeup. Hated the film. It played *one day* in Los Angeles.

The seeds of a new life. Speaking at a stroke center in Tennessee.

With Felicity Crossland.

With Colin Leslie Fox, my blessed friend, during the madwoman days.

Doctor Patricia Neal. How about that!

In the Abbess's garden at Regina Laudis. She's the photographer.

94

95

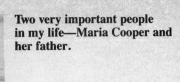
Two very important people in my life—Maria Cooper and her father.

96

At sixty-one.

97

CHAPTER FIFTY

remember seeing an article headlined: SUDDENLY PATRICIA NEAL WANTED TO LIVE. It would have been more correct to say that suddenly I realized I was, in fact, living and was starting to like the experience again.

I was becoming aware that my stroke had opened a whole new audience to me. I was no longer being watched just as an actress, but as a public survivor whose progress was important to the morale of others. After the *Life* piece came out, magazines and newspapers from all over the world began hounding us for stories. Soon I was doing an interview every week, it seemed.

Since those lovely reporters had to trek all the way to the wilds of the English countryside, it seemed only fair to feed and entertain them a bit. I remember getting one writer involved in a crossword puzzle that Val had assigned. "If you help me," I whispered, "will it be cheating?"

We worked together for several minutes when I needed a word for "brave."

"How about Pat Neal?" he graciously offered.

I checked. "I thank you," I said, "but it doesn't fit."

A week did not go by without a flood of letters pouring into Gipsy House. Many were from movie fans who wanted to express concern and get an autographed slip of paper back. But far more were from people who asked our help and advice. Roald took this very much to heart and composed a long letter outlining his program of volunteer therapy and adding Valerie's insights. This letter was sent out by the hundreds.

I began to use the typewriter again—with my left hand —so I could keep up with my friends. Everything was in capitals because I could not manage the shift. Imagine my long-awaited pleasure when I pecked out DEAR SIR LAURENCE. THANK YOU FOR YOUR KIND LETTER.

I was making a comeback of sorts with the children, at least in terms of storytelling and reading. As long as I stayed away from *Pigling Bland* I was all right. But I still did not have authority in the house and Papa showed no signs of giving it back to me. During this period, Tessa confided in Sonia Austrian that she wanted to get out of the house because "there are just too many babies here." She was nine now and feeling pressures beyond her years. Much, much later Sonia told me that Tessa regarded me as one of those burdensome babies.

Very rarely was there a disagreement between Papa and me, but this was primarily because I did everything he told me without question. I remember that Christmas I decided to send cards, which he felt was absurd. He told me I was not to, but I wanted to so I bought some. I bought a lot, as a matter of fact. He had hired a secretary to help me with my letters and I set her to addressing this great mound of cards. Papa was furious. He was so completely distraught that he threw everything on my desk into the fire. I thought he had lost his mind. Much later, I noticed my treasured note from Maria was gone and realized it must have been destroyed with the cards.

"What can I do with him?" I implored Val.

She reminded me of something I truly knew. "You would never make it without him."

My sessions with Valerie were continuing on an almost daily basis. No longer working with me just by her wits and intuition, she was collecting a reservoir of information that would eventually help thousands of stroke victims. And she was also collecting anecdotes about her pupil. Here's a favorite; the two of us were talking to an interviewer:

> VAL: You see, *I* can talk. Pat does not have this verbal fluency . . .
> ME: I can talk.
> VAL: But you don't find it easy.
> ME: Yes, I do.
> VAL: But you can't formulate abstract ideas.
> ME: I don't have any abstract ideas.

On New Year's Day, 1966, Papa gave the press an update on my progress. "My wife said today that she feels certain she will be working within twelve months." I felt nothing of the sort and was dismayed that he continued to press me to go back to work. He even got the Oscar down off the shelf and placed it smack in the middle of the sitting room window.

Millie Dunnock, believing the press releases, visited with the intention of getting me interested in acting again. But she gave that up when she saw me. Instead, she graciously warned me that if I did go back to acting, I would have to play roles that were "appropriate to your condition." That did not appeal to me one bit. I was better off at home.

I even gave away the wee replica of Oscar that I constantly wore around my neck. It was at Papa's insistence, but I did so happily—I thought. He was always asking me to give away pieces of jewelry, usually to friends or neighbors who had done me a service, and I never argued. I remember now seeing Claudia Marsh removing a piece of her jewelry and giving it to someone simply because Charles had asked her to.

The wee Oscar, by the way, was restored to me years later and I do wear it today.

Roald got an offer from the producer Cubby Broccoli to do the script for the next James Bond film. It came when we were at the peak of financial worry and Roald accepted immediately. He seemed to feel screenplay writing was less difficult than short stories and he adored sending his drafts to London in a paid-for, chauffeur-driven Rolls-Royce. I used to pretend jealousy that *he* was now being courted by the moguls instead of me. Or was jealousy what I was really feeling?

Still, there seemed to be something in the air for me. Mike Nichols was the first to send out a feeler. The man I had advised not to go into the business was now a major director in Hollywood and wondered if I might be up to doing a part in his new film. It was called *The Graduate*. I told him that I wasn't sure if I could remember lines and I still had a limp. He said that Herbert Marshall had a wooden leg and no one ever noticed it.

Of course, I couldn't have done it on a bet. I don't think anyone could have touched what Annie Bancroft did as Mrs. Robinson. But there was no doubt about it, I did like the feeling of being asked again.

Peter Sellers called, too. He promised to find something for me in his next film, whatever that was to be.

The BBC suggested I repeat my role in the Strindberg play that I had done on American television some years before, the one in which I didn't speak a word. This seemed the most likely possibility, but, although the stroke was a year behind me, it was still too early to consider seriously.

In the spring, the British Motion Picture Academy again named me best foreign actress, this time for *In Harm's Way*. I could not have been more surprised. The ceremonies were held at Grosvenor House in London and I felt up to going. Leslie Caron made the presentation. It was one long walk to the stage and then a laborious eight-step climb to the rostrum. But the waves of love I felt from the audience made it more than worth the trip. I had not heard applause for a long, long time.

You Only Live Twice, the Bond movie, was shot on location in Japan in the summer of 1966, and Papa asked me to join him for two weeks while he was there. He hoped the trip would be a great treat for me, giving me a holiday from my lessons and broadening my horizon, which had narrowed considerably since the stroke. I did go. But I have only the vaguest impression of that country, mostly just memories of sleeping on tatami mats and buying out department stores. And being left standing more than once with a door swinging in my face.

It was just like old times.

During the weeks before Papa got back, I took hold of my home again. I could tell the children to wipe their feet before coming into the house. I could talk to Tessa about her Brownie meetings and give Theo permission to stay overnight with a friend. What is all this fuss about acting? I thought to myself. All I wanted was to be a mother who pots around the house, fusses with her children, tattles with the neighbors over tea and goes shopping. "It's marvelous to go shopping now that Papa's so rich," I told friends. "Do you know he made more money writing that one movie than I ever made in my career?" Of course I would always add, "although *I* won the Oscar."

One night we had the worst thunderstorm I have ever experienced. It seemed endless. My bedroom door swung open and four frightened children descended on me, crawling wildly over me and burying themselves under the covers next to me. I lay there with them all huddled close and actually *thanked* God for the first time in many months for the healing gift of that storm.

Darling Peter Sellers came through with that offer. It was a cameo part in a movie called *What's New, Pussycat?* It was not at all right for me, and although I was grateful, I turned it down. But it gave me a reason to think about activating Harvey. If I was going to get offers again, I should have an agent to say no for me.

Papa returned like Marco Polo just in time for his fiftieth birthday. Sonia and Geoff were with us then. Sonia's first words when she saw me looking so well were, "Well, Tennessee hillbillies don't conk that easy, do they?" Roald adored that line. He filed it away for future use. He had something up his sleeve.

I didn't know what until early the following year. Papa had agreed that I would give a speech in New York in March at a charity dinner for brain-injured children. It would be my debut. Just ten or fifteen minutes, he promised—nothing to perform, I would have my script right there in front of me. Just the right challenge.

"I don't want to do it," I told Val.

"Don't be obstinate," she answered. "Let's give it a go."

Although she truly thought it was too early for me to appear in public, she wouldn't counter Roald without first making sure we tried our very best. But I couldn't believe he seriously intended to have me go out in public and give a speech with less than a month to prepare.

I had already agreed to return to Hollywood for the Oscar ceremonies in the spring, but that would require just a couple of words and I looked forward to it without worry. This dinner was something I dreaded, and I balked at rehearsing the speech Roald wrote for me.

"You'd better get with it," Papa warned. "If you make a botch of it, it'll be curtains for you. All those film moguls will just say, 'Well, that's it, she's through.' "

"And they'll be right! I *cannot* give a speech! I *cannot* remember lines!"

"But you agreed to do it, Pat."

"I did not! You agreed for me!"

"That's hardly the point. The point is that they are counting on you."

The terrible fear of making a fool of myself in front of all my friends began to creep up on me as the days slipped by. I decided I should try to read through the speech.

At first I'd lose my place and stumble over the same words time and time again. But somehow a new energy that I hadn't known before began to overtake me. I plunged in like a professional. The speech never left my hands. I'd work on it all day with Val and read it to Papa and the children every night at supper.

A week before the dinner, we held a kind of dress rehearsal, inviting a dozen or so family and friends to Val's home as a kind of captive audience. Papa had decided that he would not accompany me to New York, that it should be Val, and that was good of him. I liked the idea that Val would share the spotlight. She prepared a short speech to introduce me that evening. I coached her for a change because she was terribly nervous. Astonishingly, I was not. I got through the thirteen-and-a-half-minute trial run smoothly.

I was amazed by the show of interest that greeted me in New York. Flowers and messages from everyone filled our suite at the Waldorf. We had three days in town before the night of the banquet, and nearly all the time was taken up with interviews. Of course, I was asked if I was eager to return to motion pictures. "No," I answered candidly, "I don't want to return to films."

"An Evening with Patricia Neal" was what they called it. The Grand Ballroom at the Waldorf was unbelievable. It seemed that everyone I had ever known and loved was there. Faces that created a mosaic of my past. Lillian. The Premingers. Sharman Douglas. Sonia and Geoff. The Cusicks. Ed and Marian Goodman. Anne and Eli. Lee Strasberg. Gadge. Millie and Keith. Even Beatrice Straight and Peter Cookson.

Valerie was introduced first. She was divine.

Our village is not an important place on anybody's map. But we, like you, love Pat. We started her on a voyage of rediscovery. Everything she had learned throughout her life was still there. It was still available—provided we could reach it. No matter how difficult it was, Pat kept her humor. "Who was Adam?" I asked her. "He was a man," she said, "who had a tempting woman and an apple in his throat."

In the wings I felt perfectly calm and ready. Even when I heard Rock Hudson introduce me and I walked across the stage, I didn't have the slightest trace of fear. The thundering applause was like a warming quilt wrapping itself around me. Everyone in the room was on his feet. A *standing ovation*. I remembered the phrase.

But when I reached the podium, my leg was trembling so badly I thought I would collapse. *Stop shaking!* I commanded almost audibly. And it did. In fact, it has never done it since.

I thank you. I thank you. I thank you. I hope what happened to me never happens to any of you. It was *evil*.

That last just slipped out. It wasn't meant to be part of the speech and it got a tremendous laugh. You see, in Valerie's introduction, she had specifically mentioned that *evil* was a pet phrase I had stopped using.

This thing burst in my head and from that moment on two people took over my life. First there was Roald, who knew what had happened and immediately telephoned exactly the right person, a neurosurgeon. He was the second person. He saved my life—he did—he and that splendid UCLA hospital in California. It wasn't only a fine operation. It was a brave one. I know very well that the doctor thought I would conk out in the middle of it. But Tennessee hillbillies don't conk that easy.

Before I realized it, I had finished the speech. People stood and wept and cheered. I knew then that my life had been given back to me for something more than I had imagined. Mind you, I had no idea what that could possibly be. But I knew at that moment that Roald the slave driver, Roald the bastard, with his relentless scourge, Roald the Rotten, as I had called him more than once, had thrown me back into the deep water.

Where I belonged.

4 | WHAT REMAINS
IS LOVE
1967–1983

CHAPTER FIFTY-ONE

returned, triumphant, to Gipsy House, where I played the tape of my speech at the Waldorf over and over until I thought Papa would go out of his mind. He said I was just in love with myself. He was right. Hearing the speech again and again was like a series of injections of hope. All those months of work with Val had paid off. I had only to turn on the tape machine to prove it. It made it easier to look at the script lying on the table.

The Subject Was Roses was a play I knew. A beautifully written work by Frank Gilroy, it was about an Irish family in the Bronx just after the war, and it had won the Pulitzer Prize. I remembered when it was offered to me to do on Broadway. The production with Irene Dailey, Jack Albertson and Martin Sheen had been acclaimed and won the Tony. Its producer, Edgar Lansbury, and director, Ulu Grosbard, had approached Roald to see if I would be up to returning to work in the movie version. He assured them that I was.

I hated the idea, but that did not stop anybody.

I liked the play when I first read it, and I liked the script for the film. I loved the character of Nettie. I understood her frustration with her husband and her maternal struggle for her child. She was a woman with calluses on her ego. I knew I could play her. I knew it would be a good thing to do. I just did not have any confidence that I would be up to it. Papa, of course, had no doubt that I would do it. And Val also encouraged me. It got to the point where Edgar and Ulu decided they should come over and have a look at me.

They brought Frank Gilroy with them and spent the day at Gipsy House. I remember I made a gorgeous lunch for them. I also looked pretty damned good. Roald made sure of that. He insisted that I put on makeup. When the day was over, they all agreed they wanted me to do the film. They assured me we wouldn't start until early in 1968, which would give me several months to work on memorizing the lines.

The contract was negotiated by Harvey, and he was so thrilled that he didn't even mind working with Roald. Still, there was no celebration when I signed the contract.

Those lovely heights I thought I had reached when I listened to my speech disappeared very soon. I was terrified of the work to be accomplished and the possibility —no, the probability—that I would not be able to do it. I was secretly pleased that everyone knew I didn't want to do the film in the first place, so that if I failed, Roald and Val would get the blame. The bottom line, however, was that I was putting off making a real effort to work.

I had plenty of excuses to procrastinate.

The Motion Picture Academy had invited me to present the Oscar for the best foreign film at the Academy Awards ceremonies that April. It would be my first appearance in Hollywood since the stroke, and I was anxious to do it. Thanks to K. T. Stevens, who offered to look after her, Tessa made the trip with me.

If the ceremony did not have the same crystal ecstasy as that moment at the Waldorf, it was nonetheless another look through a prism of grace. Imagine my happy surprise when an old friend showed up to do my hair for the show. It was Gertrude Wheeler. I wore a divine evening dress that I had bought in one of our village shops. It was not expensive, but it looked like a million dollars.

When I was introduced, the entire auditorium—"my people"—stood up for me. The applause continued for I don't know how long. Harvey gleefully told me later that the ovation cost the network "forty grand." Whatever it cost, it was wasted on my daughter. She was astonished, K. T. told me later, that anyone would applaud Mummy.

As if my welcome back to Hollywood had not been spectacular enough, I had a surprise visit from an actress whom I had never met but had deeply admired for a long time. Katharine Hepburn had heard from mutual friends that I had always wanted to meet her, and she called and came by "for just a few minutes." We spent hours together, and for a recovering stroke victim, I must say I talked her ears off. I told Katharine Hepburn everything that had ever happened to me in my life, and this great lady listened and listened and listened.

I was home only a few weeks when Roald and I made a short visit to Paris—my first in fourteen years. We stayed with Annabella. Then we had a series of visits from old friends—Valerie French, the Goodmans and the Cusicks, and Barry Farrell, who had returned to work on his book—all of which gave me more excuses not to study. Finally, the whole family went to France on holiday for the month of August. Marian and Ed Goodman and their daughters came with us. So did Angela Kirwan and Barry. The more the merrier. Anything to keep from facing the script, which I dutifully took with me.

When the holiday was over, Papa put his foot down. "You are an actress. You were born to be an actress. You will never be fully recovered until you face working again." Reluctantly, I began to study with Val.

With an artful knack for dramatic coincidence, death came once more on November 17. Roald's beloved Mormor died on the fifth anniversary of Olivia's death. It was unexpected. We knew she was ill, but at that moment it was Roald we were more concerned about; he was in the Oxford Hospital for one of his many back operations. He was too ill to attend his mother's funeral. I barely made it myself because I was very sick with the flu. Mormor's funeral was held on the same date Olivia's had been. It reminded me that seven years had passed since bad things had started happening to us. If there was indeed a seven-year curse, maybe it would stop now.

Roald was always a good doctor. But he was a lousy patient. When he went down, the ground heaved as though a great tree had been felled. Mormor had always been especially needed during Roald's many times in the hospital. She would spend hours and hours at his bedside comforting him. I tried my best to show the same tenderness of heart during his ordeal, but he would just close his eyes and suffer alone. Unfortunately, there were nasty complications and the wound from the operation would not close. Roald lost a lot of blood and had to have several transfusions. A second operation was, thank God, successful, and he slowly mended with the loving help of our Nesta Powell, who nursed at the hospital.

Mormor was cremated, as was the practice in the Dahl family, and after Roald recovered, we took her ashes back to Wales. I have often wondered—if I had been able to take on the mantle of Mormor's great maternal role with Roald, would things have turned out differently between us?

We brought home her favorite cactus and put it in our greenhouse in her memory. It grew to an enormous height—right through the roof—and thrived until the day I left Gipsy House. Then it mysteriously died.

In spite of my reluctance, Val worked with me for several hours each day on my lines for *Roses*. She was determined that I would be ready to do the film.

"When you call upon a jackass, he kicks," she reminded me. "We've spent two and a half years preparing you for this. What's your answer?"

"I want to be a thoroughbred!" I replied, and down deep, I meant it.

It was a great relief when Val agreed to come with me to New York for the filming. Still, I did not, did not, did *not* want to get on the plane for New York. It had little to do with stage fright, or even the lingering resentment that doing the movie had not been my decision. It had a lot to do with leaving my children and my home, a primal feeling that left me brooding with a heavy heart on the flight over.

There were a few things to do before rehearsals began. First I had to go through what seemed like hundreds of interviews, during which really only two questions were asked. "Are you happy you're going back to work?" and "Do you think you can do it?"

The answer to the first was that I did not want to do the film, that my husband was making me do it and that I would be perfectly content not to do anything but stay at home.

The answer to the second was, "I hope so."

I also wanted to see an old friend, Peter Cookson. I was anxious to mend a long-ago-torn fence. I had come across his letters and felt such tenderness when I reread them, not for our past relationship—God knows we were not meant to be—but for a special young man, so vulnerable in his love.

Peter and his wife, Beatrice, accepted my invitation to come to supper, and when we finished the meal, she and Val graciously left Peter and me alone. I was finally able to tell him how sorry I was for what I had put him through all those years ago. Peter assured me that his presence at the Waldorf on my big night had said whatever needed to be said.

Just before the film began I was invited to receive the Heart of the Year award from President Johnson at the White House. Barry Farrell and the *Roses* publicist, Lars McSorley, flew to Washington, D.C., with me. Shortly before our scheduled arrival, the plane developed serious trouble. The wheels would not go down and the captain announced that we were returning all the way to Kennedy Airport because "they had better fire-fighting equipment." Well, that cut it. Poor Barry broke out in a cold sweat. He thought his life was over. So did most everyone else on board. Oddly enough, I was not frightened. I was certain that we would make it and set about relieving the tension.

"I think we all deserve a free martini," I declared. The surprised stewardess quickly brought a tray.

"I'd like to propose a toast to you and you and you," I announced grandly, "and to all the people we're leaving behind."

I'm not sure they appreciated my gallows humor, but they drank to it.

Even when we were preparing for a crash landing, I remember knowing that we would be saved, that someone up there, maybe even a loving God, still had something in mind for me. When we felt *wheels* hit the ground, everyone sent up a cheer. Then I noticed there was one other passenger who had not despaired. Lars, a publicity man to the end, had been busily writing out press releases.

I was thrilled to meet the president of the United States but not in the least nervous. That is, not until my car turned into the west portico of the White House and the guard asked for identification. I had none. Not my passport or any other official paper. All I could produce for identification was my checkbook! I was mortified, but he smiled and said, with a twinkle in his eye, "Oh, I recognize you, ma'am," and let us pass.

President Johnson was very kind to me. He pointed out that we shared this honor from the American Heart Association. He had been its recipient in 1959, following his heart attack. I remember we got kind of folksy and compared hospital stories. He asked what my first memory was when I came out of my coma and I told him it was probably my husband smoking a cigarette. He said that his was just as basic. Shortly before his surgery, Lady Bird had ordered three new suits from his tailor—a blue, a gray and a tan. He said he woke up from the operation thinking he would like to be buried in the blue one.

On the first day of rehearsals for *The Subject Was Roses,* I seethed in a cold anger toward Roald and Valerie. I could not believe that they had put me in this position. I liked my costars, Jack Albertson and Martin Sheen, but I couldn't thaw out that day. My stroke had put me in another rhythm for the past three years, and my clumsy body was out of the acting habit. Jack and

Martin were repeating their stage roles and were letter-perfect in their lines. Even Val knew every word in the script. I was totally stymied by trying to remember even a few. The second day brought no change in my attitude. I could find no excitement in me for acting. I wanted to go home.

On the third day I actually felt myself responding a little to the words. Gilroy's dialogue was so real. It was the kind with which I would have had no difficulty in the past. I began to work more earnestly with Val on the set and every night in our hotel suite. We rarely left the room, not even for meals. I was going to prove to myself that I could do it again.

But by the time we got into the actual filming, something else was at play. There was such appreciation from Jack and Martin, I began to realize I was doing it for them, too. And for Ulu, a director of great considerateness who made me feel that everything I did came from the soul of Nettie Cleary, and all he had to do was select the treasures. I was finally again part of something for which I was needed and effective.

Jack and Martin were really extraordinary. They were kind and patient and convinced me I could not fail. We were forming special relationships with tiny affectionate threads. The day Martin and I did the polka scene—the son whirls his mother around the room in one of the film's happier moments—he was apprehensive that my bum leg would give way and I'd take a tumble. At every turn he would whisper, "Hey, I'm the one who's supposed to lead!"

I have a special place in my heart for Jack. He would constantly entertain me with his jokes. And, I mean, he had a warehouse of them. He would always begin by asking if I had heard the one about this or that, and I would always tell him it didn't matter if I had, I wouldn't remember it anyway.

The filming was done entirely in the New York area with one location at the Jersey shore, just a few miles from Point Pleasant, where Eugene O'Neill used to live. People who came to watch us were not only fans who wanted to see a movie being made. Many were stroke victims, some in wheelchairs, some relearning to walk and talk, and all seemed to take pride and pleasure in the fact that their Patricia was making it again. The outside world was becoming an intimate place for me.

Press interest in my comeback did not wane after the coverage of my arrival. In fact, it seemed to accelerate during production. It was soon clear that the press was not going to leave me alone. Scads of requests to interview me on the set came in, and there was some discussion of whether I should accommodate the press while I was working. I had no objection to keeping the set open. My basic training in Hollywood had come during a time when performers believed that courting the press was a professional responsibility, and I always considered it part of my job. I found interviews stimulating. They made me think and talk and develop confidence.

Roald interrupted his work on a new film, *Chitty Chitty Bang Bang,* to come over for the 1968 Gala for Brain Injured Children at Madison Square Garden, which I had helped plan with my friend Sharman Douglas. I think he also came to have a look at what I was doing.

Roald watched the filming of one of the major scenes between Jack and me—one that follows a happy night on the town, which the husband mistakes for a reconciliation. The wife has the wonderful line, "One nice evening doesn't make everything different." We shot the scene over and over from every angle, and I didn't miss a word. When we finished, I walked over to Roald.

"Well, what do you think?" I asked. "Am I any good?"

"You're marvelous," he answered. "Marvelous." Then he did something that he rarely did in public. He put his arm around my shoulder as we walked to my dressing room.

"It's all because of you, Papa," I told him. "You're a great man. I love you more than anyone in the world." And I meant it.

* * *

Ever since the start of the film I had been dreading Nettie's long, long scene with her son. In the old days I would have wept with joy for the chance to do a five-page monologue. Val and I had prepared for this scene for months, and I was sure I knew those lines, but I also knew that Ulu planned to shoot the entire scene in one take, and that terrified me.

When the night of the shooting came, the fear of forgetting those lines became such physical terror my guts were in a knot. I remember we shot on the roof of a real tenement somewhere in the city. God, it was so cold we were wrapped in blankets and had to use hand warmers. Val was at my side, but we both knew there was no more rehearsing. It had to be in me.

I saw teleprompters, which had my lines written on them, on both sides of the set. Now, I thought, I can act and stop worrying about remembering.

When the camera began rolling I felt the flush of fear turn into energy, and the words came. I may have glanced at the prompters, I can't remember now. But before I knew it, we had done the scene—the whole scene in one take, and I had not stopped.

We shot it several more times from different angles, and each time it went well. When in the early morning hours Ulu called a wrap, the crew burst into applause. Ulu and Martin and I were one big hug.

I was a working actress again. I could do anything now —with help.

CHAPTER FIFTY-TWO

*T*he Subject Was Roses turned out to be one of the most satisfying experiences of my career. I had been sure I could not do it, but I not only did it, I did it well.

Not that I had doubted my talent. No, I had never once during my illness believed the stroke had affected the talent. Memory and movement, yes, but my brain never stopped understanding how people think and feel. I did limp and my right hand felt awkward, which bothered me when I saw the film, but it was not all that noticeable to others. At the beginning I struggled with every single line, and by the time the production ended I could master five pages without the help of a monitor.

I remember one sequence written for the film in which Nettie "runs away" for a day. She takes a bus and goes back to the little beach town where she spent her honeymoon. Most of the day she just walks along the shore, thinking. Ulu kept the camera on me as he talked me through the scene. There was no dialogue, but the audience must feel what she is feeling. I don't usually quote reviews, but I couldn't have been more pleased when one reviewer said, "I have never seen acting in a purer form than that walk down the beach." The *Time* critic wrote, "She no longer indicates suffering, she defines it." I forget who those gentlemen were, but I thank them for that.

On October 13, 1968, *The Subject Was Roses* premiered in New York City. Roald made a rare appearance as my escort. The moment I entered the theater, there was a standing ovation. It was amazing. I was being applauded *before* I performed or even uttered a word. I was a hit—just for being alive.

Two days later, MGM premiered the film again in Los Angeles and decided to have the banquet before the screening so I would not get tired. I not only stayed through the film, but remained into the wee hours at the post-premiere celebration, basking in my new role as a living legend.

Before I left Hollywood I tried to call old friends. Unfortunately, names just would not shake loose from my brain and I would sometimes forget whom I was calling before I got an answer. I had just seen Paul Newman's film *Rachel, Rachel* and had to tell him how much I adored it. I called, and when he picked up the phone, I remember saying, "Oh—what *is* your name?—You did it beautifully."

One of the most touching memories I have of those few days is of Barbara Stanwyck, and she probably wouldn't remember it at all. When we were introduced in the bar at the Beverly Hills Hotel, she took my hand and said, "You're gorgeous."

"Oh," I laughed, "you finally saw *The Fountainhead?*"

But this great lady was having none of my joke. She looked me squarely in the eye and said, "I admire you very much." And I thank her, too, for that.

The trip for the premieres turned out to be one of my longest stays in America since I had lived there, and it brought me back to my roots.

First, I went to Texas to see my brother, Pete. Pete had grown into a fine man. He was a teacher now, and I was so proud of him. He and his lovely young wife, Charlcie, had just had their first child, Celia Ann. They were so thrilled because a photographer was following me around recording my reunions for a magazine piece. Pete got some great baby pictures—free. Then I went on to Atlanta to see Mother, NiNi and George, my lovely young niece Ann Neal, and my strapping nephew Dutch, who was already starting college.

Although I don't recall any great emotional scenes, our reunion was, for all of us, nothing less than a miracle. For my family and friends, I had returned from the grave. I even had a yellow watermelon. One of the most fabulous things in the world to me still is a yellow watermelon.

I stopped in Chicago to fulfill a promise I had made to Henry Betts, the head of the Chicago Rehabilitation Institute, to speak at the ground-breaking ceremonies for their new hospital. I shall never forget that day. It was very cold and dark as I lifted the first shovelful of dirt. But when I started to speak, the sky was suddenly pierced by a shaft of sunlight. It was as if the light spoke an imperative: This hospital will be a great success.

Following the speech, I was taken to talk with some of the Institute's patients. More than half of the seventy people there were stroke victims, many paralyzed and confined to wheelchairs or stretchers. I found I was very comfortable with them. We were all damaged. And when I saw determination and the will to go on in their eyes, I felt proud of them.

My message that day was a simple one: Rehabilitation is not pleasant and it takes work, work, work. And then I shared my story. When I finished, a very old, severely impaired woman struggled long moments before she was able to say, "You are an inspiration to all of us." I was so deeply moved that I could not answer. Had that light also said something to *me?* Was I to stand as a promise that no one ever had to accept defeat?

I returned to England and got my wish to stay home. There were no great job offers after *The Subject Was Roses,* even though I had again been nominated for a best actress Oscar. I told interviewers I was a housewife and mother again and loved every minute of my needlepoint-and-tatting domestic life—even though I now had the help of a maid, a cook and a secretary who was also my driver. I did cook a meal once or twice a week and took a special delight in gardening. One of the best things I did was weed.

With the money Mormor had left us, Papa had a fabulous covered swimming pool built that had its own dressing rooms and kitchen. It was the first such pool in Great Missenden, and it was a rare day, indeed, when half the village population under twelve was not splashing around in it. Papa also used it a lot, but I did not. I could swim, but now it seemed like therapy and not recreation.

For all outward signs, we had returned to a normal life again; in some ways it was even better than normal. During those years Roald's career blossomed. He was now the prosperous one. All his children's books were internationally popular, and that year, 1969, *Charlie and the Chocolate Factory* was sold to the films. The Gipsy House walls now boasted Matisse, Picasso, Bacon and Popova, and our furniture bore the names of Chippendale and Gibbons, none of which, I'm shocked to say, was ever insured. Papa just did not believe in it. Success did not mellow my husband. Quite the contrary, it only enforced his conviction that although life was a two-lane street, he had the right of way.

Friends were getting the Dahl treatment on a regular basis once more. Sonia Austrian confided that when we were in New York, she had called to say she might drop by to see me and Roald had demanded that she make an appointment. She thought that was a bit much. So did I. And the dear Dulantys, who had been our friends for years, dropped out of our lives because of a fight with Roald. Roald told me the argument was over nothing. But how could nothing have caused Brian to throw him out of the house?

I left the weeding for a quick trip to the Oscar ceremonies. I did not win, but Jack Albertson did. And well he deserved it.

Pat and Roald, Barry Farrell's book, was about to be published. Roald and I had not exercised our approval rights because we trusted Barry completely. But Roald's agent had seen galleys and insisted that we take a look. I was appalled. Not only had he included details of our home life that were nobody's business, but also it was clear he had not understood me at all. I felt cut to pieces. Papa objected too, to a lesser degree, and contacted Barry at once to request cuts and changes. Barry was furious, insisting that we had ruined his book. He remained angry with us for years, and I have always regretted that he died before we could make peace between us.

About a week before we were to take our annual vacation in Norway, Papa had a nose operation to correct his breathing. He seemed to be pretty well mended, so we kept to our plan. The day after we arrived, that nose began to bleed. Nothing would stop it. I remember thinking of *Cyrano de Bergerac*—"When it bleeds, the red sea!" The poor man had to be rushed to the hospital, where they kept pushing things into his nostrils while he screamed his lungs out. I remained with him all night, sleeping on the floor of his room. He stayed in the hospital for the duration of our holiday and I dutifully visited him twice a day. Once I brought him a great bunch of grapes. He loved grapes, and I was sure he would be pleased. "I don't want your grapes," he growled. I protested that they were good grapes and cost a lot of money in Norway and shoved them into his hand anyway. Do you know what he did? He threw the damn things right out the window! I didn't know why he was so angry.

I think now that he was already growing tired of me.

CHAPTER
FIFTY-THREE

n 1970 I appeared for the first time on the *Good Housekeeping* poll of the most-admired women in America. I was alongside Pearl Buck, Golda Meir, the Kennedy women, Mrs. Martin Luther King, Jr. and Mrs. Gandhi.

How ironic, because at home I had the affection of my children and the concern of my husband, but I had not regained the dignity and respect of a mother and wife by any means.

Outside my home I was impaired but again at the top of my profession, and as awesome and frightening as it seemed, my mere presence could be an inspiration. I could be applauded before I said a word. Yet my darling Tessa wondered, in all innocence and sincerity, why anyone would applaud Mummy.

Because inside my home, I was merely impaired.

I had not reentered my family as I had hoped. They were disappointed in me for not fulfilling their needs and I hated myself for feeling inadequate. My children always had plenty of love for me, but they regarded me as a peer with whom they vied for Papa's attentions. Or they totally ignored me.

I remember a lovely dinner ring Roald had given me. One day I discovered it was missing and I recalled seeing Ophelia playing with it. I was sure she had made off with it. Even though she was in school, I was so annoyed that

I walked there and asked to see her immediately. When I questioned her about it, she said she had lost it. But I could see it made no difference to her one way or the other. All the children were like that. They felt that they could get away with anything with me. It was as if I didn't matter.

It is difficult to write about this now, because I do not want to impose guilt on my children. At the same time, I cannot say honestly that I was to blame.

I was still not considered adequate to center the life of our maturing family. Any decisions about the children and their futures were still made by Papa, and I was informed of them. All the girls were now at Godstowe and Downe House—Roedean was a bust with our Tessa —and Theo was now going to Caldicott because Roald had held to his conviction that our son be kept in a regular school. "I want a mother for my children," he had demanded of the doctors after the stroke, but he no longer felt any need for one.

Roald did not give me authority, and I would not take it because I feared my inadequacy would be exposed. I could forget something, some connection, a phone call or a date, or else my physical clumsiness could cause a problem. I might just screw things up.

I found it impossible to maneuver the stairs with a tea tray. So when I knew Papa wanted tea, I would put the cup down on the step, three ahead of me, and then climb up after it. Of course, by the time I got to the top, the tea was no longer hot and he wouldn't want it. It got to the point where Roald did not wish me to do anything for him.

I desperately wanted to serve my children, but mine was in no way the selfless, hidden service of a healthy mother who does her job and never has to be noticed or thanked. I felt I deserved a mother's respect and consideration and resented their indifference. I was still wrestling with my own selfishness, which many individuals recovering from a long illness must do. And I was, emotionally, very much a child and needed constant reassurance and attention. When I didn't get it, I could conjure the blackest of moods.

I would even slink back into that state of mind where I simply did not give a damn about trying to keep anything together. Then the family would just move on without me.

In the old days we used to hike up Beacon Hill. It was not an undemanding feat and I always shared the thrill of the conquest and the great view from the top. When we went after my stroke, the children ran after Roald and left me standing by the car to wait. Not once did they turn back, and not one of them suggested waiting with me. I was left there, and it hurt.

When they returned they were flushed with excitement, but no one offered to share one bit of the experience with me.

Granted, by then I was so mad I was as hard as a stone —hardly an appealing welcome.

I could only hope my children would turn out all right, because I felt I had no way to influence them. My illness and its wounds had been presented to them as a weakness —something to overcome, but not to reflect on or learn from. There was no reverence for that sort of thing in Roald and he transmitted his feelings well to young minds.

For seven years I was securely a part of that "most-admired" list. But at home, I felt a sense of danger. I was being x'd out of my family.

CHAPTER
FIFTY-FOUR

Roald simply could not abide my career standing still. He wrote a movie for me based on Joy Cowley's novel *Nest in a Falling Tree*. It was about a woman just my age, a recovered stroke victim who has had to learn to walk and talk and live all over again. If it sounds especially tailored to me, the coincidence was purely intentional. The similarity, however, ends there; the character gets involved with a homicidal maniac. Roald dashed off to Hollywood to set up the financing. This began a procession of films throughout the 1970s in which I would play a woman having to deal with serious illness in one way or another.

We were not often in touch during this trip. He was "so busy" that he asked me to wait for his calls and not try to reach him. Sort of a don't-call-me-I'll-call-you arrangement. So I was astonished when he arrived home with a beautiful new set of capped teeth.

Before the film started we took our annual vacation in Norway, and I was surprised to find a letter waiting for Roald at the Strand Hotel in Arendal. It was from a strange lady he said he had met at the Beverly Hills Hotel during his trip. I was slightly miffed, but agreed when he insisted we give a big supper party at Gipsy House for this same lady, who was coming to England with her father.

Our guests of honor turned out to be a tall shapely

woman for whom the word "broad" seemed aptly coined, and her short fat daddy, who looked and sounded like Al Capone.

During the evening, the "gangster's daughter" directed all her attention to Roald. She did not stop making cute remarks to him, which met with his appreciative laughter and which angered me—noticeably. I became very cold to her, and she was cold to me. My debonair husband seemed to enjoy this, as did our other guests, who were tittering at the show. By the time the "lady" left, I was really pissed. Later, of course, I did what I always did, I just let it go. I trusted my instinct completely when I was acting. I rarely did in real life.

Roald's movie, eventually released in 1971 as *The Night Digger*, was filmed in a crumbling old mansion on the road to Windsor Castle. I received no salary for it. It simply would not have been made had I demanded anything close to my fee. Both Roald and I took expenses only, but would have shared in the profits had there been any.

It was a very difficult picture for me. Valerie came to help with the lines, but my coworkers did not have the generous spirit of Jack Albertson and Martin Sheen and I sensed their impatience when I stumbled.

I also remember distinctly, on more than one occasion, hearing them making fun of me. Brain-damaged people can sense when someone is mocking them. We grow antennae.

All in all, *The Night Digger* brings back hard memories, and I didn't get a nickel for doing it.

Fortunately, I had no time to brood. Roald had written a TV documentary called "Stroke Counter Stroke" to help educate brain-damaged people and their families about our process of rehabilitation. Valerie and I both worked in it, and so did Roald. He's a wonderful writer but, I must say, one terrible actor.

I began to get invitations to attend conferences in England and America on the subject of strokes and how to cope with them. Before long, the invitations included requests to speak, which Papa urged me to do even though these engagements would take me away from home frequently. He wrote a wonderful, very simple speech for me that retold the story of my stroke and the subsequent months of rehabilitation.

From the very first, I loved doing it. I really *loved* talking to people. We set up a program. If they could pay my fare, I was on my way. I could afford to do it for free in those days.

Valerie's own book, *A Stroke in the Family,* was published and became very well respected in its field. She had established The Chest, Heart and Stroke Association in England, thus extending her healing gift to thousands of others. I was pleased that Val's work, which had gotten short shrift, was beginning to get the recognition it deserved.

Best of all, I was asked to present an award to both Roald and Valerie from The Speech Rehabilitation Institute at the Plaza Hotel in New York. The recognition was for their intensive home therapy experiments, which had saved my own life and were now being introduced in America as The Patricia Neal Therapy Extension Program. There are now many stroke centers in the United States and England utilizing their revolutionary system.

There was a note of sadness, too, at this time. One morning I picked up a newspaper and turned first to the obituary page, as I admit I always do. Peter Douglas's wife, Virginia, had died of cancer. I was heartbroken for Peter and wrote him at once.

While we were in New York I received my first Hollywood job offer since *The Subject Was Roses*. My old friend Fielder Cook sent me a script called "The Homecoming." It was for television, a Christmas story about a rural Virginia family during the Depression. It was perfect for me.

So I became Olivia Walton. The character was almost renamed Mary, but I told Fielder I really wouldn't want to do it unless I could keep the original name. I intended it to be an homage to my beautiful firstborn.

I had no idea how difficult that would be. The writer, Earl Hamner, who based the story on his own family, had previously sold a script about them to Warner Brothers. It was called "Spencer's Mountain." So in addition to the story, Warners owned the *names* of the characters. Earl got them to look the other way. I kept the name.

I found it surprisingly easy to slip back into southern speech patterns. It helped, of course, that I was surrounded by unreconstructed southerners on the set. Fielder was from Georgia. Earl is a Virginian. And one of my costars, Edgar Bergen, claimed his parents emigrated from *southern* Sweden.

Because the producer was fearful of asking me to work outdoors in the rugged location scenes, I was scheduled to finish my part early and in Hollywood. But I insisted on going on to Wyoming with the company. I wasn't paid for the extra time, but I loved the cast so much I didn't want to leave. Besides, I had always wanted to see Jackson Hole in the winter.

As long as I'd known Fielder I had wanted to work with him but never had. I thought of him as the John Ford of television. In addition to the wonderful Richard Thomas, who played my eldest, there were seven nippers in the cast, and each one became very special to me. Little Kami Cotler, who played my baby daughter in the film, sent me Christmas presents for years.

The Homecoming was not shown in England, so I was thrilled to arrange a private viewing for family and friends at the local hall in Great Missenden. I was rarely thought of as anyone other than Mrs. Dahl in the village, so whenever friends saw me on the screen, it was as much fun for them as seeing a member of their own family.

I received an Emmy nomination for my Olivia Walton but lost to Glenda Jackson, a lady whom I had never met. The show continued, of course, as the long-running series "The Waltons." Why didn't I do the series? Simple. No one asked me.

My next job was for darling Lionel Jeffries in a film called *The Boy,* which was released as *Baxter.* I played a speech therapist who works with a mentally disturbed boy. It was a film I thoroughly enjoyed doing, especially because I could tip my hat to the people who had helped bring about my own recovery.

I made a good friend in Lynn Carlin, who was also in the cast. Coincidentally, she was a friend of Maureen Cookson, Peter's first wife, the lady I shot down in Denver all those years ago. When the film finished, I begged Lynn to let her friend know how deeply sorry I was. Lynn did, indeed, deliver my message—not long before Maureen Cookson died of cancer. I was grateful when Lynn assured me I had found forgiveness with her.

I went back to Hollywood, but this time not for movies. I was asked to read a commentary for a medical film about cancer in women. I wanted to do that for Maureen Cookson and Virginia Douglas.

In the spring of 1972 Papa, Valerie and I were all invited to participate in stroke conferences in the South. Since our expenses would be paid to Savannah, I insisted that we continue on to Knoxville and Williamsburg. I especially wanted to bring my two teachers, Valerie and Emily Mahan Faust, together. I so wanted them to like each other, and they did. Emily's husband, Hugh, was most smitten with Val and behaved like a schoolboy, while dear Emily watched and smiled.

You might think I had more guts than brains to bring my husband back into the cradle of my family, but things could not have gone more smoothly. It remained for Aunt Maude to be the one member of the Neal family to win the heart of Roald Dahl. Not that she needed it, but she had the help of our Uncle Sid Peavley's Kentucky moonshine whiskey. Roald discovered gold. He just had to bring some back to England to serve Gipsy House guests after dinner. To surprise him, I also packed an extra bottle. I was the one who got the surprise. At home I discovered to my great horror that somewhere over the Atlantic Uncle Sid's hooch had exploded in my suitcase.

CHAPTER FIFTY-FIVE

Felicity Crossland was good-looking. When she appeared at the door of Gipsy House one morning carrying a huge box with Ambers Dress Shop written on it, my first impression was that she knew how to please.

Felicity was a free-lance coordinator working for David Ogilvy's advertising agency at the time. In turn, the agency worked for General Foods, my new boss.

I had not done commercials before, but I didn't mind the idea at all. Roald had negotiated a good fee for my services as the spokeswoman for Maxim Coffee for one year, which would be upped for a second year "if it all worked out."

I said I would do it if I could test the coffee to see if I liked it. This pleased Jane Maas, the tiny, lovely advertising lady under whose wing I had been placed and who would guide me through four years of pitching coffee beans on television. There was a new legal regulation for celebrity endorsements that demanded we test the product for several months before a commercial could be filmed. This rule went into effect shortly after an actor who was appearing in commercials for a shaving product was asked on television if he really liked the stuff. The actor had answered that he didn't know because he had never used it.

Roald had to drink the coffee, too, because he would

be referred to in the spots. Coffee had to be a "husband-pleaser" or it did not sell, and Maxim felt *I* was the lady who could best convince American women that I would *never* do anything my husband did not like—including giving him a lousy cup of coffee. Fortunately, Papa and I really did like Maxim.

Jane came to England for the filming of the first two commercials because she thought it would be easier for me to be near home. I must say I was treated like the *grandest* of *dames* doing the most important film of the century. General Foods fetched me in limousines, gave Roald script approval and arranged the shooting schedule to suit me. I didn't even have to leave the house for wardrobe fittings.

The first commercial found me poised to serve Roald his morning coffee. The second was an after-dinner scene in which I purred that this was my favorite time of the day, when the children were in bed and I could be alone with my husband. And, of course, a good cup of coffee.

It was for this scene that Felicity Crossland had brought me a selection of dresses from which to choose. Or actually, for Papa to choose, since he was approving everything. All told, she had made three trips to Ambers on her search, but insisted she gladly would have made ten more.

The box contained an absolutely gorgeous brown silk evening dress with a shirt-style top and yards of pleated paisley skirt that Felicity felt would be the perfect outfit for me. I certainly agreed. The young lady obviously knew her job.

During the filming, which was in a graceful old house in London that she had also found, Felicity rarely left my side. While I sold coffee in my beautiful brown dress, she sat on the floor staring up at me, her eyes dewy with admiration. I thought, what a lovely girl.

Roald complained that there was far too much fuss and feathers about doing a commercial, but he admitted he liked the Maxim people, especially Felicity, whom he felt was the most professional one in the bunch. When it was over, he insisted we take all of them for a big celebration at the Curzon Club.

The Maxim commercial did succeed as we had hoped. American women liked me and began writing in, asking that I be shown in my own kitchen. The agency went for it. Because the rest of the commercials were shot in New York, where I now would be at least four times a year, a set "re-creating" my own home was constructed.

It seemed all of New York recognized me on the street because of my new association with coffee. I remember even "21" brought out jars of Maxim with hot water, making a special exception whenever Sue Conrad and I lunched there.

Sue was one of the young account executives at Ogilvy & Mather, a sweet girl who was never too busy to look after my personal needs. She would have remained only that, had it not been for British Airways. Sue and her beau, David, meant to drop me off at Kennedy, but my flight was delayed and they offered to wait with me. We had a drink and became better acquainted. When my plane finally took off, five hours later, we were not only better acquainted, I had talked them into tying the knot. They were married on January 20, 1973, my birthday.

Felicity—or Liccy, as she was nicknamed—soon became a familiar face at our house. She was Catholic, divorced, and lived in a flat in London near the Albert Bridge. Tessa even stayed there overnight with her. Felicity was very well bred, from high English society. In fact, her blood was tinged with blue.

Little by little she ingratiated herself with thoughtfulness and favors. She always brought gifts, mainly for the children, who adored her, but I remember one wedding anniversary when Roald surprised me with some dresses. They were nothing at all like what he would have chosen, and I thought I recognized Felicity's fine eye in them. When we had problems with our nanny, Felicity arranged to send us a Spanish woman who had worked for her. I, in turn, introduced my new friend to the chemist and the shopkeepers in Great Missenden, and included her in our family outings to London.

And quite often she joined Roald and me at the Curzon Club. I did not really like gambling all that much, not since college when I won a poker game with a whole trainful of soldiers on furlough. Now I usually just played the slot machine with a careful eye on my shillings. In Felicity, Roald had finally found someone who adored the tables as much as he. Felicity absolutely loved to gamble, and she usually wound up a winner.

CHAPTER FIFTY-SIX

My relationship with at least one of my children was about to be altered—and all because I blurted out a question without thinking.

Darren McGavin's wife, Kathie, sent me a script they were producing called *Happy Mother's Day—Love George*. It was a so-so little thriller, but it had three good roles for women. I said yes to one of the parts and Cloris Leachman, a friend since Northwestern, happily said yes to another. When Kathie told me the third role, that of my daughter, was yet to be cast, I asked, "What about my Tessa?"

The idea went down well with everyone but Roald. He was horrified that I would even think of suggesting our fifteen-year-old leave school, especially to make a film. But Tessa was ecstatic. And persuasive. Darren went to England to hear her read for it. After only one reading, Tessa got the part.

The filming began in Nova Scotia almost immediately, which did, indeed, necessitate Tessa's leaving school. I was surprised by Tessa's natural talent. I was equally surprised that I had little, if any, of the stage mother in me. I let Tessa find her own way with the director, which paid off—if not in her performance (which I thought was better than mine), then certainly in a new mother-daughter bonding.

It looked as if Tessa had found what she wanted to do

with her life, and I was overjoyed. When she returned to Downe House, she was immediately chosen for one of the leads in the school's Shakespearean play. But during rehearsals she abruptly left school—just walked out and never returned. I always suspected that because she was now looked upon as a "movie star," the pressure she felt was just too much. I suggested getting her an apprenticeship at the Barter Theatre, where I had begun thirty-one years before, as much to keep her in an educational atmosphere as to prepare her for an acting career.

The mother-daughter team continued with an appearance on a television show called "Movin' On," which featured another Northwestern alum, Claude Akins. We also did a Maxim commercial together. Tessa took my advice and signed up for a summer at the Barter.

But Roald was ultimately right. Acting was not Tessa's cup of tea. She had talent but was just not driven. She tried modeling for a while, but it wasn't until she had a family that Tessa found her true calling. Just recently, she delighted all of us by revealing an exceptional writing talent. Her first work, a book for children, will soon be published.

I got my own invitation to go back to school. Knoxville High School's class of '43 was planning its thirty-year reunion and wanted the actress who played the lead in *And Along Came Spring* to be the guest of honor. The school was graciously asking almost a year in advance to make sure I would be able to come. I assured them nothing would keep me from being there.

With the Maxim campaign into its second year and thriving, I found myself returning to America every three months.

It was during one of these stays in New York that I met Maria Cooper again.

After receiving her note during my recovery, I had scrawled an answer in my revolting handwriting: "I very much want to see you." Although we had exchanged polite phone calls a few times when I came to New York, the promised meeting never seemed possible. Until one day, when she suddenly agreed to come for breakfast.

I was so excited. It seems silly, but I kept wondering what I should feed her. I decided to have the hotel send up sweet rolls and English muffins, marmalade, crispy bacon and orange juice. I waited for her knock as if I were waiting for the curtain to open on a play I thought I'd never see.

None of my preparations could have anticipated her gift. When at last Maria arrived, she spread her arms open to me. She held me and the years of emptiness between Gary and me were over.

It was a morning of breakthrough for us both, and perhaps for the first time since my stroke, I intuited an amazing grace that my illness had given me. Somehow, a memory that once had the power to wound me now passed benignly through my head. I was not able to understand it at that moment. That would come later.

Maria finally asked, "Is it true that you were pregnant by my father?"

"Yes. I am so sorry I didn't have it."

"It's my loss, too. I'm the only one."

Then a familiar crinkle formed around her eyes. So like Gary's. "It could have been a helluva lot of fun with you for a—shall we say—stepmother?"

"It could have been plain hell, too. Look at me now."

"I'm looking, Pat, and you're beautiful."

Before Maria left that morning she said, "Promise me one thing. That you will write to my mother. You must do that. She is now Mrs. John Converse."

"I wouldn't know what to say."

"You will," she said, jotting down an address, and she left.

CHAPTER FIFTY-SEVEN

t was one excited and happy Patsy Neal on her way to Knoxville to relive lovely carefree days three decades past. For nine months there had been periodic calls to remind me to save the May 19 weekend for the Class of '43 reunion. Over half of the 395 graduates would be there, some coming from almost as far away as I. My only concern as I headed to America was my speech. Papa, who had little tolerance for this kind of nonsense, flatly refused to write one for me. I would be on my own.

As usual, I changed planes in Atlanta and anticipated a short, joyous visit at the airport with my brother and his family. Pete and Charlcie were waiting, but their faces were somber as they pulled me into the privacy of a cloakroom. "We have something to tell you," Pete began, but before he could get out another word his eyes welled with tears. Without knowing why, I started to cry, too.

My young nephew, Dutch, NiNi's boy, had been cave diving in Florida and had drowned. His burial would be in a few days.

There was no way I could go to the funeral. I called NiNi and promised to come see her before returning to England. The rest of the family was astonished that I would not be there, but NiNi understood. I had to take that plane to Knoxville. The reunion had been planned around me. It was almost a professional commitment. I had given my word.

I was glad I went. I was the center of attention the entire two days and I shamelessly enjoyed every moment. I don't think any group had followed my life and career more closely than the people back home. With my not-so-right head, they knew more about me than I did.

I do not remember one word of what I passed off as my speech, but Anne Fonde Walter, our generous hostess, told me I said that what I remembered most about those days thirty years ago were the football games, Glenn Miller and Kathryn Stubley's bosoms.

In 1973 we also lost our dear Leslie Hansen and John Logsdail, my two brothers-in-law. Death was not new to me, and as I moved toward my half-century mark, it began to fetch family and friends with an ever-decreasing shock. Death now came as a matter of course.

At nearly fifty I had no illusions about myself as a late-blooming glamour girl. When I was home, I was what I was, an English housewife. I bought my clothes at Ambers in Amersham, kept the same hairstyle and had long since given up wearing much makeup. But I was noticing sags on my face that were getting serious. These were not caused by age. My stroke had left one eye and one side of my mouth weakened and drooping. My sister-in-law Asta insisted that I consider a face-lift. She knew of a fine surgeon. I declined at the moment, but filed the suggestion away under unfinished business.

That particular business almost got finished sooner than expected. Roald and I went to Switzerland to visit Theo, who was now studying there, and we had a terrible auto accident in a snowstorm. My face smashed into the windshield and I needed twelve stitches to repair my mouth. I also suffered a concussion. Roald, who carried on so, moaning over and over that he was dying, only split his gorgeous California caps. The next day we snapped pictures of each other, him with his crooked teeth and me with my puffy face, and we were hysterical. But then, he always went for the bizarre. And for a time, even this small adversity brought us closer again.

In January 1974 Roald and I went to Tobago in the West Indies for a golf tournament. It was a fabulous two weeks, the first time we had been away from home together since Japan. Roald had once been a great golfer with a scratch handicap, and he was in fine form. Outrageously witty, too. He charmed everyone at the event. Including me. We got along so well that I started to think of Tobago as our second honeymoon.

For the next many months my life slipped into a predictable back-and-forth schedule of Maxim commercials in New York, then home, stroke speeches wherever, then home. The comfortable monotony was occasionally broken by a side trip whenever I could wangle free lodging from friends like Phyllis Jenkins or Gloria Stroock Stern or Sue Conrad Pollack. But for whatever reason, I was now spending a great deal of time away from home. With Papa's blessing.

And so, in June 1974 when I returned to England, it was like so many other returns, with Papa and Theo meeting me at the airport. Except Roald was strangely cold. I had brought gifts, but he threw my packages aside and went to shoot billiards, and totally ignored the fact that I was back. I lit up a cigarette, as I now did too many times a day, and chalked it off to a bad mood. I had other things on my mind. I had finally decided to have the face surgery and was due to go into the hospital the following afternoon.

The whole ordeal was agony. I developed a cigarette cough following surgery and burst open all the stitches in my face and scalp. The angry doctor had to come back that night and redo the operation. When I was finally able to look at my new self in the mirror, I could have died. I looked like I had been beaten to a pulp.

How I welcomed the sight of old friends who didn't care about my appearance. Jean Hagen was en route to Germany when Helen Horton told her I was in the hospital. She insisted that they rush over to see me. Jean wasn't drinking now and looked the best I had seen her in years.

Unfortunately, she had another problem that made my troubles seem lightweight. My beloved Jean had throat cancer and was going to Germany for laetrile, a supposed cure unavailable in the States. But she was bubbly and bright and so much the way I remembered her from the old days.

We three were reminiscing—*cautiously,* so I wouldn't laugh and again pop my stitches—when Felicity Crossland came in with an armload of presents. All conversation stopped while I oohed and aahed over each one and told Felicity how great I thought she was. After she left, I remember Jean looking down at the pile of gifts on my bed and asking pointedly, "Isn't she overdoing it?"

I didn't think Felicity's affections were overdone at all. I was always very thick in gift giving and it was fun to have a friend into it, too.

When Roald decided that we would take our holiday in Minorca instead of Norway that summer, the whole family was overjoyed, especially when he announced that Felicity and her daughters would be there with her friend Phoebe Berens and her girls.

The families had a fabulous time together, sharing lazy days on the beach and barbecues under the stars. Roald was again his charming and sexy self in a welcome replay of the Tobago honeymoon. One afternoon, girl-talking with Phoebe, I bragged about how happy Roald and I were now, and what a great sex life we had. I remember Phoebe looked at me and then rolled her eyes up to the ceiling.

I don't know what it was—maybe it was the look on her face—but I could not shake that moment. I think perhaps it was the moment I began to wonder if something might be going on between Felicity Crossland and my good husband.

Back home, I decided it would be a good idea to just come out and ask her if she felt more than friendship for Roald. I invited her to lunch with me at the Curzon Club. But I could not bring myself to ask the question. What if I was wrong? She would be insulted forever and Roald would never forgive me if I ruined our relationship. I dropped it. It was ridiculous. Felicity was my friend. I upbraided myself for being such a nasty, suspicious tight-ass.

I successfully tried not to think about it. Then one afternoon at Felicity's house, I noticed a man's dressing gown hanging on her bathroom door. Very expensive. Made in Paris. I decided she must be having an affair with some Frenchman. I remember she was doing needle-work when curiosity got the better of me and I brought it up.

"Is he from Paris?" I asked.

"Yes," she answered.

"Is he married?"

"Yes."

"Children?"

"Yes."

"How many?"

Without missing a stitch she replied, "Three daughters and one son."

"Just like we have. Does he love his family?"

"He adores his children but not his wife."

"Will he get a divorce?" I continued.

But Felicity wanted no more. She put down her sewing and said she didn't want to talk about it.

No woman, except perhaps one who has been through this, could believe how blind I was. It's really crazy, but I simply did not want to know what was going on.

CHAPTER
FIFTY-EIGHT

After *The Homecoming* I became identified with a rather classic character—the American mother. Ironic, because I had all but lost my own sense of motherhood and it had left a void in me. But frequently actors must be satisfied with portraying relationships that are denied them in their own lives. I played two earth-mother parts in a row.

The first was in a touching drama by John Gay called *Things in Their Season*. I was a farm woman dying of leukemia, and we shot it on a real farm in Shawano, Wisconsin, with local people in bit parts. I enjoyed taking over the Koeller farm as if I really knew how to drive tractors and milk cows. My lovely stand-in, Mary Hafeman, actually did the driving for me, but that didn't keep me from feeling a real part of America's heartland. One of the nicest compliments I got was from a farmer. "You walk just like us, Miss Neal," he said. "Fast and tired."

One moment in the film stayed with me a long time. It was when Ed Flanders, that fine actor who played my husband, learns I am dying. He just says a simple, "I love you, Peg." That's all. But it reminded me that during my entire illness, Roald had not said those words to me.

The second honeymoon with Roald did not last. The first time he was unable to make love to me, I assured him it was just a phase we were going through. But that

355

phase had continued for some time now. Although not to my liking, it was bearable.

Lucy's tenth birthday was almost upon us, and my family, believe it or not, had never seen her. It seemed about time to introduce them. In April I took Lucy and Ophelia with me to visit the Neals and the Mahans, now spread from Kentucky to Georgia, Virginia and Florida. I was pleased that while we were gone, Roald and Theo would take the opportunity to weekend with Felicity and her daughters at her uncle's estate.

My girls got along fine with their grandmother and their great-aunt Maude, and especially took to Aunt Ima. Away from Papa's influence, they even liked Mother's southern cooking. Poor Mother had no idea that there was anything wrong with my marriage. I simply did not discuss it with her.

We returned home to find that Felicity was in the hospital. I understood she'd had her tonsils out. Papa picked a bouquet of flowers from our garden, I wrapped up some perfume, and we went to see her. On the way he asked if we could give Felicity a loan for the hospital bill and I readily agreed.

During our visit I couldn't help but notice a telegram by her bed that said: I LOVE YOU. I LOVE YOU. I remember thinking that was a bit much for a tonsillectomy. I remember, too, being surprised but not displeased when Roald suddenly decided that Liccy should stay at Gipsy House while she recovered.

She was with us a week. For the first two days she stayed in bed and I brought her trays. But once on her feet, she wanted to make supper and invite friends from London. With her customary efficiency, she planned not one, but two dinner parties during her residence. Liccy was the chef supreme and I was her assistant.

I was quietly watching Roald and our guests play billiards when Felicity came into the room and began pecking him with tiny affectionate kisses. I'm afraid they made little impression on me. Even when she saw me and jumped, it meant nothing. It was not that I was ignoring the implication. I was completely blind to it.

In fact, at that moment, my mind was on trying to find some way to please Roald. I had long thought that he had not gotten the recognition from his country that he deserved—an idea he shared, by the way—but I hadn't the foggiest notion of how to go about rectifying this until just then. Liccy, I suddenly recalled, had connections in high places. "I was thinking, Liccy," I said, "Roald has written so many fine books, maybe you could use your influence to get him an honor from the queen."

She magnanimously answered, "Yes, I will see what I can do."

I know it is hard to believe, but that is the way it happened. Whatever my other faults are, I do think I am honest. So does Roald. I am reminded of a dinner at Gipsy House with Elizabeth Baekeland, whom I met through Roald, and Elizabeth mentioned that she always thought of herself as 90 percent honest.

"Nonsense," said Roald, who adored percentages, "you are no more than 60 percent honest. Very few are. The only person I've ever known who is 100 percent honest is Pat."

My next mother role was in *Eric,* the true story of a young man's gallant fight against leukemia, based on the book by Doris Lund, the boy's real mother. It was a lovely reminder of how precious our time on this earth is and how important our loved ones are. My son was played by John Savage, who, shortly after we finished the film, was severely injured in a motorcycle accident. He lost his memory and his power of speech for a while, but recovered to remain a gifted actor.

An old friend invited me to dinner my last night in town and took me to the airport. Peter Douglas had not remarried since his wife died and was as warm and generous as I had remembered him. I needed to be touched again. Quite unexpectedly I said, "Peter, I have been a faithful wife for my whole marriage. But I need you and I would love to sleep with you. Would you stay with me the next time I'm here?"

Peter looked at me for a long moment and then said quietly, "I'd love to."

Soon after my return, Felicity joined Roald and me for supper at the club. I felt as if *I* had joined *them*. Felicity did all the ordering for us, as if she were the hostess. This time there was no mistaking her signals. When we went to the ladies' room together, she walked so briskly that I could barely keep up with her. As we entered, she turned and gave me such a look. I will never forget it. It said very plainly, *You have lost him. He is mine.* I was sure of it then and I am sure of it now. No one can ever tell me I misread what was written in her eyes.

All night long, pieces of a puzzle kept forming ugly pictures in my head.

I thought of the night, when Felicity was staying with us, that I had heard Roald leave our bed; I had just rolled over and gone back to sleep. Of course he had gone to her. And I thought of the time I had seen her smothering him with kisses. I should have thrown the bitch out of my house. And then I remembered how idiotically happy I had been about their lovely weekend together during my trip. God, I was such a jackass!

Tessa took me to lunch and a fashion show the next day. She was in good spirits and ordered us a lovely meal, which I'm afraid I spoiled. "Tessa," I prodded, "I simply must know something and you must tell me if you know. Are Felicity and your father having an affair?" I could tell that she was immediately panicked. I was right. She knew something. She tried everything to avoid the issue, but I would not drop it. I asked her over and over again. I tortured her with my insistence until I wore her down.

"Yes," she said wretchedly, "yes, they are."

So there it was.

I was a wreck all day, but by the time I met Roald that night in the Curzon bar, I had stopped shaking. I remember I ordered only tomato juice. Roald did not say a word to me, but then he rarely talked to me at the club, just to Eddie, the bartender. Finally we went to a corner booth and sat down. I waited while he took an eternity to order our food and wine. Then I looked him squarely in the eye and said, "I know."

He looked at me questioningly.

"You are having an affair with Felicity Crossland."

"What makes you think that?"

I had to hand it to him. He wanted to know how I knew before he wasted time denying it.

He began to slide nearer to me, which, with my bad right eye, put him out of my line of sight, forcing me to swivel my body around in order to see him.

"Don't lie to me," I demanded.

He did it again. He slid closer and I could barely keep him in my view. His eyes were literally dancing. I could tell Roald was experiencing some bizarre delight in my distress.

"Maybe I am."

I was so furious that I was shaking again. "Then leave me and go to her."

We finished our meal and drove back to Great Missenden in silence.

Roald went immediately to bed and conked out the minute he hit the pillow, just as always. I did not even try to sleep. I was raging. I flew into Ophelia's room and screamed, "Your bastard daddy is having an affair! I hate her! I hate her!" The child began to cry. She was only eleven. My mind jumped back twenty-five years to a hotel in Aspen and another desperate woman spewing venom to her child. I ran from the room, sobbing.

Roald left the house early the next morning. I heard his car start and I knew he was going to Felicity to tell her. Then I thought, No, he won't drive all the way to London, he'll find a pay phone.

Felicity called that morning. She wanted to come to Gipsy House to talk to me, but I said I had no time. I had luncheon plans with Lourdes Nichols, a wonderful Mexican lady whose daughter went to school with my Lucy, and I was not about to change them. An hour later Felicity called again and begged to see me. I wanted to be fair. I thought I should hear her out. So I said she could come for tea.

Roald was in the garden when Felicity arrived. As she walked to the house, I heard him say, "Call me if you need me."

I bolted to the door and yelled, "*I* will call you—if *I* need you!"

When Felicity came in, she sat down in Roald's chair, threw her head back in an overly dramatic gesture and started to cry. I wasn't greatly moved, but then, I have never cottoned to lousy acting. When she kept it simple I found her apologies genuine, even touching.

"I can understand your loving Roald," I told her, "because I love him, too. But how could you have pretended to be my friend and come into my house? How could you invite your friends here who obviously knew about you and Roald? How could you make such a fool of me?"

Roald joined us, and the two of them agreed that I was making far too much of it. They felt, for my own good, that I should have an affair, too. I didn't tell them then—although I did later—that I had had thoughts of infidelity myself.

I asked Roald point-blank, "Do you want to marry her?"

"No, I do not," he snapped.

Felicity flinched as if she had been stabbed. She turned and left the house.

But not before she said her polite goodbyes. I think she even thanked me for tea.

Later, I went to my closet and pulled out the brown silk dress she had brought that first morning. I tore it from its hanger, carried it to the outside incinerator and put it on the fire. Over and over I smashed it down with the poker. Then I faced Roald and screamed in his face, "I burned it! I burned it!"

He didn't give a shit.

But when I look back, I regret it in the worst way. It was, damn it, a really super dress.

I needed desperately to talk to someone. I called Helen Horton and asked her to meet me for lunch at the club. As I told her what was happening, I couldn't stop crying. I was so embarrassed, but I could not stop.

The waiter came, and as he served us I saw such sympathy in his face. He didn't say a word, but I have always thought that without hearing our conversation, he knew exactly what I was saying because he had served Roald and Felicity when I was out of town. Of course, I'll never know if that was true, but I felt his compassion at that moment and secretly wanted to thank him for it.

CHAPTER
FIFTY-NINE

had lived with Roald Dahl for almost a quarter of a century, and if I had not wondered about his unfaithfulness before, my thoughts were flooded now. I began to consider the possibility—or probability—that he had cheated on me before. The "gangster's daughter" was certainly on the probable side. Then there was a famous Irish writer whose intimate looks I had chalked up as merely friendly. Now I figured her for a possible. That one from Switzerland was another possible.

But even if he had been unfaithful with them all, none had lasted to threaten our marriage. Why should I think that Felicity would?

My thoughts went back to Rocky Cooper. She had known that if she waited it out, she would win. I would wait it out, too.

Roald and I got through the days as best we could. He was bored and I was ignored. The nights were more difficult. I was a wild woman and would find myself moving from bed to bed to bed, all over the house.

The children were aware of the situation, of course, but it was never acknowledged. My only support came from Marjorie Clipstone and Roald's half-brother, Louie, and his wife, Meriel. They had weathered a similar storm by a belief in the permanence of marriage as strong as my own. "Don't let him go, Pat," they urged. "Whatever you do, don't let him go." There had never been a divorce in the Dahl family. Infidelity was accepted, but not divorce.

I was sincerely grateful for their counsel, but I always wondered why they didn't get on *Roald's* back.

Marjorie heard a very angry Roald tell me exactly what he thought was wrong with me. I was lazy, stupid, a rotten housekeeper, a rotten mother, a rotten *everything* and he didn't know why he put up with this rotten marriage. I stood there and took it, but Marjorie didn't. "No, Roald," she said angrily, "you are married to a good woman. And you're tearing her down." I was so touched I began to cry. And Roald stopped ranting. Marjorie would act as a go-between many more times in the next few years.

I was literally going crazy. When I learned that Roald's sisters and their children, even the maid, knew about the affair, I felt such fury. When Else chided, "What about Gary Cooper?" I let her have it.

"That was years ago, dear Else, *before* I was married to your fucking brother!"

And each time I thought about Tessa and Ophelia, how I dragged them into it, I would feel such guilt.

At times I felt sure I was reacting like an immature, jealous schoolgirl and sometimes I knew I was a shrew. And lots of times I was just humiliated.

When I first told Marjorie Clipstone about Roald and Felicity, she said she already knew. Then she put her arms around me. "Oh, Pat," she cried, "everyone knows." From then on, I hated having to go into the village and see all my friends in the shops, knowing they knew.

All the time, Roald kept telling me to be sensible. To be kind, grown-up, forgiving.

I made up my mind to try. I could be grown-up and sophisticated—like a character right out of Noel Coward. I went so far as to plan an evening that dear Noel would have found deliciously pregnant with possibilities. I gave a supper party for Felicity.

We were six. I invited a young couple from a neighboring village. I forget their names, but he was a salesman and the reason I asked them was that they were gay and fun. Felicity brought a young man whose name also escapes me, but I do remember he soon wondered what the hell was going on.

I prepared the greatest meal of my life. And how nice I was. The atmosphere got so tense I thought we would all crack.

After supper I suggested a relaxing game of Scrabble. I've always been good at parlor games, and Scrabble was one of my best. Roald paired off with the salesman's wife and the salesman played with Felicity. Her young date was my partner. As we played, an overpowering urge to win welled up in me and I began to go for the kill. At one point I actually rose from my seat, and, glaring straight into Felicity's face, I slapped down each of the letters that gave us the game. I must say that victory was very sweet, but I can't take all the credit. My young partner, whoever he was, played very good Scrabble.

A few days later, I got the following letter from Felicity:

Because of my respect and affection for you, I am getting away from you both. In the clear light of day I realize that there is, at the moment, no happiness for any of us. Consequentially, on Tuesday I leave for France, and immediately on my return, go to Scotland. I shan't be back until the beginning of September. I feel very sad at the unhappiness which I have caused you and hope that in the fullness of time, life will sort itself out. Love, Liccy

I remember I once thought of writing to Rocky. I wanted to tell her that I loved her husband and that I admired her. I would have meant it. Maybe Felicity did, too. I wanted to believe her, and I did.

My plans to remain at home during this time of trial were quickly changed by a letter from Harvey Orkin. Harvey had a brain tumor and was dying. "Get your ass

over here," he commanded. "It's no good without you."
I left immediately for New York.

I got to Harvey's bedside with one half of my face broken out in a rash. I thought it was nerves, but it turned out to be an allergy to a plant that Theo had given me. After I told him what had been happening in England, Harvey insisted my awful condition was not caused by a plant, but by an allergy to Mr. Dahl.

It was going to be hard to lose my Harvey.

My last note from him was a little script he'd composed.

HARVEY: Wasn't that nice that Patsy was here?
FRIEND: She loves you, you know.
HARVEY: I know. I love her.
FRIEND: She knows.
HARVEY: I know.

When I returned, I found that Felicity had been true to her word. She had gone to France and the affair was on hold.

I received a script for an episode of "Little House on the Prairie" from Michael Landon, the show's producer and star. I loved it and wanted to do it very much. Unfortunately, the shooting schedule would cut across our summer plans for Norway and I just could not afford to leave the family now. I asked Irving Lazar, then my agent, to try to negotiate something, but he was sure I had lost it. I would not be discouraged. I called Michael Landon directly and pleaded my case. Dear Michael told me that I had the part, and that they would wait.

Norway was not the happy vacation I had hoped for. Tensions between Roald and me grew, until one night in the hotel's seaside restaurant I exploded. I can remember there was a huge raft in the middle of the bay heaped with refuse that was set aflame each evening for a spectacular entertainment. I watched as a tiny boat headed out to set the fire. I could not help but feel as though that huge raft of garbage was my life. When the raft burst into flame, I raced from the room. Roald followed me and I leapt at him, pummeling him with my fists. "I hate you!" I screamed. This would be the family's last vacation together.

"Little House on the Prairie" turned out to be a lovely experience. I had been a bit concerned that Michael Landon was not only the star and producer but had written the script and was the director as well. I did not know how one man could do all of that and do it well. But he fooled me good. Michael is one of the finest directors I have ever worked with. He understands actors and he understands people.

I made my promised call to Peter Douglas. The dear man thought he was coming to a seductive woman and instead found a witch. As I poured out my story I became more and more overwrought, until any thought of a romantic liaison was ridiculous. I was such a mess, but instead of fleeing, Peter kindly offered whatever help he could. He thought it would be good for me to talk to a psychiatrist friend in Newport Beach.

The doctor agreed to see me on a Saturday and we had a long, long talk. She zeroed in on my anger. Although I had many legitimate reasons to be angry, I had allowed it to change me, to make me a guilty and helpless person. Do you know there is actually a book called *Angry Book?* She sent it to me in England and I read it.

While I was in California I received a letter from Roald. After the usual chatty news about the family, he got down to business.

I would like to talk about ourselves and put something straight as possible.
    1) I love you. Surely you know that.

That was the third time he said it.

    2) I would never think of leaving you.
    3) But the fact remains that I am very fond of Liccy. I cannot help that. There is absolutely nothing I can do about it at present. I have not seen her and will not see her until after you return. Then I shall

probably look occasionally for her companionship. It is not sex. You think it is. I promise you it isn't. I am very happy right now without sex of any sort. In that respect I somehow feel utterly tired. I feel whacked out. You don't. But you are a bit younger than me. Also I am a huge fellow physically, and I believe that huge fellows, I mean really huge ones of 6 foot 5 or 6 inches, do grow physically tired earlier than others. Certainly I feel pretty tired a lot of the times these days.

4) So what I would like to do, and I think you would want, too, is to go on living with you and loving you and having you return this love *without* feeling the least bit jealous of the fact that now and again, but not very often, I meet Liccy and have lunch with her.

5) I see no reason in the world why a man of fifty-nine should not love his wife and also be allowed to feel strongly about another woman. It would be strange if he didn't.

6) All of this is obviously a rotten deal for Liccy, and I sort of hope that she won't put up with it for long. There is no future in it for her. In time, she is bound to meet someone else and that will be the end of that. But it would be wrong and cruel and unkind for me to push her right away myself. I have told her long ago that there is no chance of me ever leaving you. She knows it.

So there is no future for her with me. For her sake, though, as well as for mine, the thing should be allowed to tick over until it comes to its natural end. And the best thing you can do to encourage that ending is to be non-jealous and normal. And at all times, feel absolutely secure in the knowledge that this family will go on as long as I live.

Could I settle for what Roald wanted? I would have to try. From then on, if it was humanly possible, I would put Felicity out of my mind. If Roald saw her, it was his business and I did not want to know anything about it.

* * *

My darling Harvey died that November. I was asked to read at his memorial service and chose lines from a children's book called *The Velveteen Rabbit*. Harvey had given it to me while I was ill. Some of the words could have been written for my beloved friend: "When you are real you don't mind being hurt."

CHAPTER SIXTY

don't think my husband would divorce me if I made a bad cup of coffee.'' That was one of my last commercials for Maxim. I shall have to ask Jane Maas how she happened to think that one up.

My run was just about over. The agency called it burn-up or burn-down or wear-out, I forget which, but certainly my husband's new demands could not have endeared me to my bosses. He was now asking for a considerable amount of money for just being *referred to* as ''my husband'' in the spots.

My first acting job of 1977 was a gem. I played Senator Margaret Chase Smith in a TV drama called ''Tail Gunner Joe,'' about the old witch-hunter himself, Joseph McCarthy. I re-created Senator Smith's great stand on the Senate floor against McCarthy's tactics.

In an exchange of letters, Senator Smith told me how pleased she was that I had played her, and agreed that we had something in common. Just a few years before, that lady had been faced with the prospect of being confined to a wheelchair because of crippling arthritis. Several painful hip operations restored her ability to walk, but in a recent campaign, she had been falsely portrayed as being physically incompetent. She lost the election.

Although the role gave me only a few minutes of screen time, I got an Emmy nomination for it.

''Including Me'' was a documentary on the need to

treat handicapped people as members of society. It focused on the new federal law that guaranteed America's eight million handicapped children the same rights as other children. I was truly pleased to be asked to narrate it. I no longer resented being thought of as a symbol for the handicapped. I was even thankful that people could look at me and say to themselves: If she can do it, so can I.

My major performance was as Patricia Neal. The strong, inspirational, together lady who spoke at the stroke centers and gave the interviews and even shopped for groceries barely resembled the shaky woman I was inside. The letters I received—"I have read all about you and I do admire the way you have managed your life"— reflected that I had become very accomplished at portraying the smiling survivor.

Now and then I would drop my guard. Once a reporter asked me if I was happy and I snapped, "Let's say it is enough not to be unhappy and let it go at that."

While working on the documentary, I was given a book called *Nineteen Steps Up the Mountain,* about a California couple named Dorothy and Robert DeBolt. The DeBolts, who had six children of their own, adopted thirteen more of various nationalities and with physical and learning disabilities. It stirred memories of my sixth year, when Aunt Ima brought home a little boy from the orphanage. His name was Albert and he had purple permanganate all over his head. He stayed with us for only a weekend because Aunt Ima was not married at the time and wasn't allowed to keep him. I'll never forget how Albert clung to her and cried when he was taken back to the orphanage. I always wondered what happened to him. I thought the DeBolts were wonderful for giving all those children a home and I wrote to the publishers to thank them for putting out the book.

Children were very much on my mind now. My darling daughter Tessa birthed a beautiful baby girl named Sophie. So I was now a grandmother. A young one, mind you.

In the years between Tessa's leaving school (for which I still blamed myself) and Sophie's arrival, we'd had our differences. Tessa established her independence early, having moved into her own apartment in London, just down the street from Felicity, at seventeen.

She was a stunningly beautiful young woman and I was delighted whenever anyone pointed out how much alike we looked. I began to think the resemblance did not end with the cheekbones. There had been an abundance of men in her life already and her version of morality was too close to what mine had been at her age to give me any comfort. I wanted no heartbreak for her. I was especially alarmed over her fleeting romance with Peter Sellers. She was eighteen. He was fifty. Her relationship with Julian Holloway, the actor-son of Stanley Holloway, produced heavenly Sophie. The delighted father and the loving and conscientious mother did not intend to marry.

It was certainly a different age.

There were two reasons I signed for a little movie called *The Widow's Nest,* neither of them good. The producer charmed me into it. And it was going to be made in Mexico.

It had been almost thirty years since I had been in Mexico and I desperately wanted to return. So my first disappointment came when the location of the movie was switched to Spain. Then the producer ran out of money and none of the actors got paid.

There were also two reasons why the movie was worth doing. I was able to work with Helen Horton for the first time since *Twelfth Night* in 1945. And I met Warren Langton. This eager young writer was hired as my driver, coach and general babysitter. He became a faithful friend.

I was grateful both were there when I got the news of Jean Hagen's death. Helen especially, because she reminded me of the last time the three of us were together and how sharp Jean had been about Felicity.

There was no mention of Felicity now. Roald and I did

not speak of her at home, and whenever I was away his letters contained no comment on her. These letters were surprisingly affectionate. He was able to put loving thoughts onto a page. But after all, he *was* a writer.

When the powers at the Fort Sanders Presbyterian Hospital in Knoxville wrote to say they were building a new wing that would be dedicated to rehabilitation and wanted to name it after me, I am told I answered with four words: Great! Great! Great! Great! That is exactly how I felt. And so very proud.

Papa wrote the speech I gave at the dedication of The Patricia Neal Rehabilitation Center, and I felt the words deeply. "The work in the field of rehabilitation is a calling that requires very special qualities of patience and understanding." No one knew better than I. "They are heroes, every one of them," I told the crowd that bulged with Knoxville friends, "and this life-changing center is a house of heroes."

When I returned to see the center in full operation, I was struck to see the words "House of Heroes" engraved on a plaque in the foyer. One of the patients I met that day was Miss Ruby Bird, my high school drama teacher, who gave me a stickpin and a note that read, "A Tennessee pearl for a Tennessee pearl." I still wear that pin. And I have remained grateful to be associated with that wonderful facility, which has now been in operation for over a decade.

I received a surprise letter from Dorothy DeBolt. Her publisher had forwarded my note, and she was writing not only to thank me but to ask my help with their program, AASK, which stands for Aid to Adoption of Special Kids. I promised I would take on their crusade and, in my speeches, tried to encourage adoption of special children. A few months later I met Bob and Dorothy in their San Francisco home, and it was instant love for them and their brood.

One of their remarkable children composed a poem for my birthday. It put me in mind of Olivia. I had it framed and it now hangs in my home.

Winter

Winter is like the light wings of an angel
The air sparkles like the smile on your face
It is like a blanket of blossoms
It is like the snow of kids having fun in the snow
How could we live without winter?

> Happy birthday
> Love, JR

During the late 1970s I was continually on the go. For a lady who once froze at the thought of flying, I was spending almost as much time in the air as on the ground.

Roald eagerly supported any idea that got me out of the house. He even had one of his own. Why not turn my speaking engagements into a new career? He could write me a longer version of the speech I'd been using for my invitational appearances at stroke centers that would be suitable for engagements at women's clubs and universities. He asked his New York agent to contact the Keedick Lecture Bureau about handling me as a public speaker. Robert Keedick got back to us right away. He said the fees would not be great, but he felt there would be enough interest in me to provide a reasonable income and thought we should give it a go. Within the first month I had twenty-five speaking engagements in America.

I took a part in a miniseries called "The Bastard," which was about the American Revolution. I played a French peasant woman. I slaved over an accent that everyone thought was wonderful, and then I had to redub it. I was too French! One of my coworkers on the series was an old Warner Brothers stablemate, Eleanor Parker, who could still make me laugh.

That relationship was to continue through her son, Paul Clements, who was just beginning his acting career. I played Paul's mother in *The Passage,* an adventure drama with quite a good cast, including Anthony Quinn, whom I had known since the days of Michael Chekhov's class. I had also been among a few friends who had wished Tony bon voyage the night he sailed for Europe to gamble on a little Italian movie called *La Strada*. Tony is an inspired actor and I adored working with him.

I had another reunion during that filming. An American company in Paris was working on a series of programs about the great women of our time and asked me to narrate the presentation on Helen Keller. Ever since I played Helen's mother onstage, I had read her words with deepening appreciation. But when I spoke them, I felt a heart-to-heart response to this woman, a passionate sense of oneness with her.

When *The Passage* company moved to Nice, Papa spent a few days with me en route to Switzerland. When he left, he told me to move to a cheaper hotel and pocket the difference, which I dutifully did. It was when I changed my mind and went back to my former hotel that I caught sight of Maria Cooper. For all the great plans we try to make in our lives, truly important moments are always surprises.

Maria, now Mrs. Byron Janis, was in town for a few days, accompanying her brilliant husband on a concert tour. During our daily visits, I didn't speak a word about my problems with Roald. But Maria was amazingly intuitive. She sensed my inner anguish and asked me about my faith in God. I told her I had been struggling deeply about God since my stroke. Believing in Him again was very difficult after seeming to lose everything. Then she said, "I know an abbey you would love. You should go sometime."

Yes, I found myself thinking, that is something I would really like to do—sometime. And I slipped it into my bank of thoughts.

Back in England, Roald took me to a formal party at Sir John Woolf's office. Sir John was producing Roald's short stories as a TV series called "Tales of the Unexpected." There were scads of British stars there who had appeared in the shows. Midway through the party, an unfamiliar man with a large red album under his arm interrupted an enjoyable conversation I was having. That was a bit much, I thought.

The man was Eamonn Andrews, the host of the British "This Is Your Life" television program, and it was *my* life they were doing then and there. So that was the reason for Roald's mysterious chauffeured-limousine trips to London!

It seemed that everyone who had ever been in my life had been gathered. Mother and NiNi, the whole Neal family and Emily Mahan Faust were flown in from America. Roald's family and half of Great Missenden were there. Even Dr. Charles Carton, Kirk Douglas and Duke Wayne sent greetings on film. It was fabulous—on television.

It was a private fiasco, however. We did not have room at Gipsy House to put up my family because all the children were home on holiday. Mother was crushed. Once safely home, she let me know with an angry letter. When Roald saw it, a lifetime of antagonism between them burst like a ripe boil. He dictated a scathing letter saying *we* would never see her again. I was not prepared to cut Mother out of my life over a misunderstanding, but I still could not take a stand against my husband. The letter was sent.

We ended the 1970s with a bang of sorts. Roald, Tessa and I took Phyllis and George Jenkins to Boxing Night dinner at the Curzon—on the house. In the middle of a dinner that he didn't think was up to par, Roald stood up and told everyone in the room exactly what he thought of the food—and shot a few volleys at the building's architecture as well. The fact that it was a free do was irrelevant, he felt. The management booted us out, revoking our membership forever.

CHAPTER SIXTY-ONE

had not thought much about Maria's abbey. Then one day in early December I received a letter from her. In it was a letter from one of the sisters inviting me to visit. I was surprised at how thrilled I was. I checked my calendar for the speech dates that would take me to America and I answered the sister immediately, typing the reply myself. I did not want even my secretary to know.

The good nun and I agreed that May would be the best time to come, and a date was confirmed. I started to wonder about all sorts of things. Would they let me smoke? How could I exist without a cigarette? Where could I get my hair done?

And—what would I be asked to do?

In February I went to America to receive an honorary doctorate from Rockford College in Illinois. I happily became a Doctor of Humane Letters. It was the first of two such honors I was given. The second would come in 1984 from Simmons College in Boston.

I had not been in touch with my mother for months, ever since Roald banished her from our lives, and I was so upset about it that I developed a nervous twitch in my eye. Dear Sue Conrad invited me on a Florida holiday very near St. Petersburg, and kept after me to call my mother. I did, and Mother and I had our tearful reunion.

In fact, I fell back into the arms of my whole family again. And it was right.

In March and April I was preoccupied by travel and speeches and friends. When May arrived, I suddenly wondered what the hell I was doing, going to a Catholic nunnery.

I hired a driver at my hotel to get me to the abbey and, en route, asked him to stop off at a liquor store. I bought a bottle of wine and a bottle of vodka and some mixer and shoved them into my suitcase.

The abbey was an unpretentious place in the New England countryside, almost hidden away in a valley of pine and maple and surrounded by flowers. I was so glad it was spring.

I was taken to have a parlor with the nun who had written to me. She greeted me from behind a grille and she had the most beautiful eyes I'd ever seen. As we talked, the wooden lattice separating us almost seemed to disappear. She told me about the abbey and its traditional heritage of Benedictine monastic life. And she laid out a kind of schedule for my three-day visit. I confessed smoking was a "real sin" of mine and hoped there would not be a rule against it. The sister said that there was, indeed, a prohibiting "law" at the abbey, but that the abbess "knew from *real* sin," and she was sure a way for me to indulge my vice could be found. "Sometimes," she said, smiling, "we have to get below the law to deeper law." But she wasn't sure she could find an ashtray.

I was shown to a guest house where a small room awaited me. It had one window, a tiny desk and bureau, a simple bed with two freshly laundered towels and a washcloth folded neatly at the foot, and a crucifix on the wall. There was no closet, not even a cupboard, just a rod to hang clothes on. A small printed note had instructions telling one how to behave, what time to come to church and where and when to arrive for meals. I unpacked and stashed my booze in a drawer under some clothes.

Their tiny monastery chapel was filled with flowers, beautifully arranged by loving and knowing hands. The calming strains of Gregorian chant came from behind a large grille at one side of the sanctuary. The voices, a cappella, were clear and pure and somehow reassuring. I remember thinking it was the first time I had felt close to peace in a long time.

Meals were served to women guests in a private room. There was only one other guest at that time, a Jewish lady named Sunny. I thought the name suited her. We both were wild about the food, especially the fresh bread. And I got the recipe for their lentil soup.

On the second day I worked up the courage to talk about the struggle my marriage had become. The sister with the eyes said very little, but she listened, and just to be able to spill it out to someone was a relief.

The nuns knew all about Helen Keller, and I offered to do my reading of her works. Just before my performance, electricity went off in the whole area and I was certain they would cancel it. But I was picked up on schedule and taken to one of the barns. The sisters were there waiting, and a place was set for me near a wood-burning stove—just like the ones we used to have at Gipsy House.

The room was aglow with dozens of burning candles set in iron candelabra. Helen's speech seemed especially appropriate.

. . . Often when I dream, thoughts pass through my mind like cowled shadows, silent and remote, and disappear. Perhaps they are the ghosts of thoughts that once inhabited the mind of an ancestor. At other times the things I have learned and the things I have been taught, drop away, as the lizard sheds it skin, and I see my soul as God sees it.

On the third day the abbess took me to her garden, a beautiful spot in the woods. I remember blue flowers by a birdbath and large rocks where we sat in the shade. We talked about my life, but I carefully avoided mentioning my affair with Gary and said only that I had been deeply in love once. When I said that the agony I felt was because of the trouble in my marriage, she said I would have to go back further than that, even further back than the stroke, to find the seeds of my discontent.

Then I told her it was Gary Cooper I had been in love with, but he had been married and there was no way we could have been together.

"But there was," she corrected.

"I am sorry to tell you, my mother, it was not that simple. You see, it was sexual. You might not know what I mean."

"I am happy to tell you that I do know what you mean. It is *you* who do not know what *I* mean."

She was right. I never forgot that conversation.

Before I left the abbey I chose a flower from the greenhouse and asked that it be placed in the chapel as a remembrance for Olivia. That evening at vespers, I saw it had been placed right in front of the altar. I went back to my little room and wept.

Later when I was packing, I realized I had completely forgotten about the booze. The bottles were unopened.

An immediate blessing followed. I got a good little part in the television version of *All Quiet on the Western Front*. Again, I was mother to Richard Thomas, my John-Boy of *The Homecoming*. We shot behind the Iron Curtain, in Poland, and I was miserable. The poverty was so sad. And there was nothing beautiful. No statues. No pictures. Even the churches were closed. I think it must be so dull to be a Communist.

The lovely part of the filming was working with Richard again and meeting his wife and small son, who was the most appealing child I ever saw. He made me want to hold him in my arms forever.

I returned home in time for our wedding anniversary only to find Roald in the hospital for the latest in a series of back operations. He was having a very rough time, but he remembered to send me two divine bunches of flowers. I wanted to send a picture of them to the sisters, but I had never used a camera. Roald was the photographer in the family.

I did write to them, however, to thank them for their hospitality, and to the abbess for her time and concern. I thanked the portress for the shawl she gave me. I thanked them for the soup recipe and shared Claudia Marsh's old secret for keeping parsley fresh. I even thanked the divine man who drove me to the airport. I just could not stop thanking. And I found myself asking if I could come back at the end of my next trip to America.

On that trip I was introduced to Martha's Vineyard for the very first time. I had read about the island in Katharine Cornell's memoirs when I was young and had courted the idea of going there all my life. That summer Lucy, Ophelia and I spent ten days with Millie and Keith at their house on the Vineyard. I fell in love with the island. I knew I wanted to return.

It was a special summer for me. I look back on it as the summer my children and I began a new relationship that would continue for the rest of our lives.

Theo joined the three of us and we headed for California and our first vacation without Papa. It was a motor trip up the coast with Jean Alexander in her huge trailer. We were tourists, camping out in sleeping bags and stopping wherever we fancied. We were roughing it, and it was fun. My children and I would now share vacations and the things friends shared. It would not be the relationship I once wanted, but it was something I was willing to settle for.

It was on this trip that Warren Langton took me to see my old friend and stand-in from the Warner Brothers days, Ann Urcan. Ann, too, had suffered a stroke and had been left an invalid. She was unable to speak to me, but when I told her I loved her, her eyes filled with tears. I knew she understood.

My last stop on this summer odyssey was Louisville. When I accepted Robert and Nancy Sexton's invitation to attend a special presentation of their play called *Packard,* all about the old town and its inhabitants, I had no idea how special that evening would be. Another actor, who now worked in his son's theater in that city, had also been invited to the performance.

I had not been in touch with Victor Jory for forty years. We put our arms around each other and embraced as two old friends would. But later, when the lights went down in the Walden Theater Cabin, Victor put his hand on mine. It stayed there throughout the performance as a greeting to an old love.

It was also a farewell. Victor died some months later.

CHAPTER
SIXTY-TWO

knew before Felicity came into our lives that the only time Roald and I were really close was in a time of crisis. But I truly did not realize that my marriage could, in fact, end.

I was spending a lot of time away from Great Missenden now. I traveled extensively, both with my speech, entitled "An Unquiet Life," and my work for The Patricia Neal Rehabilitation Center and countless other stroke centers. These were taking me on a continuous circuit from England across the North American continent to Alaska and back. So having a home again in America seemed a good idea, especially to Roald.

I also inherited Tessa's London apartment. It had been empty for nine months—and with things none too good at home, it provided a small retreat in the city. Roald was all for it, of course, but I had to furnish it myself. One of the things I brought from Gipsy House was a huge painting Charles Marsh had given me years and years before.

I had admired the painting in his home. It was by a Mexican artist and depicted Christ's mother at the foot of the Cross. I remember when I first saw it, I was so struck by the mother's face. I think it is the most tragic face I've ever seen in my life.

"God, Charles, I love it!"

He told Claudia to take it down from the wall. "Have it," he said. "It is yours."

Dear Charles was the most give-away man in the world.

Each of my homecomings would find me more engrossed in searching for clues that Roald was still seeing Felicity. I didn't merely question the children about it, I interrogated them. When I got no answers, I was sure it was because their loyalties were with their father. Before the year was out, I would spy on my children by going through their diaries and private belongings. I was looking for hurt.

My darling Tessa announced that she had finally met the man she wanted to marry, an American businessman named James Kelly. It was James who called me one day in England and said he had found a fabulous house on Martha's Vineyard. It had been owned by the captain of the ship that Herman Melville had sailed on when he was a boy. That same captain became the model for Ahab in *Moby-Dick*. Was I interested?

Roald grabbed the phone. "God, yes! She's interested!" Within hours we decided to buy it.

It was early spring and nobody was on the island the first time I saw the house. Sue Conrad and Phyllis Jenkins came with me. The real estate lady met us and we walked to my new home. It was three stories, with two great dormers on the roof. It faced the sea. Chappaquiddick was directly across. The house had a white picket fence and a garden with roses already in bloom. I had never seen anything like the ten huge flowers on one stalk. Roald would love it.

Anne Fonde Walter helped me set up housekeeping. I went to Knoxville for furniture. I wanted old things that had character but not huge price tags. Warren Langton came all the way from California to do everything from painting the house to making a sign—MOBY NEAL—for the porch. It was a happy choice of name because, as it turned out, Roald came to the house only one time.

The year 1980 was one of grand reunions for me, and made me feel appreciated and loved and wanted.

The Actors Studio filled the ballroom of the Waldorf-Astoria for a tribute to 125 successful alumni, and I renewed friendships with actors I had started out with, studied with, worked with, grown with. All told, the honored group had won 378 Tony, Oscar and Emmy nominations, and I was so very proud to be among them.

I have a lovely souvenir that always reminds me of that evening, and of a wonderful lady. Maureen Stapleton was wearing a garnet brooch that night that I admired. When she learned the garnet was my birthstone, she took the brooch off and put it in my hand. She would hear no protest, nor would she take it back. It is one of my favorite pieces of jewelry.

In October I was one of the returning alumni at Northwestern University's dedication of its new speech school. The old theater where I used to study had burned to the ground. A show featuring former students, including Cloris Leachman and Charlton Heston, was produced for TV to pay off the cost of the new building. I read the letters of Helen Keller.

The loveliest moment came when I was reunited with my beloved acting teacher Alvina Krause. It had been thirty-five years since we had seen each other. When a reporter asked what I had learned from Alvina, I answered, "She taught me timing. She taught me imagination."

"Nonsense," retorted Alvina, "I taught her to stand up straight!"

A third reunion came by way of wire. At a Patricia Neal Rehabilitation Center fund-raiser called The Party of the Stars, Senator Howard Baker read a telegram from an old coworker of mine: BOTH OUR LIVES HAVE CHANGED DRASTICALLY IN THE PAST 30 YEARS. YOU'RE A PRO BOTH ON AND OFF THE STAGE. KINDEST PERSONAL REGARDS. RONALD REAGAN. When I acknowledged the wire, I reminded the newly elected president that it had been almost a quarter of a century since we had seen each other. Three years later I would be invited to dinner at the White House, where we dined on smoked fillet of trout and supreme of capon. I couldn't help wishing it had been steak.

Pat and Roald was being made into a television film,

which did not overjoy me. I liked the fact that Robert Anderson would be writing the script but I still had strong misgivings about it. It simply was not the whole story of the stroke and its aftermath. But since no one asked my opinion, I could do nothing but hope they would find a decent actress to play me.

As it turned out, I could not have cast it better myself. When I saw the film, I thought Glenda Jackson's performance was masterful. I was both grateful and very, very relieved.

Once I took up residence on the Vineyard, gossip about a separation started appearing in the British press, which Roald never bothered to deny. Instead, he would say he did not want to comment because it might "roughen up the situation." And all the time I was keeping the myth alive, telling the world "my husband is a *great* man and I love him," the only words in the speech I wrote myself.

I was visiting my nunnery regularly now, at least every three months. I felt so comfortable there. I vaguely remembered my wonder at the peace June Haver had seemed to find in the churches and nunneries in South America all those years ago. Now I was finding that same comfort. Yes, that's the word. Comfort. *"Confortáre,"* the sister had told me. To make strong. "Comfort is the spirit of God, the life-giving flow of love," she said. "To give continuity to life is part of the Benedictine mission."

I had met four postulants who were going to become novices, and was thrilled to learn that their clothing ceremony would take place during one of my visits. It is a private ceremony in which their street clothes are exchanged for the habit, and outsiders cannot attend. But they made me feel very much a part of it. Each of the women accepted my offer and wore a piece of my jewelry at the start of the ceremony. One was Fay Compton's turquoise necklace. Another was Maureen's garnet brooch. Benedictine continuity.

That same year, I had a reunion with dear Melvyn Douglas in *Ghost Story,* which was his last performance. My role, that of Fred Astaire's wife, was very small, and

I was going to turn it down. I called the producer but his line was busy. Just then my daughter Ophelia walked in and asked what I was doing. When I told her, she insisted I *not* turn down the part. She was aware of how bad things were in the marriage, and she knew how I needed to work. Ophelia got me in front of a camera again, and I'm grateful to her.

It was on the snowy New York location for *Ghost Story* that I saw the obituary of Dr. John Converse, who was survived by his wife, Veronica Cooper Converse. I recalled an unfulfilled promise and wrote a letter.

> Dear Rocky,
>
> Time passes so quickly and we endure many crises —life, death, and great, great pain.
>
> I have for many years longed to write to you and to express my deepest regret for your loss of Gary. And now I cannot contain myself—my senses are overwhelmed by the loss of your husband. Do, please do, accept my sympathy and know that I have respected you.
>
> I have met your daughter, Maria, and the pleasure of her company has greatly relieved my heart.
>
> Again, my compassion and my sincere love.
>
> As I am,
>
> Patricia Neal Dahl

I did not expect one, but I received her reply a few weeks later. It was dated April 20, my Olivia's birthday.

> Pat Dear,
>
> Please forgive me for taking so long to answer your wonderful letter. It meant so much and said so much that I wanted to get all "the other stuff" out of the way before talking to you and truly it's been right next to my bed since Maria gave it to me. Wrote you first on "Good Friday" but in rereading there was a line I didn't like the gist of . . . it was that you surely have carried your cross as have I. A priest here told me that that act lets us bypass Purgatory.

Let's hope he's right. Do, dear Pat, let me know when next you're in this city. The three of us can have lunch up here and perhaps you can buck me up if anyone can. Life is surely full of surprises—like you writing me and vice versa!!!

Affectionately,
Rocky.

P.S. Excuse this formal paper. Gotta get something more contemporary. Old Hollywood it looks like!

I felt the stirrings of an old love in my heart. The next time I saw the abbess, she told me this was what she had been trying to tell me in the garden. This was the love that remained after everything else was taken from us.

One afternoon I was invited to a special service at the cemetery, where the nuns prayed for the dead. The moment they finished singing, I suddenly said, "I have an announcement to make. I am going to become a Catholic." It was the only time in my life I ever heard applause in a graveyard.

After making my great intention known, I was frightened of what might be expected of me right away. I was relieved when one of the postulants assured me it doesn't happen all at once.

In fact, the nuns suggested that perhaps I might want Roald to come to the abbey with me before I began instruction. They felt a decision like this should not exclude him. I agreed. I also hoped a trip to the nunnery together would help us.

Roald refused the invitation, of course. But he wrote back, complimenting the sisters on their perfectly composed letter. He told them it gave him great pleasure to read it because "there was so much poor writing around these days."

Tessa and James were married in the same church in which the children had been baptized, and where our Olivia was buried. Tessa planned every detail herself, and she did it magnificently. Unlike her mother, she did not forget the music.

387

Afterward I went back to a familiar spot in the church-yard. I had forgotten to bring something for Olivia's grave, but my friend Frankie Conquy handed me a little bouquet she had done up from her own garden.

I returned to the Vineyard, and to devastating news. My sister, NiNi, had suffered a stroke, an aneurysm just like mine. It was agreed that it would be better that I not go to Atlanta. I could not drive a car and frankly would be more of a burden than a help to George, who did not need any extra baggage at this time. I kept a phone vigil for the weeks that NiNi was in the hospital. She under-went brain surgery twice and fortunately did not lose any of her faculties. George was at her side constantly, NiNi told me later, with tenderness and unembarrassed affection.

I began going to the Federated Church on the Vineyard and became acquainted with its preacher, John Schule, who asked me to give him the three words I felt were most important in my life. I wrote down *work, integrity* and *kindness*. John gave a fine sermon based on these words, crediting me from the pulpit for "firing him up." I didn't tell him I was getting fuel for that fire from the abbey.

Then I received the most surprising letter. It was from Roald, saying there was no reason for me to come home for Christmas.

What on earth could he mean? Of course I would come home for the holidays. Why should everybody come to America? It was absurd.

Since Mormor's death, our house had become the cen-ter of the holiday festivities for the Dahl family. I had always loved Christmas, but I could barely get through it that year. It was so depressing. Grotesque. Roald was colder than he had ever been. Even the children were strangely distant. Two days later, the strained atmo-sphere still remained.

I remember it was very late. Most of the family was in bed. Roald and Ophelia were in the television room. When I joined them, I noticed they exchanged quick glances. I sensed something. A setup?

Ophelia said to me, very quickly, "Mummy, you've got to know something. Daddy is still seeing Felicity Crossland."

I just stared at him. I couldn't say a word. He said a curt "That's right," and left the room.

I was frantic. I cried and I ranted. Ophelia was genuinely frightened. She kept insisting that I must have someone in America, a friend who could help me, and begged me to make a call. I did finally phone Sonia Austrian, who advised me to leave England at once and come to New York. She would put me up until I could decide what to do. Since I felt everyone wanted me out of the house anyway, I agreed. I got no sleep at all that night. I felt so hurt. And furious.

Very early in the morning, I went into our bedroom and shook Roald awake. I hissed into his ear, "I wish you were dead. I wish something would kill you!"

Later, Roald arranged for my flight to New York. It was a one-way ticket.

The whole family drove me to the airport. Theo sat quietly in the front with Roald, and the girls tried desperately to chitchat with me in the back. When we got to Heathrow Roald cashed a check so I would have some American dollars on my arrival, and the girls kept whispering to me nervously that everything was going to be all right. I kissed them all goodbye as if I were just off on another trip.

As I went through the gate, I looked back and saw the most horrendous sight of my life. Roald's head was thrown back and he was roaring with laughter.

I did not turn back again.

CHAPTER SIXTY-THREE

I will never know how I got through that flight. The flight attendant kept asking if there was anything he could do for me. But there was nothing anyone could do. I was the most miserable woman in the world.

Kennedy Airport was milling with people, but I could not see Sonia's face anywhere. I found an empty bench and put down the few pieces of hand luggage I was carrying. From time to time, I thought I noticed a look of recognition on a stranger's face, but no one approached the strained, weary woman sitting alone on that bench. The minutes ticked away. Almost an hour passed. I looked through my address book. Who would I call if I was stranded? My thoughts went to that old woman who lived across from me in that first dreadful apartment in New York years ago. Alone. Unwanted. Penniless. At that moment my worst fear was thrust on me. How could I make it *without Roald?* He had made all the decisions in my life for the past fifteen years. How could I live on my own? Would I end up like that poor creature I had found so ghastly? Then I saw Sonia rushing toward me. She had not abandoned me. She had only been caught in traffic, but I could not stop crying for relief.

Sonia and Geoff were incredibly kind to put up with the madwoman who was their "guest" for six months. Those first days I just rambled about in the huge apartment. I would talk and talk. Then I would sit and stare into the empty space of my world, which had totally disintegrated. Thirty years! Everything I had—my children, my home—all gone. And there I was, sitting in a strange apartment looking at someone else's tables and chairs, another woman's silverware. I had nothing left of my own. God, what would I do now?

I did call good friends, finally. For hours every day I was on the phone, literally screaming with rage. Everyone was utterly gorgeous to me, especially the ones who had never liked Roald. My friend Nancy Hoadley Kirkland recommended a psychologist, whom I saw a few times, but it was just not helping me. Colin Fox, bless him, took me out to plays and parties, anything to get my mind off myself. Darling George Shdanoff, who had boosted my morale some thirty years before on *The Fountainhead*, wrote now to boost my motivation for a new life.

John Pielmeier, whose new play, *Agnes of God*, was slated for Broadway, contacted me about doing the role of Mother Superior, but I was in no frame of mind to consider it. Geraldine Page played it onstage and Anne Bancroft, of course, did the film version. Annie gave me just about my only smile during this period. I still have her note:

What in the hell do you mean by "you were kicked out of England"? Even kings who abdicate don't get kicked out and besides, don't women usually kick the men out of the house for transgressions and not vice versa? It's usually the men who transgress.

I stayed with Sonia and Geoff and then with Carolyn March until I had gathered enough resources to find a place of my own in New York. It was hell to think of starting all over again, apartment hunting in Manhattan. I had enough money in my savings to get a good address with a view of the beautiful garbage boats making their way up the East River. I had only one piece of furniture at first, a sofa that I bought from the previous tenant for one hundred dollars because it was too huge to get out of the apartment. Living alone caused no problems physically. I had no trouble caring for myself and I had a wonderful woman, Manuela, to help me. But emotionally, it was horrendous. I had virtually no contact with the family in England. Alf and her daughter Astri wrote but no one else did. Of all the children, Tessa was the only one in America, and she lived in Boston. I was really alone.

Sonia insisted that I take some legal action. My mother did, too. In fact, her letters were full of legal advice. I never knew how shrewd Mother was, and if it was possible, she was even angrier than I.

I did not want a divorce but agreed I should probably get a lawyer. I reluctantly began proceedings for a separation. Two friends told me they would testify to my character, my devotion to my family, should it come to that. Oh, my God, would I have to go into court and *plead* that I loved my husband and children?

I spent the summer on the Vineyard by myself, mostly watching afternoon television. I could not concentrate enough to read a book. Ophelia and Lucy came for three months but soon grew weary of hearing their father referred to as "that bastard" every time we spoke, so they just stayed out of my company.

Lillian Hellman and Millie Dunnock both were in residence on the Vineyard and called almost every day. But they rarely came by. Lillian, of course, was quite ill then, but I don't think that had much to do with it. Friends, too, did not want to be near me. And I can't blame them. I was so difficult to be with.

I remember a summer celebration, although not what it was for, during which an auction was held and residents bid on prizes. I remember being very upset that one of the prizes was a dinner date with me. I was so frightened that no one would bid at all, or that the winning bid would be embarrassingly low. It wasn't, fortunately, but my fear said a lot about my self-esteem.

I sent for my things from the London apartment, but only a small part of what was there actually arrived on the Vineyard. I was truly crestfallen to find that my precious Mother of Sorrows painting was missing. I have never learned what happened to it.

It is not completely lost to me, however. My good friend Marge Van Dyke, whom we met when her husband Dick starred in Roald's movie *Chitty Chitty Bang Bang,* did an exact replica of it in needlepoint. God bless her for that.

I had no problems with strangers—people I would meet on the island, young people especially, who seemed to like to talk to Patricia Neal the actress. With strangers I would give my "happy survivor" performance, and for those few minutes, I could almost feel everything was all right.

But it wasn't. I was in danger.

I called my nunnery and asked to come. I needed the comfort I had found there, time away in the country to get my thoughts back into orbit, to pray.

But I brought the anger and bitterness with me and, trip after trip, used the abbey as another place to dump my misery.

The good nuns bore this burden with quiet grace and patience. I do not remember ever being made to feel guilty, but I do remember being made to feel I could change.

Which is not to say they accomplished this by means of pious platitudes. These ladies were used to dealing with hard matters.

Every morning after church, I would meet with the sister who had first written to me. She began by trying to get me to appreciate consciously what I was doing to my life and make me realize I was only writhing in self-pity. Or as she finally put it, "Stop chewing on Felicity."

And I would try. I would go back to the city each time feeling a little better. But the rage would always seep back in. I was bloated with it.

As Thanksgiving approached, I thought I would die not to be going back to England for Christmas. A most amazing invitation saved my life.

The abbess suggested that I spend the month of December at the nunnery. Not merely as a guest, she said;

if I accepted, I would live in the monastery like a pre-postulant.

"Lady Abbess, I don't want to join up, you understand?" I said.

"Believe me," she sighed, "we don't want you to, either. I don't think we could take it for more than a month."

I told her I thought it was a great honor and guessed it must certainly be an exception. She assured me it was. But St. Benedict wrote that pilgrims could come for a period of time—if they were content with the customs of the place and did not have exorbitant wants.

As my driver pulled up to the entrance I put out the last cigarette I would ever smoke. One of the priests there gave me a blessing. I felt his cross blaze into my forehead and I went inside.

I traded my street clothes for the black dress of the postulant and scrubbed off my makeup. I removed the rings from my fingers and covered my hair with a black scarf. I looked at the bare wooden walls of my cell. It was Christmas and I felt I had nothing left.

I did not live the exact life of a postulant, but I did my best. I followed a strict schedule of work and prayer. I kept silent at meals, was on time for church. I helped bake bread. And I weeded in the greenhouse. I did a lot of that. There were times during that month I felt I never wanted to return to the outside world.

But still, I could not get the thought of Felicity Crossland out of my mind. Like a venom, it poisoned the times I should have been concentrating on other things.

Time after time, I raged to the sister that that bitch— and I used the word to shock and hurt—now had thirty years of my life. That *bitch* had everything *I* had conceived. I had gone through labor for nothing.

She would ask if I really thought it was possible to go through life all for nothing. Sure as hell looked that way, I told her. She told me I could not lose what I had honestly given my body to bring into being.

The stroke was the key. She said I would never have come to the abbey or into a reflective dimension of an enclosure except for the stroke. I would be an aging actress fighting another aging actress for a guest spot on "The Love Boat."

"Everyone has to face the stroke of the Cross," she said. "Yours had to be more dramatic because you are an actress and the Lord is a very faithful husband to you."

"I built *my* husband up all over the world and he is a *shit* now."

"You are not a mother if you build someone else up and then resent him for it."

"I have lost everything, don't you understand? She has *taken* it away from me."

"You haven't lost yourself."

I was so tired of hearing that. "I have had a *fucking* stroke! I am a *fucking* cripple! I am so scared that I can't make it on my own, that I'll end up a *fucking bag lady!* Can't you see? That's why I hurt!"

"To bear suffering always has meaning."

"And I'm tired of that *fucking shit.*"

Suddenly she was on her feet. Those eyes were blazing.

"And I am tired of *your* fucking, fucking, fucking nonsense! I am so tired that nothing else matters to you. A *great* woman is *whole*. She is *for* others and, yes, Patricia, 'one hundred percent honest.' She is pure because she is penetrable. There is a part of you that has to call a spade a spade, but also a part that has to find some fertility in the rot. You want your femaleness but you don't want your Woman. I thought if I let you vomit long enough you would get it out of your system and begin asking for something. You are not asking for anything here, so you will get nothing here. Now will you get out!"

She turned and left.

I could not believe she had treated me that way. It took me a long, long time before I could cry, and then I wept my heart out.

But I could not leave.

That night at supper she came into the dining room,

and when I saw her I began to weep again. I was so desperately sorry.

She spoke quietly. "You are a great mother, Patricia. You can give life forever—if you will stop trying to keep score."

Just before Christmas, I went with the postulants to choose a tree for the abbey. The sister had asked me to choose one that I saw as a symbol of a new life, one that could relate to what was happening to me internally at the abbey. I chose a round tree. It looked like a bush with two large branches sticking out on top, like a huge tuning fork. The nuns decorated my tree to look like a burning bush, all aglow with red lights. The burning bush, I learned, was an Old Testament symbol of the energy of love that never burns out. The branches said to me that life happens when there is a dialogue, when there are two. On Christmas Eve, as I listened to the singing in the chapel, I sensed a mysterious new beginning to my life. It may have been the first time I grasped what Christmas was all about.

Before I left, I had a parlor with the abbess again. I had to know how to get over all the stupid suffering. She said that the way to get rid of an inferior suffering is to accept a bigger one.

But why would anyone want to do that?

She said, "You have to love very much. You begin by remembering, Patricia. And when you remember all, what remains is love."

When I asked if it was that simple, she answered, "Of course it's not that simple. Every step of the way we have to be challenged. And we have to make choices to remember with integrity."

To remember. I didn't think that was really possible for me any longer. My stroke had robbed me of my past and I had gotten very used to not even trying to remember. I would say that now I had a lousy memory for dates and places, and no memory at all for names, and let it go at that.

I had gotten an offer from a publisher to write my memoirs but I simply was not able to do it. My story would forever be the fairy tale in the press or the television film made from Barry's book. That bothered me, but I would have to live with it.

The abbess told me that all the postulants are asked to write about their lives in a journal in order to begin to understand who they are and what they are called to be in this life. She told me I should do that. I should take some time each day and jot down whatever moments of my life I could recall. "Do the journal first. Then, if you want to put something in a book, get yourself an editor and share what you feel will help others."

She said that if I wanted to write the journal at the abbey, she would give me the use of a small house nearby. It would take time—years—she told me, but I would have my life back.

I was filled with gratitude. When I returned to New York, my friends were grateful to the sisters, too. I had stopped vomiting flames. I was ready to look at my life honestly. I had some decisions to make and I would make them. I did not want a divorce, but I would go through with it and begin my life over. I had done it before. I would do it again.

I will not dwell on the divorce here. I will leave that to Roald Dahl, who is much better at horror stories than I am. It is sufficient to say that I lost my shirt to lawyers in America *and* England.

I would have lost more than that, but Roald actually came to *my* defense against *my* lawyers by insisting that he pay me a just amount.

But still it was a gigantic headache. Coincidentally, I landed another commercial, this one for Anacin tablets.

I went back to Gipsy House for the last time to gather the things I wanted to keep. Alf and my friend Lourdes Nichols came with me to help pack them. Lourdes started our day by reading a short chapter from her prayer book. Then we went through closets and cupboards, and, one by one, I chose the pieces of my past that I would bring with me.

I reached for the painting by our daughter and took it from the wall. It was perhaps the one thing in the house I really needed. I had the right to take it.

I looked at it and remembered my beautiful Olivia. I remembered my grief. And I remembered Roald's grief. I put the painting back. "Leave it for him," I said to Lourdes. "It would kill him if I took it."

EPILOGUE

did eventually go to work on a journal. I used a tape recorder and had my words transcribed. This is the first entry:

When I was just born—I guess hours old—my sister, who was twenty-two months old, came into the room and she looked—of course no one told children about expecting a baby in those days—that was much too early for this modern fashion to come into effect—and so she had no idea that my mother was pregnant—she came in and she took one look at me in the bed with my mother and she said, "Well, if it isn't Bill!"

As the abbess instructed, I put everything down as I remembered it. What I could not remember, a friend often could. Many came to my willow cabin and talked of times past. Some shared letters they had kept. God love my mother, Sonia and Phyllis for saving so many of mine.

It has taken five years, but, as Lady Abbess promised, I have my life back.

When my friend Maureen Stapleton accepted her Oscar, she said, "I want to thank everyone I've ever known in my entire life." Maureen may have been joking, but to say those very words is a temptation for me, too. As I wrote my book, I tried to find ways to include the names of each human being who touched my life, from Phillip Wilson, the good doctor who treated my fractured hip for free, to the designer Ana Colon, who gave me so many gorgeous dresses, to Richard Daniel, who helped me up when I fell in front of his shop and became my hairdresser that very day. I drove my editors crazy with names, names, names of those to whom I will always be beholden.

But then I remembered Harvey's last note to me—and I know they know.

I have not, until this day, told anyone about this. During one of my recent retreats to the nunnery, I awoke with the absolute conviction that the sight in my right eye had been restored. I was convinced it was a miracle.

But even though my eyesight was physically unchanged, that certainty of a new vision has stayed with me. I think it may have been the point at which the tunnel vision of my mind began to open into one of those curved mirrors that reflects not only your own face, but everything around you. I cannot say yet that I understand what it is I see, except that my perspective is changing.

At the abbey, I was deeply impressed that God was using my life far beyond any merit of my own making. The stroke had been a means of allowing me to reach so many who were suffering. He had not given me the stroke. He was giving me the strength and love to move with it. I learned that my damaged brain cannot reclaim what is dead. It has to create totally new pathways that will allow me to make choices I would never have made had I not suffered that stroke—choices that an infallible voice assures me will be blessed.

But perhaps what stays with me most significantly is that conversation with Lady Abbess in her garden. She said there is a way to love that remains after everything else is taken from us. I am seeking that way and I know, in fact, its blessing surely works.

* * *

I had that lunch with Rocky and Maria.

I never realized how much they resembled each other.

We ate an elegantly prepared fish in Rocky's New York apartment, a home alive with those wonderful colors I remembered from the house in California.

Rocky knew about Roald and Felicity and my divorce. She was right—we had shared a purgatory. I felt that when she put her arms around me.

Maria and I shared a bond, too. It was Maria who had introduced me to the abbey where I would begin to accept and work with the smallest limitation in myself. Where I would understand, through my belief in love, the value of suffering—and where I would find that remembering is the root of hope.

After lunch, Rocky showed me framed photographs on the wall—all her own work. She could easily add photography to her résumé.

One was a beautiful portrait of Gary.

This was the one man I loved passionately, the one I had fought to get. But the bond of his marriage was stronger than our passion. And I was forced to submit to that. I am now grateful that I did. If I had not married Roald Dahl, I would have been denied my children, even my life, because he truly saved me and I will be forever grateful to him for that.

At the end of our afternoon, Rocky called for her driver to take me home. While we waited, she shared moments of Gary's last days. She had been so proud of him. She marveled at the courage and commitment with which he had accepted his fate.

"I know," he had told her, and somehow he was also speaking for me, "I know what is happening is God's will."

P.N.
Bethlehem, Connecticut
Christmas Eve, 1987

PICTURE CREDITS

PICTURE CREDITS

INDEX

INDEX

Private Lives of Very Public People

____**CONFESSIONS OF A PARISH PRIEST** Andrew Greeley
64477/$4.95

____**A REMARKABLE WOMAN** Anne Edwards 67820/$5.50

____**FRANK SINATRA, MY FATHER** Nancy Sinatra 62508/$4.50

____**THE MARILYN CONSPIRACY** Milo Speriglio 62612/$3.50

____**POOR LITTLE RICH GIRL** C. David Heymann 55769/$4.50

____**HOME BEFORE DARK** Susan Cheever 60370/$4.50

____**PRINCESS MERLE: THE ROMANTIC LIFE OF MERLE
OBERON** Charles Higham and Roy Moseley 50082/$3.95

____**WIRED** Bob Woodward 64077/$4.95

____**HEART WORN MEMORIES** Susie Nelson 66044/$3.95

____**WALT DISNEY: AN AMERICAN ORIGINAL**
Bob Thomas 66232/$4.95

____**VIVIEN LEIGH** Anne Edwards 55220/$4.95

____**STAND BY YOUR MAN** Tammy Wynette 45849/$$3.50

____**SING ME BACK HOME** Merle Haggard with
Peggy Russell 55219/$3.95

____**AMY GRANT** Carol Leggett 61795/$3.95

____**THE INDOMITABLE TIN GOOSE;
A BIOGRAPHY OF PRESTON TUCKER**
Charles T. Pearson 66046/$3.95